CW01086212

# CHARLES II AND
# THE POLITICS OF ACCESS

# CHARLES II AND THE POLITICS OF ACCESS

*Brian Weiser*

THE BOYDELL PRESS

First published 2003

Published by The Boydell Press
An imprint of Boydell & Brewer Ltd
PO Box 9, Woodbridge, Suffolk IP12 3DF, UK
and of Boydell & Brewer Inc.
PO Box 41026, Rochester, NY 14604–4126, USA
website: www.boydell.co.uk

ISBN 1 84383 020 5

A catalogue record for this book is available from the British Library

Library of Congress Cataloging-in-Publication Data
Weiser, Brian, 1969–
Charles II and the politics of access / Brian Weiser.
p. cm.
Includes bibliographical references and index.
ISBN 1-84383-020-5 (hardback : alk. paper)
1. Charles II, King of England, 1630-1685. 2. Great Britain—Politics
and government—1660-1685. 3. Monarchy—Great Britain—History—17th
century. 4. Great Britain—Kings and rulers—Biography. I. Title.

DA445.W45 2003
941.06'6'092—dc21

2003012676

Typeset by Keystroke, Jacaranda Lodge, Wolverhampton
Printed and bound in Great Britain by
The Cromwell Press, Trowbridge, Wiltshire.

# Contents

# Illustrations

## Figures

## Tables

# Acknowledgements

Upon finishing this book I cannot help but feel a smidgen like Charles II did when he finally returned to England. It took almost as long to write, it occurred over many locales, and of course, I have incurred a variety of debts. That these debts, unlike those of the restored king, are intellectual and not financial I can thank Washington University, the trustees of the Stephen Koss Memorial Fund, and the Mellon Foundation which provided support for my studies. I was granted the privilege of access to a number of libraries and archives. In the United States, I had the pleasure of using the resources of Olin Library at Washington University, Avery Architecture Library and Butler Library at Columbia University, The New York Public Library, and Bobst Library at New York University, Perry Library at Old Dominion University, and the Library at the University of New Hampshire. In Britain, the Bodleian Library at Oxford, the British Library, the Guildhall Library of London, the House of Lords Record Office, the Institute of Historical Research, the Public Record Office, the Worshipful Company of Cloth-workers, and the Record Offices of Cheshire, Chester, Coventry, Devon, Norfolk, and Warwickshire all allowed me to conduct research. I would like to thank the staffs of these institutions for their assistance and particularly Dr. Frances Harris of the British Library. I would also like to thank the editors of *The Court Historian*, *Restoration*, and *The Seventeenth Century* for allowing me to republish several paragraphs and ideas from articles that I wrote for those publications.

My fascination with the reign of Charles II started in a seminar on myth and ritual taught by Richard Wortman at Columbia University. I would like to thank him for turning my attention towards monarchy, and to thank David Cannadine, J. M. W. Bean, and Linda Pollock for inspiring me to study British history.

This book began as a dissertation at Washington University in St. Louis. There, I enjoyed the camaraderie of a cadre of graduate students who were engaged in the study of early modern English literature and history: James Benedict, Anne Cotteril, Gavin Foster, Alex Garganigo, Ann Huse, Samuel Thomas, and Robert Tripp. I would particularly like to thank the faculty of Washington University. Marc Saperstein, Max Okenfuss, Nancy Berg, and Kris Zapalac all offered guidance and assistance. Hillel Kieval, Mark Pegg, and William Wallace commented on the dissertation. I have benefitted from classes taught by Richard Davis and Steven Zwicker and from their advice and insight. I owe a special debt of gratitude to Derek Hirst for his extensive knowledge, penetrating criticism, raising the bar high, and, appropriately for this book, his free and easy access.

While researching in Britain I had the pleasure of participating in seminars and conferences held at the Institute of Historical Research. Eveline Cruickshanks, Henry Roseveare, John Miller, Lyndal Roper, and Michael Hunter organized these seminars. I also benefitted from conversations with Andrew Barclay, Alan Marshall, and Mark Knights. Along with this intellectual stimulation in Britain, I also benefitted from considerable hospitality and friendship. The United Kingdom can be a lonely place, especially in the rainy winter, and I can thank Daniel Barenholtz, Uri Berkowitz, Anna Cohen, Robert Gay, Orna Hilman, Gabi Pell, Rebecca Pine, and Andrea Whyte for welcoming a Yank among their midst.

This book has benefitted from much intellectual input. James Benedict, Rachel Brenner, Joel Budd, Anne Cotteril, Derek Hirst, Lana Schwebel, Malcolm Smuts, Abram Weiser, and Erik Zitser read and commented on drafts of various chapters of this work. Dan Beaver and Peter Lake gave insightful comments to papers I delivered. Wendi Shafran gave freely of her knowledge of graphics and architecture and Andy Pressner sped the process along through his reminders of an empty space on his bookshelf.

For the past two years I have benefitted from the intellectual stimulation of my students and colleagues at the University of New Hampshire. I want especially to thank Janet Polasky, Lige Gould, and Jennifer Selwyn who guided me through the publication process.

My greatest debt is to family. Donna, Eric, Sara, and Rebecca Paul have provided me with constant encouragement. I dedicate this book to my parents. Their support has been crucial at every stage of this work.

I would like to thank Her Majesty's Stationery Office for permission to reproduce Figures 4, 8 and 9; John Bold and the late Robin Evans for Figure 5; Nancy Sutcliffe and John Bold for Figures 2 and 3; and the estate of Robert Latham for Figure 1. The originals of these illustrations appear in: H. M. Colvin, *The History of the King's Works*, Vol. 5 of 6, Plates 8b and 31a and Figure 25 (Figures 4, 8 and 9); R. C. Latham and W. Matthews (eds) *Pepys Companion*, 480–1 (Figure 1); John Milner, *A History Civil and Ecclesiastical of Winchester*, 2nd edn (1809) (Figure 10); John Bold, *John Webb*, 128, 129, 135 (Figures 2, 3 and 5).

# Abbreviations

| | |
|---|---|
| Ailesbury | Thomas Bruce, Earl of Ailesbury, *The Memoires of Thomas Earl of Ailesbury Written by Himself* (Westminster: Nichols & Sons, 1890) |
| *BIHR* | Bulletin of the Institute of Historical Reserch |
| BL ADD | British Library, Additional Manuscripts |
| BL EG | ——, Egerton Manuscripts |
| BL Stowe | ——, Stowe Manuscripts |
| Brockket | Allan Brockket, *Nonconformity in Exeter, 1659–1875* (Manchester: published on behalf of the University of Exeter by Manchester University Press, 1962) |
| Browning | Andrew Browning, *Thomas Osborne, Earl of Danby and Duke of Leeds*, vol. 1 of 3 (Glasgow: Jackson, 1944) |
| *CJ* | *Journals of the House of Commons* |
| Coleby | A. M. Coleby, *Central Government and the Localities: Hampshire, 1649–1689* (Cambridge: Cambridge University Press, 1987) |
| Colvin | Colvin, Howard Montagu, *The History of the King's Works*, vol. 5 of 6 (London: H.M. Stationery Off., 1963–1982) |
| *CSP Clar.* | *Calendar of the Clarendon State Papers in the Bodleian Library*, ed. F. J. Routledge, vol. 5 of 5 (Oxford: Clarendon Press, 1970) |
| *CSPD* | *Calendar of State Papers Domestic* |
| *CSPV* | *Calendar of State Papers Venetian* |
| *DNB* | *Dictionary of National Biography* |
| *EHR* | *English Historical Review* |
| Evelyn | John Evelyn, *Diary*, ed. E. S. De Beer, 6 vols (Oxford: Oxford University Press, 1955) |
| Gauci | Perry Gauci, *Politics and Society in Great Yarmouth 1660–1772* (Oxford: Clarendon Press, 1996) |
| GL | Guildhall Library London |
| Haley | K. H. D. Haley, *The First Earl of Shaftesbury* (Oxford: Claredon Press, 1968) |
| Halliday | Paul Halliday, *Dismembering the Body Politic* (Cambridge: Cambridge University Press, 1998) |
| Henning, *Commons* | Basil Duke Henning (ed.), *The House of Commons 1660–90*, 3 vols (London: Secker & Warburg, 1983) |

| | |
|---|---|
| *HJ* | *Historical Journal* |
| *HMC* | *Historical Manuscripts Commission* |
| Hutton, *Charles II* | Ronald Hutton, *Charles II* (Oxford: Oxford University Press, 1989) |
| Hutton, *Restoration* | Ronald Hutton, *The Restoration: A Political and Religious History of England and Wales, 1658–1667* (Oxford: Clarendon Press, 1985) |
| *JMH* | *Journal of Modern History* |
| Knights | Mark Knights, *Politics and Opinion in Crisis: 1678–1681* (Cambridge: Cambridge University Press, 1994) |
| Miller, *Charles II* | John Miller, *Charles II* (London: Weidenfeld & Nicolson, 1989) |
| MS Carte | Bodleian Library, Carte Manuscripts |
| Pepys | Samuel Pepys, *The Diary of Samuel Pepys*, ed. R. C. Latham and W. Matthews (London: HarperCollins, 1995) |
| PRO | Public Record Office |
| Reresby | John Reresby *Memoirs*, ed. Andrew Browning (Glasgow: 1936) |
| Sainsbury | Bruce Ethel Sainsbury, *A Calendar of the Court Minutes etc. of the East India Company*, 11 vols (Oxford: Clarendon Press, 1929) |
| Sainty and Bucholz | J. C. Sainty and R. O. Bucholz, *Officials of the Royal Household, 1660–1837* (London: University of London, 1997) |
| *TRHS* | *Transactions of the Royal Historical Society* |
| Wilentz | Sean Wilentz (ed.), *Rituals of Royalty* (Princeton, NJ: Princeton University Press) |

# *Prologue*
## Charles II's escape from Worcester
## and the incognito king

In September 1651 Charles II invaded England with a troop of 6000 Scottish soldiers. After some initial success, the king's army battled Cromwell's forces at the town of Worcester. Despite the monarch's personal courage, the New Model Army routed the Scots, forcing Charles to flee for his life. The young king quickly disguised himself and spent the next six weeks hiding in priest holes and sleeping in oak trees. After a series of adventures in which Charles narrowly eluded discovery, the king escaped to Europe, where he remained until his restoration.[1]

This event proved to be the formative experience of Charles's life. In times of joy such as his restoration and in times of crisis such as the Popish Plot, Charles returned to, retold, and reformulated his story of escape, drawing from it both strength and inspiration.[2] The adventure and excitement of the moment no doubt partly explains Charles's perpetual fascination with his disguise and escape, but Charles continually drew political lessons from the escape because he realized that he had lived out one of the most famous myths of monarchy: the incognito king. Investigating this legendary myth will reveal why he saw the regulation of access as one of the, if not the, most effective political implements at his disposal.

In early modern England, tales of incognito kings were extremely popular. Rulers appear in disguise in Shakespeare's *Henry V* and *Measure for Measure*. To some degree, narratives of incognito kings attained popularity because they present an extreme case of the classic comedic motif of the fish out of water. Thus, early modern English ballads praise King Alfred who, as legend has it, donned peasant clothes to ascertain his subjects' welfare. During his travels, Alfred met an old women who asked him to watch her oven. Having no culinary experience, the king burnt the women's cakes, for which he received a sound beating. Similarly amusing stories appear in broadsides which detail Henry VIII's drinking with a cobbler and James V of Scotland

---

[1] For more details on the events of the escape see Richard Ollard, *The Escape of Charles II After the Battle of Worcester* (New York: Scribner, 1966).

[2] For more on various versions of the escape story see my "Owning the King's Story: The Escape from Worcester," *Seventeenth Century*, 14:1 (spring, 1999): 43–62.

donning beggar's clothes to inquire about the welfare of his subjects.[3] Many other tales of incognito kings including some that narrate Charles's escape, however, lack any element of humor, suggesting other reasons for their popularity. Listeners and readers found favor with stories of disguised monarchs because they presented the ruler as accessible, as willing to interact in a face-to-face manner with his or her subjects. Such a presentation of kingship was reassuring to a nation that feared an increasingly distant ruler as epitomized by two related phenomena: the evil counselor and the bureaucratization of government.

From the time of William Rufus and probably earlier, the political nation worried about a single advisor monopolizing the king's ear and thereby corrupting policy and patronage for his own benefit. The idea of the evil counselor stemmed from real fears of individual favorites such as like Buckingham, Piers Gaveston, or Cardinal Wolsley, but it also grew in force because it allowed malcontents to censure the king's policy without attacking the king. In some sense, blaming the evil counselor in the place of the king was only a rhetorical device to avoid treasonous statements, but because there was a widespread belief that "the king could do no wrong,"[4] criticizing the evil counselor instead of the monarch also prevented cognitive dissonance.[5] All strata of society subscribed to the idea of an evil counselor. In 1642, Parliament rebelled against Charles I in the king's name, claiming that evil counselors misled the king. Likewise fen rioters, in Charles I's name, protested against a drainage plan which the king himself had sponsored.[6] A monarch who disguised

---

[3]  A. Gardner-Medwin, "Views of King and People in Sixteenth and Seventeenth Century Ballads" in *Bryght Laternis*, ed. J.D. McClure and R.G. Spiller (Aberdeen: Aberdeen University Press, 1983), 24–32. Some of the tales of Charles II's escape such as John Danverd's *The Royal Oake* relate a similar story about the restored monarch. When he was posing as the servant of Jane Lane, Danverd relates, Charles was sent into the kitchen, where he encountered a maid with whom he began conversing. Charles told the maid he came from 'Brumingham' and that he was a 'naylor's' son. During this conversation the spit stopped working and the maid asked the disguised king to wind it up. The king willingly did so, but wound it in the wrong direction which damaged the spit. 'The maid grew angry, asking him where he was bred, and telling him he was the veryest clownish booby that she ever saw in all her life; which railing of hers made his Majesty, notwithstanding his present misery, go out of the room smiling' (A.M. Broadley, *The Royal Miracle* (London: Stanley Paul & Co., 1907), 87, 97). This incident, however, appears neither in Charles II's own narration nor in any eyewitness account, suggesting that it is apocryphal.
[4]  Roger Whitley, in his commonplace book, wrote, "it is an old maxime the king can do no wrong," attesting to the strength of this idea even after the Civil War. (Bodlein Lib. Hist. Mss. c711, f433.)
[5]  Judith Richards quotes Henry Burton who claimed in 1627, 1628, and 1636 "that the virtuous king was indeed effectively the captive of the evil advisers." ("The Kingship of Charles I before 1640," *Past & Present*, 113 (November 1986): 76.)
[6]  Keith Lindlay, *Fenland Riots and the English Revolution* (London: 1982), 1, 54, 101, *passim*. For further contemporary testimony about the evil counselor see BL ADD 25125, 59, and Bodlein Lib. Hist. Mss. *c*. 711, 301.

himself to learn about his subjects first hand demonstrated his wariness of evil counselors.[7]

Legalism and bureaucracy, like evil counselors, were seen popularly as growing obstacles to true communication between king and subject. A ballad, "The King and the Northernman," for instance, depicts a local yokel who is conned by a lawyer and bewildered by legal terms. The Northernman, a royal tenant, journeys to London and, helped by his comic appeal, easily gains access to the monarch. The Northernman fails to recognize the king, who has taken off his shirt after bowling, a glance at the motif of the incognito king. After a series of humorous events, the king solves the Northernman's problems. By accessing the sovereign directly, the tenant brings the king over to his side against an abuse of power. The distaste for the growth of legalism is represented by the final couplet of the ballad: "And thus I end my merry song/Which shews the plain mans simpleness,/And the Kings great mercy in righting wrongs/and the lawyers fraud and wickedness."[8] Likewise, in the play *Sir John Oldcastle*, the servant of the title character makes a summoner eat the paper and wax of a legal document. During this incident Oldcastle – the representative of all good things of merry England such as keeping good beef and beer – is placed in opposition to the new bureaucracy and legalism that seem to have destroyed the face-to-face contact upon which loyalty between lord and commoner rests.[9]

Charles's experiences as a commoner attuned him to the importance his subjects placed upon the accessibility of their ruler. Upon his restoration he strove to be open and to trumpet his affability, because he comprehended that accessibility would allow him to be everybody's king, would aid him in uniting his strife-torn nation, and thereby secure his throne. On one level accessibility would allay fears of evil counselors and bureaucracy interposing themselves between subject and sovereign. On a more symbolic level, open access suggests the interlaced imagery of Christ – the most famous incognito king – and communitas,[10] of forgiveness for past sins, and of unity, ideas which Charles stressed at the beginning of his reign.

---

[7] Many stories of incognito rulers such as *Measure for Measure* and "Henry VIII and the Cobbler" depict the ruler rendering himself incognito specifically to ascertain the welfare of his subjects.

[8] "The King and the Northern-Man" in *Pepys Ballads*, ed. Hyder Edward Rollins (Cambridge: Harvard University Press, 1929), i, 538.

[9] Anthony Munday *et al.*, *A Critical Edition of Sir John Oldcastle*, ed. Jonathan Rittenhouse (New York: Garland Press, 1984), iv, 10–65. For a similar statement see David Stevenson, "The English Devil of Keeping State: Elite Manners and the Downfall of Charles I in Scotland" in *People and Power in Scotland*, ed. Roger Mason and Norman Macdougall (Edinburgh: J. Donald, 1992), 137.

[10] Victor Turner has defined communitas as a 'transformative experience that goes to the root of each person's being and finds in that being something which is profoundly communal and shared.' That the king had experienced life as a commoner inspired a sense of communitas. Turner has found that societies throughout the world engender

Later in his reign Charles fell out of love with accessibility because it proved too weak a salve to heal the deep rifts in English society that the Civil Wars had revealed and caused. However, although his commitment to open access wavered and waned, his belief in the efficacy of the regulation of access as a political implement remained strong. In the 1670s Charles II abandoned the task of uniting his nation, for he no longer believed England to be a naturally organic whole. He ceased trying to be everybody's king and instead strove to become a leader of one political party. Here he wielded access to his person as a weapon, strictly regulating it in order to galvanize his supporters and dishearten his opponents. This shift in policy required not only a rewriting of his household ordinances but of his formative myth of escape as well.[11]

Although Charles II was particularly attuned to the matter of access, historians of his reign have not been so; indeed, most assume that Charles's accessibility remained a constant throughout his reign.[12] This lack of attention is unfortunate because it ignores an integral part of Charles II's political policy and philosophy. Furthermore, it misses a rare opportunity to investigate the wider ramifications of the interaction between subject and sovereign. Because most early modern rulers pursued consistent policies regarding access, it is difficult to detect how such policies influenced society outside of the court. Charles II's frequent alterations of the regulation of access, however, gives us the chance to pinpoint changes in access and the broad repercussions of such changes, thereby gaining insight into the workings of early modern European monarchy. This book, by establishing and examining the reasons behind Charles II's shifts in access, and the way such shifts altered the economics, politics, and self-conception of the English nation, looks to shed light on both the reign of Charles II and the institution of monarchy.

communitas by ritual humiliation, in particular 'stripping of signs and insignia of status' and 'ritual levelling,' the sort of thing that goes on when the king becomes incognito. (Victor Turner, *The Ritual Process* (Chicago: Aldine, 1969), 138.)

[11] Charles dictated a new version of his escape story to Samuel Pepys in 1680. He issued new ordinances of the household in 1679.

[12] For the sole exceptions see H. M. Baille, "Etiquette and the Planning of State Apartments," *Archaelogia* (101):169–199 and David Allen, "The Political Function of Charles II's Chiffinch," *HLQ*, 39 (1976):277–290. Baille sees Charles becoming less accessible in 1683 (175). Allen mentions that the king's person became less accessible during the popish plot (280). Neither, however, assign a political purpose to this change in access nor do they examine the effects of such alterations. Alan Marshall in his recent *Age of Faction*, like Baille, sees a change in the aftermath of the Rye Plot in 1683; as I will show below, such change came much earlier and for reasons of politics, not security (Alan Marshall, *Age of Faction* (Manchester: Manchester University Press, 1999), 22).

# Introduction
## Accessibility and monarchy in medieval and early modern Europe

Charlemagne, Einhard tells us, often invited a hundred of his nobles, attendants, friends and bodyguards to bathe with him at his spa at Aachen, so dismissive of ceremony and external signs of distinction was this greatest of Frankish kings. Notker the Stammerer adds the delightful tale of Greek envoys who, when they entered Charlemagne's court, could not distinguish the emperor from his knights, since he diffused his glory throughout his court. Louis IX, Jean de Joinville relates, sat under an oak tree at Vincennes to dispense justice to all and sundry. Such stories were, no doubt, partly panegyric, but, for most of the Middle Ages, European rulers were expected to be accessible and were lauded for that trait.[1] For the king was the linchpin of government and access to the king was the key to getting things done. By the time Charles II came to rule England, Scotland, and Ireland, the accessible king became a contested ideal: material constraints had limited a ruler's ability to be accessible, and theorists had come to favor distant and sacral monarchs.

In the early modern era, the commodity of access became both more rare and more prized. As the role of the state grew and the duties of the monarch changed, accessibility became harder to maintain. The increasingly pervasive nature of royal authority rendered an audience with the king much sought after by local elites and politicians who needed to influence, and demonstrate their ability to influence, national policy. The very ideal of accessible kingship, moreover, faced renewed competition from the resurgent model of the distant and sacral monarch.

The introduction of paper, and then printing, a supply of university-trained secretaries and administrators, and the accumulation of diverse and noncontiguous realms encouraged early modern monarchs to rule by means of

---

[1] Einhard and Notker the Stammerer, *Two Lives of Charlemagne*, ed. and trans. Lewis Thorpe (New York: Penguin, 1987), 77, 141–142. Janet Nelson, "The Lord's Anointed and the People's Choice: Carolingian Royal Ritual," in *Rituals of Royalty*, ed. David Cannadine and Simon Price (Cambridge: Cambridge University Press, 1992), 171. Janet Nelson, "Kingship and Empire in the Carolingian World," in *Carolingian Culture*, ed. Rosamond McKitterick (New York: Cambridge University Press, 1994), 62. Jean de Joinville, *The Life of St. Louis*, in *Memoirs of the Crusades*, trans. Frank T. Marzials (New York: E.P. Dutton, 1911), 177.

written dispatch. Through written accounts kings and queens stayed informed of occurrences within the localities and relayed their commands, unfiltered, to their officers in the provinces. This development both enabled rulers to centralize more decisions and reduced their need to delegate authority. Such centralization, however, adversely affected the accessibility of kings.

The bureaucratic, legalistic, and written form of government required kings to become administrators, to deal with voluminous loads of paper. The famous French historian Braudel's image of Philip II as a spider at the center of an early modern worldwide web is particularly apt. Philip, who was conscious both of the need to appear accessible and his administrative duties, was torn between these two imperatives. His solution was to isolate himself from courtiers, administrators, and his subjects, entering into hermit-like seclusion for weeks on end to deal with the backlog of paperwork.[2] Henry VII of England did not share Philip II's regard for the need for accessibility. He established a privy chamber in 1495 to which few had the right of entry. This private room gave the king, according to David Starkey, the ability to devote "long, lonely hours of toil over accounts and dispatches which gave him a more detailed knowledge of the operations of his government than any other English king before or since."[3] Few kings, however, had the stamina, ability, or desire to transact personally all the business of state.

Rulers never completely solved the conflicting pressures of the volumes of paper and the desire of many suitors to influence personally the head of state. One flawed solution, prevalent in the late sixteenth and seventeenth centuries, was the institution of a favorite.[4] Only someone believed to have the complete backing of the king, an official who could act as an *alter rex*, had the authority to deflect powerful nobles in a manner which would leave them no recourse to the king. Monarchs gave favorites a plurality of patronage, no doubt from affection, but partly so that the favorite could serve as a conduit between monarch and subjects and thereby filter out any unwanted suits from the king. This arrangement had the admirable quality of diverting the animosity of those disappointed from the king to the favorite.[5] A figure similar to that of the favorite was also necessary to relieve the monarch of his administrative duties. Both Richelieu and Olivares self-servingly emphasized the need for the king to elevate one advisor. Richelieu claimed: "if the sovereign can not or will not personally keep a continuous eye on the chart

---

[2]  According to M. J. Rodríguez-Salgado, the amount of paperwork was enormous. In two weeks of February 1571 the king read and responded personally to 300 memorials. In May of that year he received 1200 petitions (M. J. Rodríguez-Salgado, "The Court of Philip II of Spain," in *Princes, Patronage and the Nobility*, ed. R.G. Asch and A.M. Birke (Oxford: Oxford University Press, 1991), 224, *passim*.).

[3]  David Starkey, *The English Court* (New York: Longman, 1987), 73–76.

[4]  For more on favorites see J.H. Elliott and L.W.B. Brockliss (eds), *The World of the Favorite* (New Haven: Yale University Press, 1999).

[5]  Asch and Birke, 22–24.

and compass, reason demands that he should give one man responsibility above the rest." Olivares opined similarly that kings should have a single minister to see that "all the material is brought before the prince in a suitably digestible form with all the considerations, so that the prince can take the appropriate decision."[6] Kings or queens who employed prime ministers or favorites as a screen for communication, whether personal or written, were restricting access as much as those rulers who sought seclusion.

The contemporary criticism of favorites for blocking avenues to the king's ear underscores the importance of access in this period of personal monarchy. As representative assemblies met less frequently, at least in France and England, personal contact with the monarch became progressively more crucial to advance policies and voice grievances. The need of local elites to influence central policy was enhanced further by the growth of the resources at the king's disposal and the ever extending reach of the central government over religion, economics, and justice. The ability to gain access to the king, moreover, became a sign of political power. As Norbert Elias has shown, such signs of political power were transformed, at least in the halls of Versailles, to an external demonstration of social status. Access to the king became crucial both to influence public policy and to demonstrate political power and social eminence. But access to the king was a finite resource. Increased demand could not be met with increased supply.[7]

Government by paper reduced further the monarch's ability to present himself to his subjects, since paper-pushing monarchs tended to spend most of their time in one capital. Simply put, if the king was to run the government by dispatch, his officials needed a central location where they could always reach him. Philip II once again serves as an example. He established his capital at Madrid, a backwater village, simply for its location in the center of his kingdom.[8] In France, England, and Bohemia, the amount of time that the ruler stayed in his main city increased. The centralization of the regime naturally rendered the king less accessible by making him less mobile. Kings could not go on extended progresses without disrupting the administration. The establishment of capitals brought an end to government from the saddle, an end to peripatetic kingship.

Not only did material constraints, the increase and change of a monarch's duties, and the multiplication of courtiers seeking personal encounters with

[6] J. H. Elliott, *Richelieu and Olivares* (Cambridge: Cambridge University Press, 1984), 49–50.

[7] Derek Hirst, "Court, Country and Politics before 1629," in *Faction in Parliament*, ed. Kevin Sharpe (Oxford: Oxford University Press, 1978), 113, 116, *passim*. G. R. Elton, "The Points of Contact," in *Studies in Tudor and Stuart Politics and Government* (3 vols; Cambridge: Cambridge University Press, 1974–83), Vol.III, 3–57. H. M. Baille, "Etiquette and the Planning of State Apartments", *Archaelogia (101)*:175–176. Norbert Elias, *Court Society*, trans. Edmund Jephcott (Oxford: Blackwell, 1983), 153.

[8] Rodríguez-Salgado, 209–212.

the ruler diminish kings' ability to be accessible; the very conception of the ideal monarch shifted. During the Middle Ages some rulers, particularly the Ottonian and Salian dynasties of East Francia, enhanced their majesty by depicting themselves as close to God, and these rulers often used decorum and distance to emphasize their divine nature.[9] But these emperors, influenced by the practice of Byzantium, were the exception, for the emperor's subjects expected their ruler to be a "commanding but approachable figure."[10]

However, in the late fourteenth century, monarchs throughout Europe almost universally no longer strove to emulate Charlemagne's or Louis IX's approachability. Instead, they used decorum and distance as a means to enhance their position. Prompted perhaps by competition with the church, social unrest from the lower orders, and the assertion of power by representative bodies, rulers formalized pre-existing social and political hierarchies to emphasize the people's obligation for obedience. A predisposition for formality may be seen at the courts of the Holy Roman Emperor Charles IV of Luxembourg (1347–1378), John II the Good of France (1350–1364), Charles V the Wise of France (1364–80) and Richard II of England (1377–1399). Richard II established a lofty style of address, created a new order of nobility (the marquess), and emphasized ceremony. At formal dinners, held three times a year, Richard sat on his throne wearing his crown, conversing with none but watching all. Formality and etiquette could act as efficient a bar to communication as physical separation.[11]

Such concern with ceremony may have come to compensate for the lack of military vigor on the part of late fourteenth-century kings. Richard II rarely campaigned and Charles the Wise was physically weak. Their courts furthermore ceased to be a collection of warriors, and attracted bureaucrats, courtiers, and lawyers. Indeed, Richard and Charles concerned themselves with the law to a great degree, Charles sponsoring an attempt to codify French law.[12] When the king and his courtiers could not use personal military valor to show their worth they turned to the imposition of deference and distance to demonstrate their social superiority.[13]

Royal courts of the late fourteenth century, though more formal than earlier medieval royal households, were still a far cry from the extremes of

---

[9] Ernst Kantorowicz, *The King's Two Bodies* (Princeton: Princeton University Press, 1981), 61–78. Nelson, "Kingship and Empire," 66. Otto III, for instance, would sometimes sit at a separate table, elevated above his fellow diners. (Jonathan Shephard, "Byzantium and the West," in *The New Cambridge Medieval History*, ed. Timothy Reuther (New York: Cambridge University Press, 1999), Vol.III, 619.)

[10] Nelson, "Kingship and Empire," 66.

[11] Nigel Saul, *Richard II* (New Haven: Yale University Press, 1997), 339–355.

[12] Here we have a nexus between a more legal-centric government and the utilization of politics of distance.

[13] Saul, 332, 358–359.

etiquette that would govern Versailles, the Alcazar, or Charles I's Whitehall.[14] For Richard II's and Charles the Wise's courts were peripatetic.[15] The constant change of venue meant that fixed protocols could not be successfully promulgated. Any rules of court, especially those dictating right of entry, needed to take into account the variety of circumstances within which the king would find himself, so such rules were likely to be vague and ineffective. Moreover, as Lord Falkland told Edward Hyde in 1633, "keeping of state was like committing adultery, there must go two to it."[16] To become fully established, rules of distance and decorum required ingrained socialization. In a traveling court, whose makeup changed constantly to include local elites, socialization was difficult to accomplish. Such socialization, however, did occur in the influential and centralized courts of fifteenth-century Burgundy and Milan.

The dukes of Burgundy created a court whose splendor was the talk of Europe.[17] Part and parcel of this glory was the establishment of etiquette which created a hierarchy based on access to the prince. Only the most high and favored could obtain an audience with the duke. Werner Paravacini lists aspects of the Burgundian court which emphasized etiquette and distance:

> the obligation to kneel before the prince, the transformation of the formal meal into a ritual, the suite of rooms one had to pass before reaching the ruler, the separation of the court into different chambers according to rank, and the strong tendency towards leveling all members of the court, in spite of hierarchy, so that they all stood in subservient relation to the prince.[18]

Burckhardt termed the court of the Sforza dukes of Milan the most brilliant since that of Burgundy.[19] The Sforza strove for images of splendor, employing Leonardo da Vinci to create spectacles and statues which glorified their rule.

---

[14] In the fifteenth century the kings of the great states abandoned the model of distant and sacral monarchy, perhaps because they participated in warfare. Henry IV and Henry V of England, Ferdinand of Aragon, and Charles VIII of France are just a few examples of kings who led their armies in battle. Warfaring kings rarely consciously employed distance as a means of generating awe. The realities of camp life made the utilization of distance difficult and these kings did not need external signs of their worth such as decorum; they received marks of distinction on the battlefield.

[15] Saul, 337.

[16] David Stevenson, "The English Devil of Keeping State: Elite Manners and the Downfall of Charles I in Scotland" in *People and Power in Scotland*, ed. Roger Mason and Norman Macdougall (Edinburgh: J. Donald, 1992), 137.

[17] The court reached its apogée under Philip the Good (1419–1467) and Charles the Bold (1467–1477). For more on Burgundy see Richard Vaughn's four-volume *A History of Valois Burgundy* (New York: Archon, 1962–1973).

[18] Werner Paravacini, "The Court of the Dukes of Burgundy: A Model for Europe" in Asch and Birke, 89.

[19] The Sforzas ruled Milan from 1447 to 1498.

Likewise the Sforza used distance to emphasize their elevation over their subjects. They were less subtle than their Burgundian counterparts. Lodovico Sforza, Il Moro (1476–1500), when holding audiences, "kept visitors away from his person by means of a bar, so that in conversing with him they were compelled to speak at the top of their voices."[20]

The very smallness of these principalities encouraged rulers to concentrate on enhancing their image by splendor, distance, and decorum. J. H. Elliott terms this phenomenon the "Avis Principle": second-rate monarchies had to try harder.[21] The fact that the rulers of Burgundy and Milan had somewhat tenuous claims to sovereignty magnified the effect of the Avis principle.[22] To counteract their questionable claims on the obedience of their subjects these princes emphasized their glory. Furthermore, the limited extent of their territory obviated the need to travel constantly throughout their domains. These rulers could set up a court in one place which allowed them to lavish funds on only one palace and to create permanent patterns which were conducive to ingrained socialization. The size and splendor, the richness and decorum, of these courts created an image which commanded respect and gave renewed impetus to the model of splendid, distant, and sacral kingship.

The appeal of sacral rule grew throughout the early modern period as well. Protestants asserted that secular rulers had control of their country's church, which encouraged the presentation of kings and queens as numinous and divine. If the image of the king were to replace sacred icons, then kings needed to act like images of saints in hagiographic tales: when they communicated with their subjects it should be seen as miraculous.[23] Furthermore, the changing nature of warfare obviated the need for the king and his nobles to participate actively in battle. Once artillery, muskets, and mercenaries took over from knights in armor, there was no pressing need for the king to lead the army, and the idea of the sovereign in battle seemed unnecessarily risky. Like their fourteenth-century predecessors many early modern kings, and their courtiers, needed a means to express their worth when they could not do so in cavalry charges, and they did so increasingly by means of etiquette.[24] Philip IV of Spain, for instance, ached to lead his troops into battle, but he was

---

[20] Jacob Burckhardt, *The Civilization of the Renaissance in Italy* (New York: Harper & Row, 1958), 59.

[21] Elliott, in Wilentz, 151.

[22] The dukes of Burgundy held their title from the kings of France. These dukes, although theoretically vassals of the French king, had no feudal obligation to the Valois. The Sforzas's path to power could be termed Machiavellian in the most pejorative sense of the term.

[23] The strong Catholicism of the French and Spanish kings may explain why these monarchies only adopted models of sacrality in the seventeenth century. Indeed, Louis XIV's permanent settlement at Versailles occurred in the same year that he issued the Four Articles of the Gallican Church against the Papacy (Baille, 191, *passim.*).

[24] This argument echoes that of Norbert Elias in *Court Society*, 148–154.

persuaded against this by Olivares. Philip found an outlet for his desire for glory as a patron of the arts and by strictly enforcing etiquette. The king of Spain personally edited and altered the *etiquitas*, rules which governed behavior at court. J. H. Elliott claims that Philip "developed to perfection that impassive *gravitas* which served at once to distance himself from his subjects and to instruct them in the proper rules of comportment."[25] Through his attention to the details of etiquette, the Spanish king, in the words of his contemporary Alonso Carrillo, rendered the court "a school of silence, punctiliousness, and reverence."[26]

Rulers of composite monarchies, such as Philip IV, seemed particularly anxious to restrict access in order to elevate the person of the king and thereby subsume the differences between their disparate realms. Kings noted for inaccessibility virtually always strove to unite their disparate realms. Olivares advised Philip: "the most important piece of business in your monarchy is to make yourself king of Spain: by which I mean that your majesty should not be content with being king of Portugal, of Aragon, of Valencia, and count of Barcelona, but should secretly work and plan to reduce these kingdoms of which Spain is composed to the style of law of Castile."[27] Louis XIV's move to Versailles coincided with his attack on the Huguenot state within the state.[28] Charles I implemented a policy of "thorough" in his three kingdoms. Rudolf II, the Holy Roman Emperor, was an adherent of universalism who attempted to preserve the unity of Christendom, and after 1599 allied himself firmly with counter-reformers.[29]

The reasons behind the connection between uniformity and etiquette are various. For some kings, particularly Rudolf II and Charles I, there was an almost liturgical element. In the minds of Rudolf and Charles, order at court led to an ordered polity.[30] But there were more practical reasons as well. If a ruler desired to establish uniformity, he needed to reject any entreaty of a locality looking to customize the law to the needs of their region. Making access difficult would discourage the various realms from importuning the king, thereby both saving him from the trouble of constantly hearing and rejecting their entreaties, and preventing him from any inclination to gratify their request. In this era of "personal monarchy" the relationship between subject and sovereign became less personal. Of course, the king's

---

[25] Elliott, "Power and Propaganda in Spain of Philip IV" in Wilentz, 164.

[26] Alonso Carillo, *Origen de la dignidad de grande* (Madrid: 1657), 12. quoted in Elliott, "Power and Propaganda," 164. The personal military role of William III of England and Friedrich Wilhelm I of Prussia may explain their distaste for ceremonious kingship.

[27] Elliott, "Power and Propaganda," 159.

[28] Baille, 191.

[29] R.J.W. Evans, *Rudolf II and his World* (Oxford: Clarendon Press, 1973), 65.

[30] See Julian Davies, *The Caroline Captivity of the Church* (Oxford: Clarendon Press, 1992, 18–24) for the correlation between Charles's attempts at order at court, order in church, and the establishment of an hierarchical order throughout the countryside.

subjects often took issue with what they saw as their sovereign's studious disregard for their concerns. Philip IV's attempt at a Union of Arms failed, Louis XIII faced revolts in La Rochelle, his son experienced the Fronde, and Charles and Rudolf met worse fates. When Charles II was restored to the throne eleven years after his father's execution, the matter of access, the question of the relationship between subject and sovereign, loomed large.

# 1

# *The meanings, ideology, and symbolism of access*

An easy access makes a part of the mildness and duty of a prince; Princes must be familiar (sometimes) with their servants, but the rarer the better. Their affability is commendable, but it must keep a distance from contempt.[1]
(*From the Commonplace Book of Roger Whitley, MP for Cheshire*)

## Access: towards a more nuanced model

Both Charles II's contemporaries and modern historians have viewed access in a binary manner: rulers are seen under the simple rubric as being either strict or easy of access. Contemporaries, such as Roger Whitley, used the terms "easy access" or "distance." Historians, like David Starkey, separate English monarchs into those who practice a politics of participation and a politics of distance. For Starkey's purpose, explaining the relationship between the structure of the court and the nature of high politics, such a binary view works well.[2] But access, in the sense of the ability to come into contact with the king, was a more nuanced phenomenon. Investigating the practices of late sixteenth- and early seventeenth-century rulers will reveal some of the components of access.

Spain's Philip II seems, at first glance, a classic example of a monarch who employed distance. He instituted complex protocols to distance himself from his subjects in an attempt to inspire awe.[3] When building his new palace, Alcazar, Philip followed Burgundian architectural tenets, separating the king's rooms from the public chambers where the court met. Yet Philip II's belief in the king's role as servant of the people dissuaded him from abandoning completely the traditional accessibility of Castilian kings. He set aside part of the day to receive petitions and let suitors speak to him as he walked to mass.[4] Philip, in effect, severely restricted the ability of courtiers to enter

---

[1] Bod. Lib Hist. c. 711, pp. 566–567. Hereafter referred to as Whitley's Commonplace Book.
[2] Starkey, *English Court*, 7–9.
[3] Evans, *Rudolf II*, 48.
[4] Rodríguez-Salgado, 218, 219, 221.

into his physical presence, while encouraging his subjects simultaneously to communicate with him.

Louis XIV presents the exact opposite case. The sun king wrote in 1662, "If there is one characteristic particular to this monarchy, it is the free and easy access of the subjects to the prince."[5] Certainly, a large variety of courtiers were able to enter into the king's presence. But once in his presence the ability to interact with the king was almost nil. Orest Ranum describes the interaction between the king and the *corps intermédiaires* as having become "so ritualized that they were almost emptied of political discourse the *corps* could congratulate Louis, thank him, or present him with a gift but little else . . . the king ceased almost to give them the courtesy of his presence." In fact, he continued to allow them the ability to enter into his presence; he simply took away the ability to interact with the king once in his presence. It was not only the *corps intermédiaires* who suffered such a fate. At the court of Versailles all subjects of conversation with the king were limited to "births, marriages, deaths, the king's health, the weather, French victories, literature, gardens, music, plays, and the *faux pas* of others."[6] Louis, in short, was free and easy of access when considering the component of physical proximity, but not if one considers access to include the ability to interact with the king.

The practices of Louis XIV's father reveal another component of access. Louis XIII saw himself as an agent of justice, not a servant of the French people, and therefore had no compunctions regarding the restriction of access.[7] In order to assert his authority the "just" king consciously employed social snubs: refusing to let suitors enter his presence, declining to return a subject's salutation, averting his gaze, or not allowing someone to speak to him.[8] Thus, like Philip II, he limited the ability of suitors to enter into his presence and, like Louis XIV, he limited the ability of his subjects to speak with him. Such closed access at court enabled the intendants, royal representatives sent to govern the countryside, to speak as mouthpieces of the monarch, without fear that some courtier, by appealing directly to the king, would undercut their authority. Louis XIII, hence, limited not only physical proximity, and the ability to interact, but also the very conduits by which subjects could reach the king.[9]

Charles I of England, like Louis XIII, restricted access in the sense of physical proximity, the ability to interact, and the conduits by which his

---

[5] Quoted in Allan S. Weiss, *Mirrors of Infinity* (New York: Princeton Architectural Press, 1995), 67.

[6] Ranum, "Courtesy, Absolutism and the French State," *JMH* (September, 1980): 449.

[7] Alan Lloyd Moote, *Louis XIII: The Just* (Los Angeles: University of California Press, 1989), 2–3, *passim*.

[8] Ranum, 431.

[9] Louis XIV multiplied the effect of closed access by monopolizing the disposal of patronage under his person, rendering access to his person the *sine qua non* of political existence. Using patronage as a lure, Louis XIV attracted the nobility to Versailles, thereby

subjects could communicate with him. As Judith Richards establishes, Charles I rarely showed himself in public, refrained from touching for the king's evil, and discouraged suitors from presenting him with petitions.[10] The reign of Charles I is particularly interesting because it highlights the importance of analyzing to whom the monarch restricts access. Charles, interestingly, rarely if ever used access as a means to alienate those who did not agree with his political ideas. In fact, he assigned the enforcement of the regulation of access to the Earl of Holland and the Earl of Essex, respectively Groom of the Stool and Lord Chamberlain. These two Puritan lords opposed Charles's religious and foreign policies. Henry Rich, Earl of Holland, for instance, continually supported Puritan causes, feuded with Archbishop Laud, kept a Puritan chaplain, and joined the parliamentarians during the English Civil War.[11] Charles was content to allow these lords such intimate access because he did not consider the regulation of access to be a tactical political tool, but rather a device by which he could establish harmony at court, thereby creating a situation where "government and order may spread with more order through all parts of our kingdoms."[12] Such an opinion was, of course, fatally flawed.

From these four rulers' policies emerge four components of access: physical proximity, ability to interact, the nature of the conduits between the king and his subjects, and the bias upon which access is granted. Such a distinction will prove useful in understanding how Charles II shifted the regulation of access in order to further his ever-changing political agenda. However, before analyzing Charles's changing approach to regulating access to his person, it is first necessary to determine popular expectations of how a monarch should regulate access.

## Contemporary wisdom

Charles II's contemporaries had conflicting desires concerning how a monarch should regulate access. Roger Whitley, for instance, carefully qualified maxims which call for easy access.[13] Such reservations about access stem from the

---

leaving the intendants as the sole interpreters of the royal will, and the main means of contacting central authority. As Orest Ranum points out, after the Fronde, the intendants became the virtual avatars of the king; slights to them fell under the rubric of *lèse-majesté*. Through his manipulation of access *le roi soleil* delegated the power of his person to thousands of officials, whose position derived solely from him, thereby creating the implements for absolutism (Sharon Kettering, "Brokerage at the Court of Louis XIV," *HJ* 36 (1993): 72).

[10] Judith Richards,"His Nowe Majestie and the English Monarchy: The Kingship of Charles I before 1640," *Past and Present*, 113 (November, 1986): 70–96.

[11] Barbara Donagan, "A Courtier's Progress: Greed and Consistency in the Life of the Earl of Holland," *HJ* (Vol. 19:2, 1976): 317–353.

[12] LC 5/180, 1 quoted in *The English Court*, 258.

[13] See above, p. 13.

dual nature of kingship. Kings, as Ernst Kantorowicz has amply shown, were often compared to, thought of, and portrayed as sacral figures. In *The King's Two Bodies*, Kantorowicz demonstrates that during the latter Middle Ages descriptions of the king as *imago dei* replaced descriptions of the king as *imago christi*.[14] Portrayals of the king as *imago dei* suggest splendor, transcendence, aloofness, and strict justice. Depictions of the king as *imago christi* imply that the king should be accessible, merciful, and forgiving. In the Baroque age these two models still co-existed and ideal monarchs were portrayed as combining both attributes. James I in his political testament *Basilike Doron* advised his son, "Ye shall not be so facile of accesse giving at all times as I have bene: and yet not altogether retired or locked up like the kings of Persia appointing also certain hours for publick audience." In reality, however, monarchs found it difficult to walk the tightrope between decorum and accessibility. As Roger Whitley recorded in his Commonplace Book, monarchs had to choose between models, between a politics and imagery of participation or of distance:[15] "A prince must be either exceedingly affable or severe either to contain or terrify their stubborn subjects."[16] Or, as Machiavelli said, a prince should know "whether it is better to be feared or loved."[17]

In the Baroque age most elite theorists, like Machiavelli, extolled restrictive access.[18] Francis Bacon's *History of the Reign of Henry VII* claims "that keeping a distance which indeed he did towards all" provided the key for the first Tudor's success. Likewise, Shakespeare has Henry IV berate his son Prince Hal for eschewing politics of distance and embracing instead "vile participation."[19] After the English Civil War, many continued to extol the benefits of severely restricting access to the king. The Marquis of Newcastle, Charles II's guardian, declared in his advice to the young king, "Sertenly there is nothing keepes up a king, more than seremony & order, which makes distance, & this brings respecte and duty & those obedience which is all."[20] Samuel Pepys, in his *Diary*, testified to the effect too much closeness could

---

[14] Ernst Kantorowicz, *The King's Two Bodies* (Princeton: Princeton University Press, 1981), 87–97.

[15] Here, I use David Starkey's terminology. See his introduction to *The English Court*.

[16] Whitley's Commonplace Book, 574.

[17] Machiavelli, *The Prince*, ch. 17. Although Machiavelli generally sided with those who thought fear more effective. In ch. 3 of *The Prince* he does extol the benefits of open access in mixed principalities. "The Subjects will be content," the Florentine theorist claimed," if they have direct access to the king" (Niccolo Machiavelli, *The Prince*, ed. Q. Skinner and R. Price (Cambridge: Cambridge University Press, 1988).

[18] See Machiavelli, ch. 23.

[19] Quoted in Starkey, *The English Court*, 7–9.

[20] Marquis of Newcastle, *Ideology and Politics on the Eve of the Restoration: Newcastle's Advice to Charles II*, ed. T. P. Slaughter (Philadelphia: American Philosophical Society, 1984), 45.

have on an observer, "hearing him [the king] and the duke talk and seeing and observing their manner of discourse; and God forgive me, though I adore them with all the duty possible, yet the more a man considers and observes them, the less he finds of difference between them and other men."[21]

Pepys's comments remind us of the contemporary belief that distance breeds awe and intimacy contempt. Indeed, much of the monarch's authority came from his claims of sacrality and divine right. As the Marquis of Newcastle advised Charles II, the pursuit of a politics of distance reinforced the image of the king's sacrality in his subjects' minds:

> & not make your selve to cheape, by to much Familiarety, which as the proverb says, breedes contempte but when you appeare, to shew your Selfe gloryously, to your People; Like a God, for the Holly writ sayes, wee have Calld you Godds- & when the people sees you thus, they will Downe of their knees, which is worship & pray for you with trembling Feare, & Love, as they did to Queen Elizabeth."[22]

Such advice contradicted a vision of the ideal monarch with deep roots in popular culture. Stephen Justice, in his study of the tumultuous events of 1381, maintains that the rebels' claims that the king was on their side came not from an attempt to avoid charges of treason, but from a deep-seated belief that the king took up the cause of the oppressed.[23] The process of petitioning the king and the legal device of the plaint formed the basis of the commoners' trust in the king. Justice deems the petition "the proper remedy for those who had few remedies of another sort. The petitioner conventionally addressed himself directly to the king, who was, in form if not in fact, the dispenser of grace . . . there was a legal form of access to the king's political person that might be said to encourage . . . an identification with him by those who felt aggrieved." The plaint, Justice explains, "broadly implied that the king and the complainant were allied against extortionate lords and ministers, that in fact the king, through his justices, *automatically* took the side of any party victimized by the arrogance of power."[24] The implications of the plaint must have strengthened the power of the old motif, the evil counselor.

The Protestant Reformation could only have enhanced the English wariness of an evil counselor. Inspired by Kantorowicz, Linda Levy Peck has shown that early modern Europeans often drew their ideas about kings from theodicy and their images of the divine from their perceptions of monarchy. In Jacobean and Carolingian England, Peck asserts, suitors referred to Buckingham and other patronage mongers as "saints" and conversely

---

[21] Pepys, vi, 170 (July 26, 1665).
[22] Newcastle, 45.
[23] For a French example of this belief see Joinville, 167–181.
[24] Stephen Justice, *Writing and Rebellion* (Berkeley: University of California Press, 1994), 60–61.

"systematically borrowed images of the baroque court and its patronage to describe God, heaven and Christ."[25] Peck has found that even Puritan divines employed "Catholic" language to describe the court and Baroque language to describe heaven, yet such language does not fit comfortably with the strongly anti- papist sentiment within England. James VI made the pejorative connection between restricting access and the Catholic Church. In his advice to his heir Henry, James – then King of Scotland – wrote,

> Acquaint yourself so with all the honest men of your Barrones and gentle-men, & be in your giving accesse so open and affable to every ranke of honest persons, as may make them pearte without scarring at you, to make their own suits to you themselves; and not to employ the great lords, their intercessors, for intercession to saints is Papistry: so shall ye bring to a measure their monstrous backes.[26]

Charles I did not take his father's advice, opting to employ the politics of distance as a means to inspire awe and create order in his realm, with dire consequences.

Some of the witnesses to the English Civil War saw Charles I's restrictive access policy as a reason for the king's difficulty in gaining support.[27] Similar observations may have induced Edward Hyde and James Butler, Duke of Ormonde, to convince Charles II to pursue a policy of easy access. Hyde, Charles II's chief advisor during the exile, constantly nagged the itinerant king to establish and maintain an extensive correspondence with loyalist supporters. Soon after the Restoration, Hyde touted Charles II's affability. In a speech to the House of Lords on December 23, 1660, Hyde claimed: "he [the king] hath given us a noble and princely example by opening and stretching out his arms to all who are worthy to be his subjects at once in his arms and himself in theirs."[28] James Butler, the Duke of Ormonde, showed his favoring of easy access by his example. Edward Cooke, in a letter to Lord Bruce, described Ormonde's court when he was Lord Lieutenant of Ireland: "and after till dinner gives free access to all the people; and so for an hour after dinner; then into his closet . . . I never was in love with a court before."[29] Even without the advice of Clarendon and Ormonde, Charles's own experience brought him to an appreciation of the benefits open access would bring to his realm.

---

[25] Linda Levy Peck, "Benefits, Brokers and Beneficiaries" in *Court, Country and Culture*, ed. B.Y. Kunze and D.D. Brautigam (Rochester: University of Rochester Press, 1992), 109–127, esp. 114–115.

[26] James VI, *Basilikon Doron*, ed. James Craigie, *Scottish Text Society* (3rd series (16), 1944), 85.

[27] For more on this idea see David Stevenson, "The English Devil of Keeping State: Elite Manners and the Downfall of Charles I in Scotland" in *People and Power in Scotland*, ed. Roger Mason and Norman Macdougall (Edinburgh: J. Donald, 1992), 126–145.

[28] *Journal of the House of Lords*, Vol. 11, 238.

[29] HMC Ailesbury, 165 (September 13, 1662).

## A king in the woods and at foreign courts

Unlike any other monarch of his age, Charles II's experiences before he gained the throne gave him a unique insight into the dynamics of access. While other monarchs (for instance, his great-grandfather James V) may have masqueraded themselves for a few hours or days,[30] Charles knew what it was like to be a commoner. During the six weeks that Charles II spent disguised as a common servant to escape Cromwell's army, he was able to interact with his subjects as their peer. In his exile, heads of state recognized his dignity in ceremonies, but he lacked the financial resources to maintain the trappings of majesty. Oliver Cromwell's Secretary of State, John Thurloe, received reports that "Charles Stuart" walked alone through the winding streets of Cologne with his head uncovered.[31] When one loyalist presented the king with a pack of hounds Charles could not afford to maintain them, but he could not offend the supporter by giving them away either.[32]

Many of his contemporaries believed that Charles II's experiences shaped his opinions about access. One correspondent to the Earl of Manchester wrote on the eve of the restoration that he hoped the king's troubles had taught him "a wise good lesson . . . how to pity."[33] Others, particularly foreign observers who were amazed at Charles's accessibility during the first decade of the reign, believed that his accessibility came from habit. On December 30, 1661 the Venetian resident reported to the Senate that "[the King] in short seems practically unable to shake off the habits formed under necessity during so many years of private life and which please him better than the actuality and pomp of royalty."[34] Lorenzo Magalotti, an Italian who visited England in 1668, recorded court opinion as saying "that his courtesy and affability are not so entirely the effect of royal magnanimity that some little part of them may not be due to the habit formed in his youth of adopting the humble manners of a poor and private nobleman."[35] Magalotti's allusion to royal magnanimity suggests that Charles's views of statecraft played some role in the king's structuring of access.

His experiences in the woods of Boscobel and foreign courts shaped Charles's political views as well as his habits. His fascination with his story of escape suggests that he appreciated the commoners' desire for an accessible king and his stay in foreign courts would only have strengthened this appreciation.

---

[30] Gardner-Medwin, 29.
[31] Antonia Fraser, *Royal Charles* (New York: Knopf, 1979), 140.
[32] Ronald Hutton, *Charles II King of England, Scotland and Ireland* (Oxford: Clarendon Press, 1989), 89.
[33] HLRO, Earl of Manchester MSS, Willcocks Selection, Section 2 (May 15, 1660).
[34] *CSPV*, Vol.33, 84.
[35] Lorenzo Magalotti, *Lorenzo Magalotti at the Court of Charles II*, ed. and trans. W. E. Knowles Middleton (Waterloo, Ontario: Wilfrid Laurier University Press, 1980), 27.

Charles's stay in France probably had the most impact on the young king. Charles resided in Paris or St. Germaine between June 1646 and June 1648, January 1649 and September 1649, and October 1651 and July 1654. During this period, few observers could have predicted the power Louis XIV would soon command. France was in the grips of the Fronde, a revolt which would have brought bad memories to the English exiles. Charles II must have seen how limiting access to the monarch spurred on the Fronde. Both Anne of Austria and Mazarin insisted that "to listen or to be received were courtesies which they alone could grant or decline."[36] This lack of access led, in part, to Mazarin's being vilified as the evil counselor. Parisians stoned the windows of Mazarin's mansion (the event which gave the Fronde its name) and hung his likeness in effigy throughout the streets of the capital.[37] Anne and Mazarin realized the alienating affect of their distance and tried to win people to their cause, but their subjects were not impressed. One anonymous diarist wrote, "it is believed that all these caresses are done according to maxim and that the metamorphoses of the state is not yet complete."[38] The chaos of the Fronde, the advice of Clarendon and Ormonde, and his own positive experience of dealing directly with his subjects must have brought the young king to question the efficacy of the politics of distance.

## A too public monarch? Sex and access

In the late winter and early spring of 1660, few in England knew much about Charles Stuart, the man whom they designated to restore monarchy and order to their turbulent nation. Curiosity and apprehension brought many in England to scurry to find out about their new king, reading histories of his life and characters of his person, such as Samuel Tuke's *Character* that described the new monarch as "handsome, graceful, serious, learned, shrewd, and of good morals for some time."[39] Soon, however, they would learn about their king in intimate detail, in too intimate detail.

Despite Tuke's wishful thinking, Charles was anything but of "good morals for some time." Even before his restoration he had engaged in a number of affairs and fathered at least one illegitimate son. But his "immorality," while troubling to contemporaries who feared divine retribution, was not striking; indeed, mistresses were common for monarchs in the latter half of the seven-

---

[36] Ranum,"Courtesy," 445.

[37] *Memoires of Le Grande Mademoiselle Duchesse de Montpensier*, trans. Grace Hart Seely (New York: The Century Company, 1928), 105.

[38] Ranum, "Courtesy," 444.

[39] Tuke's *Character* was published on April 30, 1660, Thomason. As quoted in Ronald Hutton, *The Restoration: A Political and Religions History of England and Wales, 1658–1667* (Oxford: Clarendon Press, 1985), 111.

teenth century. Perhaps the best example of its commonality is that of Frederick III (I) of Prussia who, although a strict Calvinist, thought having a mistress as essential to a king's dignity. He named the wife of Wartenburg, one of his ministers, mistress in title, trying to obtain the prestige of having a mistress without endangering his soul by engaging in any extra-marital affairs. It was the incredibly public nature of Charles' sexuality, however, that astounded contemporaries. In the theatrical age that followed his restoration, the rampant sex drives of the monarch, his brother, and his chief courtiers took center stage. Pepys's *Diary* is riddled with intimate details of the king's sex life. The king's mistress Castlemaine, Pepys hears, "rules him [the king]" by employing "all the tricks of Aretino that are to be practised to give pleasure – in which he is too able having a large ——."[40] Not only did those with connections at court comment on the size of the royal genitals, even outsiders like the Italian visitor Magalotti could claim to have heard that the Queen

> is more than usually sensitive to pleasure. She finds the king provided by nature with implements most suitable for exciting it, and it is said that her ecstasy is then so extreme that after the ordinary escape of these humours that the violence of pleasure presses even from women, blood comes from her genital parts in such great abundance that it does not stop for several days.[41]

One can hardly imagine a more intimate access to the king's body.

The public nature of his sexuality had a powerful effect upon historians' evaluation of his reign, not least of which was enhancing the king's reputation of laxity, affability, and accessibility. Such a reputation is certainly warranted by historical evidence. Evelyn's *Diary* connects the king's sexuality, laxity, and accessibility.

> An excellent prince doubtlesse had he ben lesse addicted to Women, which made him uneasy & allways in Want to supply their unmeasurable profusion . . . his too Easy nature resign's him to be manag'd by crafty men, & some abandoned & prophane wretches, who corrupted his otherwise sufficient parts.[42]

The effect of the king's sexuality upon his reputation for accessibility was, however, much more complicated, for the king's *amour* was subject to two very different, albeit both negative, interpretations.

Some saw the public nature of the king's sexual activity as impinging upon his ability to project a sacred image. How could a king project majesty when so much was known about his sexual habits? Pepys certainly comments that too open a display of dalliance diminished the king's dignity. On February

---

[40] Pepys, IV, 137 (May 15, 1663).
[41] Magalotti, 55.
[42] Evelyn, IV, 109.

1, 1663, Pepys reported, "this day Creed and I, walking in White-hall Garden, did see the king coming privately from my Lady Castlemayns; which is a poor thing for a Prince to do."[43] As Evelyn and Pepys indicate, Charles's sexual adventures and the public nature thereof made it impossible for him to fully exploit his majestic dignity.

But it was just as common to place the king's sexuality on the same continuum as effeminacy, Catholicism, tyranny, and inaccessibility.[44] Too much sex, in early modern minds, caused men to lose their vigor and manhood.[45] Such a loss of manhood resulted from and brought about an inability to control one's self, a classic and classical characteristic of a tyrant.[46] The satirical poem written in 1667, the "Fifth Advice to the Painter," ties sex with tyranny and Catholicism:

> women have grossly snar'd the wisest prince
> that ever was before or hath been since:
> . . .
> Paint in a new piece painted Jezebel;
> give't to adorn the dining room of Hell.
> Hang by her others of the gang for more
> Serve up Alice with Rosamond, Jane Shore.
>      stay painter! now look, here's below a space;
> I'th' bottom of all this , what shall we place?
> shall it be Pope, or Turk, or prince, or nun?[47]

The symbol of tyranny (The Turk) and Catholicism (The Pope) are seen as the source for the king's being ensnared by women. Rachel Weil has asserted that opponents of Charles linked tyranny and Catholicism to debauchery. Both were also linked to inaccessibility. Even James VI in *Basilike Doron* claimed that Catholics believed God to be accessible only through the use of intermediaries and noted the inaccessibility of the prototypical tyrant the King of Persia.[48] People prone to see connections between tyranny, popery, and inaccessibility would also see Charles's mistresses as evil counselors

---

[43] Pepys, IV, 30 (February 1, 1663).

[44] Rachel Weil, "Sometimes a Scepter is Only a Scepter," in *The Invention of Pornography*, ed. Lynn Hunt (New York: Zone, 1993), 145.

[45] See John Spurr, *The 1670s*, Oxford: Blackwell), 208. Ian Frederick Moulton, *Before Pornography* (New York: Oxford University Press, 2000), 16 . Such a lack of vigor was noted by contemporaries. Pepys claimed that during the Dutch War the king had lost his ability to have an erection, hearing: "the Kings greatest pleasures is with his fingers being able to do nothing more" (Pepys VIII, 368 (July 30, 1667)).

[46] See e.g. Plato's *Republic*, Book IX.

[47] Alice, Rosamond, and Jane Shore were all famous mistresses of prior English kings.

[48] James VI, *Basilikon Doron*, ed. James Craigie, *Scottish Text Society* (3rd series (16), 1944), 85.

who, instead of monopolizing the king's ear, monopolized his prick, which – according to John Wilmot, Earl of Rochester – would be to more effect. As Rochester's famous satire infamously details:

> His Sceptter and his Prick are of a Length,
> And she may sway the one, who plays with th'other
> And make him little wiser than his Brother.
> Restlesse he roalles about from Whore to Whore
> A merry Monarch, scandalous and poor.[49]

During the exclusion crisis some radical pamphleteers suggested assassinating the mistresses just as previous patriots had killed other evil counselors such as Buckingham.[50]

But Rochester's poem suggests simultaneously that there is no monopolization of the king's private parts; "he roalles about from Whore to Whore:" no one mistress controls Charles II. Dryden makes a similar contention in the beginning of *Absalom and Achitophel* where he describes the sex life of David/Charles:

> His vigorous warmth did **variously** impart
> To wives and slaves; and, **wide** as his command.
>
> (*Absalom and Achitophel*, 8–9)

One need not fear that Charles is monopolized by any one mistress, that any one women controls him; in this and in other matters, Dryden seems to contend, Charles is open to all.

Non-royalists also commented on the variety of the king's mistresses and their competition with each other. A few exclusion crisis era satires depict Charles's vilified French mistress Portsmouth having cat fights with Nell Gwynn or Castlemaine. These tracts, however, do not imply that a multitude of mistresses means a lack of monopolization of Charles. In fact, in *A Dialogue between the D of C and the D of P . . . With the Ghost of Jane Shore*, Castlemaine accuses Portsmouth of monopolizing the king, "With which thou didst subdue our monarch's heart/and wouldn't not let me with thee share a part."

Like the story of his escape from Worcester,[51] the image of the overly sexed monarch was a contested battleground subject to diverse interpretation, and such interpretations were influenced by Charles II's policies of access.

---

[49] John Wilmot, Earl of Rochester, "A Satire on Charles II" in K. Walker (ed.) *The Poems of John Wilmot: Earl of Rochester* (Oxford: Blackwell, 1984), 11–15.
[50] Weil, 152.
[51] See my "Owning the King's Story," *passim*.

# 2

# *The architecture of access*

## Charles II's palaces

In 1682 Lord Arlington, who had served Charles II as Secretary of State and currently held the position of Lord Chamberlain, walked to the king's newly constructed bedchamber in the Volary buildings of Whitehall. When he reached the door a groom of the bedchamber stopped the Lord Chamberlain. The groom explained that since his majesty was in his closet, the groom was unable to ask the king's leave for the Lord Chamberlain to enter the bedchamber, and that Arlington therefore had to wait in the antechamber until the king exited his closet. Arlington was aghast. He petitioned the king for redress for this insult to his honor and abridgement of his privileges. The measures taken to resolve this dispute demonstrate that this was no minor quibble. Charles appointed a special subcommittee of the Privy Council including his then chief ministers Halifax and Rochester to decide the matter. The hearings took place over the course of an entire year and the record of testimony exceeds seventy pages in the Lord Chamberlain's record book.[1] Such extensive effort testifies to the importance of access to contemporaries.

Charles II recognized the significance of access and capitalized upon it, for the regulation of access was one of the most potent weapons in the political arsenal of the restored monarch. As long as Charles believed in the inherent unity of his realm, he utilized open access to diffuse tension and to deflate factional warfare. When he recognized the depth of the political and religious divisions in his land, Charles opted to become a leader of one party, and he therefore restricted access to bolster his supporters and dishearten his opponents. The following chronological study of the royal residences will clearly delineate how Charles altered his pattern of residence, constructed new royal buildings, remodeled the physical structure of his palaces, and reformed the etiquette that governed his court, all in an attempt to transform the patterns of access; that is to say, the nature of communication between sovereign and subject.[2]

---

[1] See below, pp. 46–48.

[2] Architectural historians have dealt admirably with the palaces of English monarchs, but they rarely concern themselves with the political ramifications of architectural decisions. See e.g. John Bold, *John Webb: Architectural Theory and Practice in the Seventeenth Century* (Oxford: Clarendon Press, 1989); Mark Girouard, *Windsor, the Most Romantic*

The active role the king took in architectural matters suggests such concern with access. The nature and style of royal residences were decisions which the king made personally. A proposal written in 1667 by an employee of the Office of Works assumes that royal architects conferred constantly with the king.[3] Charles was particularly aware of both planned works and ongoing construction. On a number of occasions, he conversed with John Evelyn about architecture in general and the royal palaces in particular.[4] Once, when talking with the diarist, the king called for crayon and paper and drew a plan for a new palace at Whitehall.[5] (Evelyn did not think the monarch an adept draftsman, but he kept the picture as a rarity.) Charles also visited work sites to inspect his builders' progress.[6] Memoir-writers recalled Charles II's devout interest in his buildings and often made morbid associations between the unfinished palace at Winchester and the king's premature death. Roger North recalled that Charles II, a few months before he died, had asked Christopher Wren if he could hasten the erecting of Winchester to finish it in one year. Wren replied, "Yes . . . but not so well, nor without great confusion, charge and inconvenience, and however diligent they were, he feared disappointments would happen. Well, said the king, if it be possible to be done in one year, I will have it so, for a year is a great deal in my life."[7] The identification by these writers between the king's palace and his body suggests that contemporaries and the king considered the way his palaces represented its chief inhabitant.

## That maze of accessibility: Whitehall

At the beginning of his reign, Charles used accessibility to unite his divided realm. He found Whitehall conducive to this agenda. Of Charles's residences, Whitehall was the easiest to reach. Anyone who had business with Parliament or in the city could readily visit the king's main palace. The attractions of

---

*Castle* (London: Hodder & Stoughton, 1993); Peter Thornton, *Seventeenth Century Interior Decoration in England, France and Holland* (New Haven, Yale University Press, 1978); Simon Thurley, "The Lost Palace of Whitehall," *History Today* (January, 1988); Thurley, "A Country Seat Fit for a King: Charles II, Greenwich, and Winchester" in Eveline Cruickshanks, *The Stuart Courts* (Stroud, UK: Sutton, 2000), 214–39; Thurley, *The Royal Palaces of Tudor England: Architecture and Court Life, 1460–1547* (New Haven, CT: Yale University Press, 1993); Thurley, *Whitehall Palace: An Architectural History of the Royal Apartments, 1240–1698* (New Haven, CT: Yale University Press, 1999).
[3] The anonymous proposal is in PRO Shaftesbury Papers 30/24/7/601. See Colvin, 11, 22.
[4] Evelyn, III, 297–303 (October 1, 1661), 435 (January 24, 1661).
[5] Evelyn, III, 466 (October 28, 1664).
[6] He visited Windsor for that express reason on February 16, 1676/7 (*HMC Rutland*, v.2, 37). He also visited Winchester while construction was under way (see Appendix).
[7] Colvin, 23. See also below, p. 52.

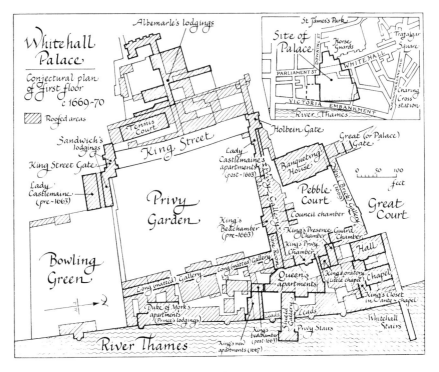

**Figure 1** Whitehall: that maze of accessibility

the only metropolis in England and the capital's abundance of lodging made visiting Whitehall appealing and relatively easy.[8]

In the early 1660s a prospective suitor would find few obstacles on the way to the king. At the main palace gate, porters stopped "those who pressed with rudeness or disorder, carried unfit weapons, divines not wearing their robes and those of inferior quality who came muffled, masqued or otherwise disguised."[9] If allowed through the gate, visitors passed freely into the great court to the covered gallery and then to the great chamber where two yeoman ushers stood guard. The presence or audience chamber lay to the east of the

---

[8] Visiting the king at other palaces could be arduous. When the king was in residence, lodgings in Windsor were difficult to obtain, even for courtiers. Whenever the king traveled to Windsor, the knight harbinger ordered the mayor to proclaim "to all the inhabitants of Windsor and Eton that they presume not to . . . let any of their lodgings or stables without . . . [the Lord Chamberlain's] order or a billet from . . . his Majesty's knight harbinger" (PRO LC 5/140, 462; LC 5/137, 395; PRO LC 5/137–145, *passim.*). Viewing palaces other than Whitehall appears to have required a trip specific for that purpose. James Yonge took such a trip in 1681 when he visited Windsor, Hampton Court and Whitehall (*The Journal of James Yonge*, ed. F. N. L. Poynter (London: Longman, 1863), 169–173).
[9] BL Stowe, 562, 1.

great or guard chamber and occasionally witnessed the king dining in state. South of the presence chamber, separated by a corridor, lay the king's privy chamber. A household order of 1667 allowed everyone except "footmen, mean or ordinary persons" to enter both the privy and presence chambers.[10] It is unclear what regulations governed admittance to the Vane Room which served as a withdrawing-room until 1663 and was located across the privy gallery from the privy chamber. The book of orders for the government of the bedchamber (issued in 1661, 1673, and 1678) restricted everyone except princes of the blood and servants of the bedchamber from entering the king's bedchamber without explicit leave,[11] while only those pre-approved by the king were allowed in the closet. Evidence exists, however, which suggests that in practice the orders regulating the bedchamber were not strictly enforced before 1680.[12]

Although regulations governed the formal route to the king's staterooms and bedchambers, Whitehall's design encouraged informal meetings. Originally the London residence of the Archbishop of York, it grew in an almost organic manner as courtiers and other royal servants added rooms and buildings haphazardly to the twenty-three-acre complex.[13] The result was a chaotic sprawl. Samuel Sorbiere, a French physician visiting London in 1665, described Whitehall as "ill built and nothing but a heap of houses, erected at divers times and of different models which they made contiguous in the best manner they could for the residence of the court."[14] John Miller has likened Whitehall to a "great rabbit warren of apartments, cubby holes and corridors maybe two thousand rooms in all – through which courtiers and politicians scuttled like rats in a granary."[15] The size of the palace meant that most of the chief courtiers and ministers had apartments in the actual complex; this enabled them to be in near constant attendance upon his majesty.[16] Furthermore, Whitehall's disorderly construction provided many paths which suitors used to bypass the formal progression of entrance.

---

[10] PRO LC 5/138, 342 (December 2, 1667). Stricter regulations were issued in 1673 and again in 1679; see pp. 38, 42–45.

[11] PRO LC 5/201, 34.

[12] PRO LC 5/201 74. See pp. 46–48 for specifics.

[13] During Charles II's reign, for instance, the Lord Chamberlains issued warrants to over twenty people to enlarge existing lodgings or to build new ones (PRO LC5/137–145, *passim.*).

[14] Quoted in Susan Foreman, *From Palace to Power* (Brighton: Alpha Press, 1995), 27. Lorenzo Magalotti had a similar impression: "It is more remarkable for its situation than for the nobleness of its structure, being nothing more than an assemblage of several houses, badly built at different times and for different purposes." Quoted in John Martin Robinson, *Royal Residences* (London: Macdonald & Co., 1982), 171.

[15] John Miller, *James II: A Study in Kingship* (Hove: Wayland, 1977), 38.

[16] Colvin, key to Plate 36.

Besides making physical access to the king easier, the unorganized nature of Whitehall's construction suggested a sense of openness to visitors. Instructive parallels exist between palaces and the gardens that lay outside them. According to the Duke of Saint Simon, the ideal French garden, like that of Versailles, tried to "tyrranize nature by making shrubs and plants part of a geometric scheme."[17] Eighteenth-century English gardens reacted against the French garden; English gardeners took as their guiding principle to leave nature undisturbed. Contemporaries and historians have often pointed to the symbolic connotations of these gardens, making analogies between absolutism and the French garden and a government of consultation and the English garden.[18] Likewise, architectural historians have often noted the absolutist connotations of planned unified ranges.[19] Constructing such a building demonstrates the builder's desire to impose his will upon nature; it shows a reluctance to compromise. On the other hand, Whitehall's chaotic structure implies a willingness to negotiate with the forces of nature. The viewer of this central palace infers that the king lacks either the desire or the ability to bend his castles to his will and consequently that the monarch would be more open to the idea that he must confer with his subjects instead of simply ordering them about. The disadvantage of this unplanned structure, however, is that it did little to engender respect or awe of the monarch. When Lorenzo Magalotti, a companion of Prince Cosimo of Tuscany, viewed Whitehall in 1669, he condemned it as having "nothing in it from which you could suppose it to be the habitation of the king."[20]

Initially, Charles appears to have enjoyed the bustle and chaos of Whitehall. In the first two years of his reign he almost never left his main palace: he spent only six nights away from Whitehall in 1661 (See Table 1). His father and brother tried to impose order upon the maze of a palace by strictly regulating access and by vigilantly controlling the keys to their private

[17] Louis XIV intended the gardens of Versailles to represent his absolute power not only by exhibiting his mastery over nature, but also by forcing visitors to view it through his own perspective. Louis XIV wrote *Manier de Montrer le Jardins de Versailles* which imposed upon all viewers an exact itinerary to follow when visiting the gardens. In some sense the king's presence was seen as creating the garden: the fountains worked only when Louis was in close proximity. Allan S. Weiss, *Mirrors of Infinity* (New York: Princeton Architectural Press, 1995), 33.

[18] Weiss, 14–15, 23–26, 33, 61, 67, *passim*.

[19] See, e.g. Bold, *John Webb*, 145–146. See Figure 2 for an example of a palace constructed of unified ranges.

[20] Quoted in Robinson, 171. Charles, of course, understood the ignoble nature of his main palace; in 1661 he toyed with the idea of a massive rebuilding of Whitehall which would render the entire structure in the likeness of Inigo Jones's banqueting house. These plans, however, were never more than a passing fancy. The lack of finances, the difficulty of displacing the courtiers who lodged in Whitehall, and perhaps an ambivalence towards making such an authoritarian statement dissuaded the king from any concrete moves towards a complete rebuilding of his main palace. Bold, 11, 145, 146.

**Table 1** Days of the year Charles spent in his principal residences

| Year | Whitehall | Hampton Court | Windsor | Newmarket | Winchester |
|------|-----------|---------------|---------|-----------|------------|
| 1661 | 359 | 1 | 3 | | |
| 1662 | 280 | 85 | | | |
| 1663 | 325 | | | | |
| 1664 | 361 | | | | |
| 1665 | 180 | 18 | | | |
| 1666 | 322 | | | | |
| 1667 | 365 | | | | |
| 1668 | 324 | 2 | | 10 | |
| 1669 | 325 | 12 | | 19 | |
| 1670 | 293 | | 18 | 33 | |
| 1671 | 298 | | 41 | 11 | |
| 1672 | 334 | | | 14 | |
| 1673 | 356 | | | | |
| 1674 | 259 | | 92 | 14 | |
| 1675 | 271 | | 66 | 18 | |
| 1676 | 336 | | | 26 | |
| 1677 | 332 | | 1 | 18 | |
| 1678 | 309 | | 41 | 11 | |
| 1679 | 258 | 2 | 79 | 17 | |
| 1680 | 191 | | 133 | | |
| 1681 | 183 | | 131 | 34 | |
| 1682 | 177 | 4 | 130 | 48 | |
| 1683 | 176 | | 127 | 36 | 24 |
| 1684 | 173 | 3 | 139 | 22 | 25 |

quarters,[21] but, upon his accession, Charles did neither: he allowed the few orders regulating access that he issued to be ignored and gave out keys to his lodgings with reckless abandon. In 1661 alone, the royal locksmith received orders to cut over 150 double keys (which opened ordinary doors in the palace and the staterooms) and at least ten treble keys or pipe keys (which opened the ordinary doors, staterooms, and the king's bedchamber).[22] Charles's contentment with Whitehall lasted only as long as he adhered to a policy of open access.

[21] Kevin Sharpe, *The Personal Rule of Charles I* (New Haven, CT: Yale University Press, 1992), 216. PRO LC 5/201, 38. BL ADD 5017, 8.
[22] PRO LC 5/137; orders to the locksmith were written in the back of the volume, unfoliated and in reverse.

## Away from the throng: Greenwich

In late 1662, spurred by a change in advisors and the failure of his attempts at unifying the disparate factions of his nation, Charles no longer strove to maintain open access. Deeming his accessibility as yielding only marginal results, he concentrated on his private pleasures.

In 1662, 1663, and 1664 the king stayed away from Whitehall for considerable periods of time, traveling to Bath, Oxford, and Tunbridge Wells; these trips were not royal progresses designed to present his person to his subjects outside of London, but rather vacations to escape the throngs at court.[23] As the lady Countess Dowager of Devonshire wrote to Lord Bruce in August of 1663, "the king goes his progress to the Bath with the Queen, the Duke, and Duchess of York. They design a very merry journey and yet no great court, for no carts are warned to come in, neither do I hear of any officers that are appointed to go."[24] Even at Whitehall, Charles kept his distance. The royal brewer reported to Pepys that the king was being "led away by half a dozen men, that none of his serious servants and friends can come at him."[25] The brewer also believed that the king's elimination of public dining days came not from a desire to save money as the administration claimed, but because the "crew that are about him will not have him come to common view again, but keep him obscurely to themselves."[26] The brewer must have lost considerable revenue due to the retrenchment of household expenses and his sentiments were no doubt sour grapes. But the king's decision not to appear as often in public, even if his primary reason was to save money, shows that he no longer placed a premium on displaying himself to or interacting with his subjects.

Charles's changing the location of his bedchamber in 1663 supports the assertion that the king was looking to avoid the crush of suitors.[27] Before 1663, the king's bedchamber was directly to the east of the Vane Room,[28] faced the privy garden, and was across the hall from the council chamber. This position was easily accessible by the privy and long galleries. The Galleries, the site of much of the king's art collection,[29] attracted strollers: Evelyn records that in September of 1663, "Being *casually* in the Privy Gallery at Whitehall, his Majestie gave me thanks before divers lords & noble men for my book of

---

[23] See Appendix.

[24] Ailesbury, 170–171 (August 21, 1663).

[25] Pepys, v, 56 (February 22, 1664).

[26] Ibid. For general discontent on taking tables away see Ailesbury, 170–171 (August 21, 1663); *HMC Finch*, Vol.1, 274 (September 3, 1663).

[27] Colvin found the first reference to the "king's new bedchamber" in January of 1664. Colvin, 267.

[28] The Vane Room served as the withdrawing-room. It got its name because it was below the weather vane.

[29] *London Survey*, xiii, 84.

Architecture and Sylva again,"[30] and Pepys often walked for hours on end in the hallways.[31] The bedchamber's proximity to so much traffic made reaching the entrance of the inner sanctum easy, and the identity of those who did so public knowledge.

As part of his general policy of restricting access in 1663, the king moved his bedchamber away from the privy gallery to the Turks gallery[32] (see Figure 1). Between the king's new bedchamber and the long gallery lay two ante-chambers which separated the king's private quarters from the traffic of the long gallery, enabling him to restrict access.

Charles was not satisfied with the moderate restriction of access he gained by remodeling Whitehall and taking short journeys to the countryside. He wanted a residence away from the bustle of central London, and in 1663 he began to build a new palace at Greenwich. John Webb, Inigo Jones's protege, drafted a design which, not surprisingly, celebrated the baroque image of monarchy. Like the plans drawn for Whitehall in 1661, the original plans for Greenwich Palace demonstrate a desire to show mastery over nature by creating a unified and geometric building in three ranges.[33] The existing Queen's House would be virtually ignored and serve merely as part of the prospect. Charles II, partly from a lack of funds but also partly due to a lack of desire to create such a baroque and absolutist statement, balked at such an ambitious project. His primary motivation for the new building was not to create a baroque image of grandeur, but to have a private get-away.[34] As such, he commanded Webb to change his plans, opting to incorporate the existing structure of the Queen's House into the palace. Because of the lack of unity of the new design, the building would have been less imposing than Webb's original conception.

Financial straits caused Charles first to slow down and then to bring an end to the construction of Greenwich Palace; Webb finished only one of the two new ranges and did not alter the Queen's House.[35] The single range, however, tells us a great deal about the kind of palace Charles was contemplating in 1663. The block relies "on large statements, emphatically made. The giant order is employed, with no sign of hesitancy at the centre and ends of the

---

[30] Evelyn, iii, 386 (September 28, 1664); emphasis added.

[31] In January, 1662/3 Samuel Pepys reported that he went "to White-hall where I spent a little time walking among the courtiers, which I perceive I shall be able to do with great confidence, being now beginning to be pretty well known among them" (iv, 1). For another example see Pepys viii, 591 (December 27, 1667). Even after Charles II moved his bedchamber away from the two corridors, traffic in the galleries was so dense that the king felt the need to restrict entrance to the privy gallery ( PRO LC 5/140, May 13, 1673).

[32] Colvin, 267.

[33] Colvin, 141.

[34] For an alternate interpretation see Simon Thurley, "A Country Seat Fit for a King."

[35] The range still exists and now houses the University of Greenwich.

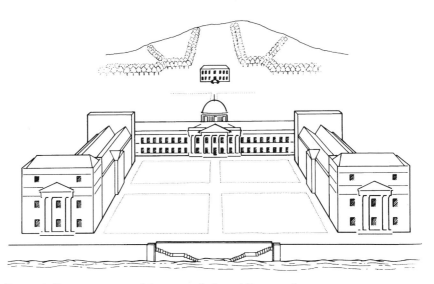

**Figure 2** Reconstruction of the original plan of Greenwich

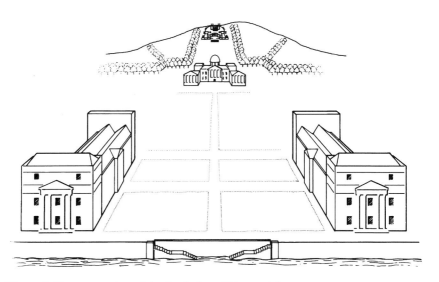

**Figure 3** Reconstruction of the final plan of Greenwich

**Figure 4** King Charles building, Greenwich

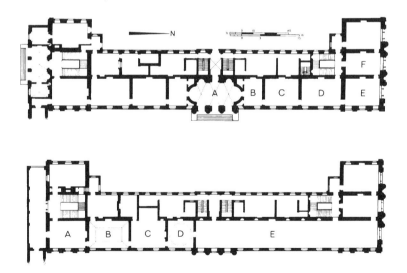

**Figure 5** Greenwich Palace interior
*Top*: Ground floor. A Entrace vestibule; B Waiting room; C Anteroom; D Dining-room; E Withdrawing-room; F Cabinet room. *Bottom*: First floor. A Presence chamber; B Privy chamber; C King's bedchamber; D Cabinet room; E Long gallery.

facade."[36] The size and grandeur of the block exudes confidence and stability (Figure 4). The range's exterior was created in conscious imitation of the Escorial's *estilo desornento*, and the interior reflects the Spanish regard for privacy.[37] Webb placed the staterooms *en suite* and *en filade*: entrance to one room could be obtained only by passing through the previous one (Figure 5). This arrangement would have limited the scurrying around that occurred at Whitehall thereby enhancing the king's ability to live privately.

Unfortunately, the Second Dutch War, the plague, and the fire diverted the king from this project. Furthermore, the closed access of these years gave birth to the perception that Charles disregarded his subjects. To remedy the situation, after the war, Charles turned to a policy of open access which obviated his need for a new building along the banks of the Thames.

## Accessibility and informality: Newmarket

Under the influence of the disparate advisors of the Cabal, Charles tried once again to represent himself to his people as an accessible king who would listen to their complaints and who was above the political fray. Charles altered his palaces, the regulation of access, and his pattern of residence in order to be more accessible and to project an imagery of informality and accessibility.

The construction of a new set of personal apartments for the king in the Volary buildings[38] (commenced in 1668) was one of the first concrete signs of Charles's return to a policy of open access.[39] For the remodeling

---

[36] Bold, 140.

[37] Rodríguez-Salgado, "The Court of Philip II of Spain" in Asch and Birke.

[38] So-called because the location had previously been the site of the king's aviary (Colvin, 269–270).

[39] Simon Thurley claims, by contrast, that Charles "was profoundly influenced by what he saw at the French court whilst living in Paris at the Louvre, and particularly by Louis XIV's use of his bedchamber as a pivotal room in public court ceremonial," and built this new bedchamber in order to "institute(d) a daily levee and receive(d) guests of distinction." Thurley's article does not have footnotes, and therefore the evidence upon which he bases his argument – other than Charles's choice of French furniture – is unclear (Simon Thurley, "The Lost Palace of Whitehall," *History Today*, January, 1988, 51. ) It is almost certain, however, that he was influenced by H. G. Baille's seminal article "Etiquette and the Planning of The State Apartments in Baroque Palaces." Baille muses that Charles II's practice of receiving in his bedchamber may "have been due to his stay in France, but also his policy of being accessible to as many people as possible" (Baille, *Archaeologia*, Vol. 101, 175). Charles may have been influenced by the relatively open access of the pre-1660 French court, but considering that Charles II lived in France during the midst of the Fronde, it is unlikely that he was inordinately impressed with French ceremonial. In fact English contemporaries do not refer to their king's rising as ceremonial or term it a "*levée*". According to the *OED*, the first appearance of the word "*levi*" occurs in John Dryden's *Marriage a la Mode* (1672). The characters in the play, however, use the word to

Charles chose Hugh May, a proponent of Dutch neo-classicism.[40] Dutch neo-classicism differed considerably from the contemporary French style. Dutch inspired architecture tended to be more bourgeois, more accessible, less grand, and less imposing than its French counterpart. John Summerson has described Dutch neo-classicism as "agreeable, easy, and economic to build." For instance, instead of using a grand columnar order to ornament a building, Dutch neo-classicist architects used a less powerful and less expensive pilaster.[41] With the hiring of May to design the bedchamber of his main palace, Charles harnessed the imagery of Dutch neo-classicism to his agenda of promoting himself as an accessible monarch.

The new bedchamber's location, as well as its design, enhanced Charles's ability to interact informally with his subjects. The Volary bedchamber was in close proximity to the queen's chamber (Figure 1). Charles, we can safely assume, did not move his bedchamber in order to be closer to his wife; rather, he was attracted to the new location because formal etiquette bound the

disparagingly describe the French court (Act II, i). On June 26, 1680 Henry Sidney took care to mention that he attended the king's risings, and after hearing the king was angry with him on June 22, noted that he dressed the king on June 24. But this care came from Sidney's position as master of the robe, not from any great concern on Charles II's part or Sidney's with the ceremonial of the levée (Henry Sidney, *Diary of the Times of Charles II*, ed. R. W. Blencowe (London: Henry Colburn, 1843), Vol. 2 of 2, 77, 206–207.) Evelyn attended the king in his bedchamber while he was dressing but it was to conduct business, not to take part in any particular ceremony. Specifically, Evelyn met with the king in his bedchamber on April 20, 1665 to discuss how to treat various prisoners of war and on October 14, 1670 to converse about his drafting a history of the Dutch War (Evelyn, iii, 406, 562). Although attending the king when he was dressing may have been a sign of intimacy, never is there a glimpse of the sort of ceremony which occurred surrounding Louis XIV's risings. James II, however, had *levées* (see *Diary of Dr Thomas Cartwright Bishop of Chester 1686–7*, Camden Society First Series (1843), p. 3 (October 7, 1686). Baille's other suggestion – that Charles II received people in his bedchamber as part of his policy of accessibility – carries more weight. Charles's choice of Hugh May as the architect in charge of the remodeling of Whitehall also contradicts Thurley's assertion of French influence. It is interesting to note that Thurley may have backed away from his assertion about Charles II's adoption of French ceremony. In his *Whitehall Palace* (106–111) Thurley claims that in 1661 Charles, influenced by the French use of the bedchamber as a ceremonial focal point, arranged for a bed with a canopy and rails to be placed in the bedchamber. In this work, however, Thurley never directly claims that Charles actually used the bedchamber in a manner similar to the French kings.

[40] Eltham House, his first work (completed in 1662), is distinctively akin to Van Campen's *Mauritshuis*. John Summerson, *Architecture in Britain 1530–1830* (New Haven, CT: Yale University Press, 1993), 173.

[41] Summerson, 173. For more on Dutch neo-classicism see Katherine Fremantle, *The Baroque Town Hall of Amsterdam* (Utrecht: Haentjens, Dekker & Gumbert, 1959); J. J. Terwin, "The Buildings of Johann Maurits van Nassau" in *Johan Maurits van Nassau-Siegen, 1604–1679*, ed. E. van de Boogaart (The Hague: Johan Maurits van Nassan Stichting, 1979); Jacobine Huiskèn, *Jacob van Campen: The Classical Ideal in the Golden Age* (Amsterdam: Architectura and Natura Pers, 1995).

monarch less in the queen's suite than in his own chambers. Ambassadors, whose meetings with the king in state apartments were particularly governed by protocol, frequented the queen's chamber to meet with the king in a less regulated setting. In the two years following the king's move, the Venetian ambassador mentioned four specific times when he conversed with the king in the queen's chambers and one time when the French ambassador spoke to the king in the queen's chambers.[42]

The new chamber also abutted the Thames and the privy stairs. This location allowed the king to invite people to see him in secrecy. Visitors, virtually unseen, could take a boat to the privy stairs on the banks of the Thames and then proceed to the King's bedchamber with only William Chiffinch and the other pages of the backstairs being aware of it.[43] A number of unsavory people entered this way,[44] and one wonders if Sir Balthazar Gerbier had Whitehall in mind when he claimed "In some Palaces and Noble-mens Houses, Too many staires and back doores (as the old English Proverb) makes Thieves and Whores."[45] Besides providing easy access for his nocturnal adventures, the move to the Thames-side apartments allowed Charles II to restrict the press of people seeking him, without narrowing the range of people whom he could see informally.

Such a presentation of a more accessible and informal majesty coincided with the beginning of the king's visits to Newmarket in 1668 (See Table 1). He delighted in Newmarket because the relaxed formality of the extended hunting trip allowed him to interact more intimately with his subjects. Sir John Reresby later recorded that

> The king was so much pleased in the country, and so great a lover of the diversions which that place did afford, that he let himself down from majesty to the very degree of a country gentleman. He mixed himself amongst the crowd, *allowed every man to speak to him that pleased*, went a hawking in mornings, to cock matches in the afternoons (if there were no horse races) and to plays in the evening, acted in a barn and by very ordinary Bartholomew fair comedians.[46]

---

[42] *CSPV*, vol. 35, 227–230; vol. 36, 57, 78, 87, 154.

[43] During the exclusion crisis the king kept up ties with the opposition by seeing them in this secretive manner. Knights, 351; David Allen, "The Political Function of Charles II's Chiffinch," *Huntington Lib. Q*, 39 (1976), 286–287. According to Allen, Chiffinch did not act on his own initiative, allowing only those people whom the king specifically asked for to be brought to the king through the backstairs. Allen, 287–288.

[44] *HMC Bath*, 169.

[45] Balthazar Gerbier, *A Brief Discourse Concerning the Three Chief Principles of Magnificent Building* (London: 1662), 14. The supposition that Gerbier was thinking about Whitehall is supported by the fact that the next sentence in his tract refers directly to Whitehall.

[46] John Reresby, added 259; emphasis *Memoirs*, ed. Andrew Browning (Glasgow: Jackson, 1936).

Charles, in effect, mixed freely among his subjects, as he had done when he disguised himself after the Battle of Worcester.[47]

The king's desire to appear familiar with his subjects helps explain his choice to live in a house which was not fit for a king. When Evelyn visited Newmarket on July 22, 1670, he admired the arches which William Samwell had designed in the cellars, but he considered the rest of the house "meane enough, & hardly capable for a hunting house." What particularly irked Evelyn was the house's location, "plac'd in a dirty streete; without any court or avenue, like a common Burgers; whereas it might and Ought to have been built at either end of the Towne, upon the very Carpe, where the sports are celebrated."[48] What seemed beneath a monarch's dignity to Evelyn was to Charles a chance for informality and openness. His subjects appear to have responded to this openness; petitioners acted on the impression that they would receive a favorable reception at Newmarket.[49]

## Decorum, dignity and hierarchy: Windsor

In 1673, prompted by the Earl of Danby, Charles turned decisively towards a politics of partisanship. In doing so he slowly moved away from his adherence to open access. Open access was a valuable tool to create a society in which disparate factions and conflicting ideologies could co-exist peacefully. By allowing various interest groups to believe that they could communicate with the king, open access decreased the desperation of those out of power and encouraged them to wait for the tides to turn in their favor. Charles's switch in 1673 from endeavoring to create a coalition of Presbyterians and Anglicans to leading the royalist Anglicans in their suppression of nonconformity obviated the need for open access. Now, Charles restricted access to send a message that he would no longer brook opposition and to reassert the court's place as a symbol of order, an ideal very close to the royalist-Anglican heart.[50]

---

[47] It is no mere coincidence that Newmarket was the site where Charles II dictated his account of the escape to Pepys.

[48] Evelyn, July 22, 1670.

[49] I have found a large number of instances where subjects pressed their suits at Newmarket. Norf. RO WKC 7/6/68, 7/6/69; King's Lynn RO MRFO 430/2, March 13, 1681; *HMC Rutland*, vol. II, 69 (April 10, 1682); *HMC Ormonde*, September 29, 1679; *HMC Kenyon*, 411, September 5, 1681; *HMC Fleming*, 171 (September 18, 1680); BL EG 3338. I have also found two cases of individuals going to be healed for the king's evil; see Corie, *Correspondence*, 12; Rye, *Extracts*, 16 January 1674/5.

[50] Caroline Hibbard has characterized Anglican views as emphasizing "harmony, decorum, unity through conformity and proper hierarchy" ("The Theatre of Dynasty" in *The Stuart Court and Europe*, ed. M. Smuts (Cambridge: Cambridge University Press, 1996), 170).

Charles's first step was to bring decorum and order to the maze of Whitehall. On May 13, 1673, Lord St. Albans, the Lord Chamberlain,[51] sent warrants to the ushers.[52] These warrants proclaimed the king's dissatisfaction with the lack of regulation in his household; they particularly emphasized that the ease of entry into his privy gallery led to "indecencies and inconveniences." The privy galleries teemed with people who did not belong. The staterooms were consequently empty. The new warrants tried to remedy the situation by insisting that "the way be by his guard chamber, presence and privy chamber." To ensure that no one disobeyed these orders, the king commanded that stock locks be placed on "all the doors that have entrance into the said galleryes" and that a gentleman usher of the privy chamber constantly guard the privy gallery.

A concern to ensure dignity and order emerges from these warrants. Restricting access to the privy gallery would increase the king's dignity both by preventing the disorderly wandering about that occurred there and by rendering the state chambers, which were designed to inspire a sense of the king's majesty, a place of concourse.[53] To encourage courtiers to frequent the staterooms, the king charged specifically that the chambers be cleansed of all unpleasant odors.[54] In order to endow these staterooms with the favorable aura of exclusivity, Charles commanded

> that the footmen of all persons be prohibited to come in as sometimes they have done and that all pages are to stay in the guard chamber and to come no further and no strangers that have not the appearance of gentlemen or the knowing by some of the court are to be suffered to pass into the house.[55]

The warrants of 1673 were not the only instance of Charles's endeavoring to establish a more orderly household. The following year, Charles urged for more decorum in the chapel and at public healings.[56] For the next five years, Charles issued a number of ordinances designed to ensure propriety

---

[51] The Lord Chamberlain was the chief officer of the household above stairs and "responsible for the ceremonial, social and artistic life of the monarch and his court." J.C. Sainty and R.O. Bucholz, *Officials of the Royal Household, 1660–1837* (London: University of London Press, 1997), vol. I, xxii.

[52] PRO LC 5/140, 248–249.

[53] The warrant to the gentleman ushers of the privy chamber enjoins the "reducement of the privy gallery to some order," and the warrant to the gentleman ushers' daily waiters voices a concern for the "dignity of his house" (ibid.).

[54] "That you appoint that in the guard chamber there be noe tobacco taken in smoke that there be noe ill savour of beere or any thing else for the inconvenience of the passages that way out that in the morning the doors and windows be left open and some thing burnt in the roome to take away the scent of the watch of the night" (ibid.).

[55] Ibid.

[56] LC 5/140, 453 (March 13, 1673/4), 492.

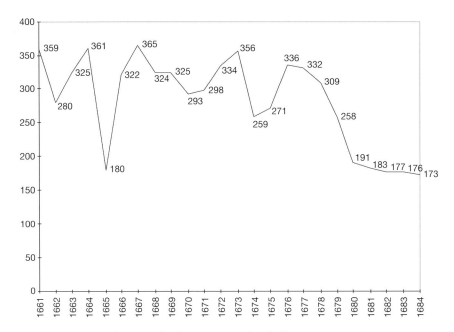

**Figure 6** Days of the year Charles spent at Whitehall

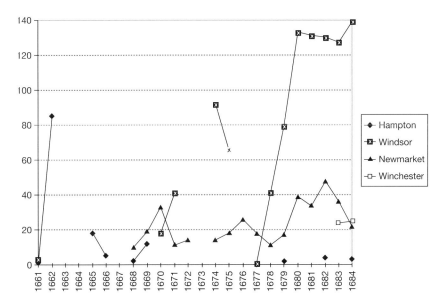

**Figure 7** Days of the year Charles spent at other principal residences

and order[57] in the palace, culminating in a systematic set of protocols issued in 1679.[58] Whitehall, however, was ill suited to restricting access to the king and to creating an environment of order, decorum, and grandeur. To remedy this situation, Charles spent progressively more time away from Whitehall.

Figures 6 and 7 chart the monarch's pattern of residence. They demonstrate that around 1673, Charles decided to spend less time in London. Certain factors beyond the king's control influenced where Charles chose to stay. The realities of early modern plumbing meant that the king could not stay in one place for too long.[59] Plague meant that Charles II spent much of 1665 in places such as Isleworth, Salisbury, and Oxford. During times of war and when Parliament was in session, the king needed to stay close to London. Furthermore, he could not reside at palaces which were undergoing construction, which explains his absence from Windsor in 1676 and 1677. With these caveats in mind, the alteration in the king's pattern of residence becomes starker. While London was growing ever more popular, Charles began to disassociate himself from city life.

Charles II's improvements to Windsor underscore his shift towards a more distant style of governing, access, and communication. Charles made his first extended trip to Windsor in 1670. According to the *Gazette*, the king was "extremely satisfied with the pleasantness of that princely seat," and he returned the following year.[60] The third Dutch War prevented the king from returning until 1674, when, after an extended stay, he decided to remodel the castle extensively.

Hugh May, appointed comptroller of Windsor in 1673,[61] oversaw the construction. May's work in 1674 and 1675 – while having some elements which encouraged interaction with the king – made significant steps towards securing order. The layout of the Windsor rooms resembled the royal apartments of Whitehall in 1668 (Figure 8). The king's chamber abuts the queen's chamber and the backstairs borders the King's closet. This arrangement facilitated Charles II's ability to meet people informally.[62] The state rooms, however, were designed *en suite* (although not *en filade*). This design regulated access by acting as "a linear filter," thereby allowing only three ways to reach the king.

The outdoor appearance of May's additions was very austere. The undecorated style clashed with the gothic appearance of the castle, but also

---

[57] PRO LC 5/141, 2, 24, 26, 30, 35, 298, 317, flyleaf.

[58] See my "A Call for Order," *The Court Historian* 6:2 (September 2001): 151–156.

[59] BL ADD 36988.

[60] Girouard, 28. For similar sentiments in 1674 see Colvin, 316.

[61] Although his appointment pre-dates Charles II's formal decision to refurbish Windsor, the king was probably already considering remodeling the castle when he gave May the post.

[62] Portsmouth, the king's mistress, had lodgings immediately underneath the king's which were easily reachable by the backstairs.

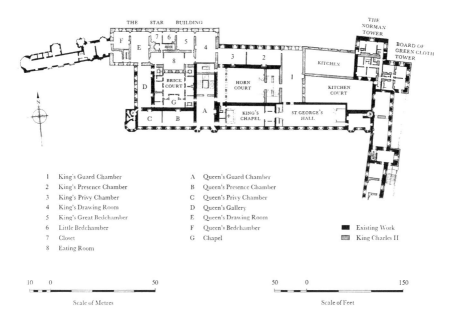

| 1 | King's Guard Chamber | | A | Queen's Guard Chamber |
|---|---|---|---|---|
| 2 | King's Presence Chamber | | B | Queen's Presence Chamber |
| 3 | King's Privy Chamber | | C | Queen's Privy Chamber |
| 4 | King's Drawing Room | | D | Queen's Gallery |
| 5 | King's Great Bedchamber | | E | Queen's Drawing Room |
| 6 | Little Bedchamber | | F | Queen's Bedchamber |
| 7 | Closet | | G | Chapel |
| 8 | Eating Room | | | |

■ Existing Work
▨ King Charles II

10  0 — 50
Scale of Metres

50  0 — 150
Scale of Feet

**Figure 8** Plan of Windsor Castle

reflected Charles's residual discomfort with presenting himself as a baroque monarch.[63] By 1676, however, Charles had become an avid proponent of splendid display; he hired Antonio Verrio and Grinling Gibbons to decorate Windsor's interior. This pair designed grandiose rooms decorated with conscious ostentation. George IV remodeled the castle and little of Verrio's work survives today, but plates in W. H. Pyne's *Royal Residences* display portions of the Italian artist's paintings. The architectural historian Mark Girouard describes these paintings as importing the "new baroque techniques of apotheosis" and "launching Charles II on clouds of glory in its ceiling."[64] Contemporaries also thought that Verrio presented the king as divine. James Yonge, who saw Verrio at work, described the deification of the king on Windsor's ceilings. Yonge called the staterooms "the finest in nature, most incomparably furnisht and painted. Many rooms that were high and archt had the king, queen and misses, pictured in chariots in the clouds, as were the gods of the heathen."[65] Yonge does not record that he saw any allegorical message in the paintings, but it seems that they did more than vaguely identify the monarch with the divine.

[63] His recent lack of success in controlling Parliament would cure him of any delusions of absolute power (Hutton, *Charles II*, 280–320).
[64] Girouard, 31.
[65] Yonge, 171–172.

Unfortunately, Pyne's watercolors do not show us all the detail of Verrio's work. In particular, the watercolor of the king's presence chamber depicts the room from a perspective which hides the ceiling. This is particularly unfortunate because Pyne describes the ceiling as "an allegorical representation of the re-establishment of the Church of England, on the restoration of Charles II in personifications of England, Scotland, and Ireland attended by faith, hope and charity. Religion is seen triumphing over superstition and hypocrisy, who are driven from the face of the church."[66] Anyone familiar with religious polemics of the time would identify superstition with the Roman Catholic Church and hypocrisy with the nonconformists.[67] The placement of this picture in the presence chamber demonstrates a claim that Charles would no longer tolerate either Catholics or radical Protestants to enter into his presence. This symbolic message had some teeth; as of November, 1674 Charles prohibited Roman Catholics from having access to his person, court, and its precinct.[68]

At the time when Verrio and Gibbons were completing their work at Windsor, Charles II issued systematic ordinances regulating access to his household.[69] The orders, issued a few days or weeks before March 8, 1679, were not simply a collation of existing practices, but rather a mandate for reform. The ordinances refer to specific problems which they aim to rectify. For instance, after citing "a very great indecence and irreverance [which] hath been committed of late by a throng of persons that assemble there [in the chapel] and talk aloud, and walke in time of service," the king commanded that none presume to walk or talk there in time of divine service under penalty of banishment from court.[70] Each change in practice that the protocols commanded had the same thrust: to restore dignity and order to the court.

To this end the new ordinances both stiffened the rules and strengthened the means of restricting access. Previously, "strangers who have not the knowledge of someone of the court" could not enter the presence and privy chambers.[71] Now, only "gentlemen of quality as are fit to have access to that

---

[66] W. H. Pyne, *History of the Royal Residences* (London: 1817).

[67] It is tempting to believe that Pyne refrained from showing this painted ceiling (the only one missing in his collection) because he did not want to reproduce such a cry for persecution.

[68] *HMC Fleming*, 166 (November 3, 1674).

[69] Stowe, 562. The Ordinances contained in BL Stowe, 562 are printed in *A Collection of Ordinances and Regulations for the Government of the Royal Household* (London: 1790). These orders are generally thought to have been issued in the first decade of the king's reign and are therefore considered to be just a compilation of existing practice. As I demonstrate in "A Call for Order," however, the orders were issued in 1679, and therefore were issued to reform existing practice.

[70] *Ordinances*, 358.

[71] LC 5/140, 248–249.

chamber" gained admittance to the presence chamber. The privy chamber was open solely to those qualified by place and to gentlemen of quality who came *specifically* to address the king, but not to "idle persons." Furthermore, the gentleman ushers were commanded "to take continuall and especiall notice of all persons being within the said chamber, and in case they shall perceive any person not meete or worthy to be therein they shall incontinently expell and avoyd him for the same."[72] The king realized that "Execution is the life" of these regulations; he therefore made the regulations not only more rigorous, but also easier to enforce.

Previously, household regulations had been vague and indeterminate; the question of who could enter was left largely to the judgement of the gentleman ushers and other court functionaries. Ushers who had no specific orders were susceptible to making an exception for those who cajoled, pressured, or pleaded entrance. The new orders listed specifically who could enter the privy chamber[73] and, like bouncers scanning a list at a nightclub, ushers could refuse admittance simply by pointing to the orders which were now posted in each of the staterooms.

The king also made structural changes in his main palace to enable the ushers to better perform their duties. He issued new locks for Whitehall and, in contrast to his laxity in 1661, vigilantly controlled who had keys.[74] Furthermore, he ordered a new building to be erected which connected the Vane Room to the Volary buildings.[75] Before this connection existed, it was impossible to proceed continuously through the staterooms to the king's bedchamber; courtiers could justify taking a variety of approaches to reach the king. Now anyone who wished to reach the king needed to transverse the guard, presence, and privy chambers as well as a number of withdrawing-

---

[72] *Ordinances*, 355.

[73] The order read, "No person of what estate or condition soever shall presume to come into Our Privy Chamber, but the Nobility and privy councellors, our servants of our bedchamber, our servants of our privy chamber, the gentlemen ushers daily wayters, querries, officers of our guards, and such who by the duty of their places are to attend us in our privy lodgings, and servants of like rank and quality that attend our dearest consort the queen, our dear brother and sister the duke and dutchesse of York, and our deare cousin Prince Rupert, when they attend their person; or such other persons whom we have *particular* business with at that time, our clerks of our councill, officers of our navy or army *who have occasion to attend us for our service*, master of our ceremonies, Master of Request, physicians, or any gentleman of good ranke and note who have *occasion to addresse themselves unto us*; but no meane, idle, or unknown persons shall be permitted to passe into the privy chamber upon any pretence whatsoever" (*Ordinances*, 361; emphasis added).

[74] The king allowed only himself, the groom of the stool, the gentlemen of the bedchamber-in-waiting, the groom of the bedchamber-in-waiting and Mr. Chiffinch to have possession of treble keys. PRO LC 5/143 January 24, 1677/8, 11–31.

[75] PRO LC 5/143, 194.

rooms and antechambers.[76] At the door of each chamber, ushers could weed out those who did not belong.

The new ordinances sought to reform not only admittance to the state-rooms, but also the behavior of courtiers within those rooms. The king wished to abolish the laxity which previously marked the court. In particular, the new ordinances call for an end to courtiers displaying contemptuous familiarity with the king or with symbols of his authority. The new ordinances enjoined the gentleman ushers to

> reprove all such as shall be so hardy as to behave themselves unreverently before us, either in speech or action in pressing too near our person, or approaching the state, or to sit down upon the stooles or foot stooles under our state or leane upon the same . . . no person of what degree soever shall presume to stand under our cloth of estate or upon the half pace; or to leane upon the table, or upon the cupboard, nor to sitt after the salt is upon the table . . . and when we are at table no man shall presume to tread upon the carpet or half pace.[77]

Such commands seem somewhat out of place in our picture of the restoration court of wits and ribalds, but, in the midst of the exclusion crisis,[78] Charles, in imitation of his father, embarked on a crusade to use distance and a reassertion of hierarchy to generate respect for the monarchy.[79] Like the hierarchical structure of the masque which Charles I so favored, where "the closer one sat to the monarch the better one's place was, an index to one's status, and more directly to the degree of favor one enjoyed,"[80] The ordinances command

> that in our going and coming thence all men keep their rankes orderly and distinctly and not break them with pretence of speaking one with another, or for any other occasion whatsoever; but proceed both for our honour and their owne reputation that being one of the most eminent and frequent occasions whereby mens ranks in precedency are distinguished and discerned.[81]

---

[76] A warrant for furnishing the state apartments issued in April, 1682 lists the following rooms as part of the staterooms: presence chamber, privy chamber, lords room, Fane [vane] Room, new withdrawing-room, anteroom to the bedchamber, eating room, bedchamber, room within the king's bedchamber, stool room, room between the old bedchamber closets on the garden side. PRO LC 5/144, 213.

[77] *Ordinances*, 358.

[78] James, Duke of York was sent in exile to Brussels in February, 1679.

[79] This policy of Charles coincided with his political moves. see Hutton, *Charles II*, 366–368.

[80] Stephen Orgel, *The Illusion of Power* (Berkeley: University of California Press, 1991), 10. The attempt to pattern his court after his father's was conscious. The king told Lord Arlington in 1682 that he "would have [his] bedchamber governed by the rules and practice of the king [his] father of blessed memory" (PRO LC 5/201, 15).

[81] *Ordinances*, 358.

Charles II, for the first time in his reign, endeavored to create a court whose actions reminded participants of the nation's hierarchical structure, his position at the top of that structure, and the distance between him and his subordinates.

The protocols exhibit a realization that the barriers which monarchs create between themselves and their subjects tend to erode under the constant press of courtiers. The discussion of the regulations of the privy chamber, for instance, is prefaced with the statement "we find it [the privy chamber] much changed from the antient institution."[82] To prevent an erosion of his new regulations, the king created mechanisms to insure their resiliency. The order that the protocols be posted in all of the staterooms endowed these regulations with the fixity of writing. In case no one bothered to read the posted regulations, the king ordered that the protocols be read aloud twice a year in each stateroom and that transcripts of the book of orders be issued to all the head officers of the chamber and household.[83] The matter was not left to household officials. The final paragraph of the ordinances commanded that the Privy Councilors send for the books of orders and "note, search, and examine, whether there hath been any default in due executing the contents; and that found, shall proceed to the reformation, correction and punishment, of such as shall be found culpable or negligent therein."[84]

Charles appointed officers dedicated to implementing strict access and enhancing the dignity of the monarch. Henry Bennet, Earl of Arlington, had served as Lord Chamberlain since September, 1674. Bennet's prior tenure as resident in Spain (1657–1661) deeply influenced his outlook of how a court should be organized; at the court of Philip IV he acquired a strong respect for stateliness, magnificence, order, and decorum.[85] Charles II probably knew Henry Savile's predilection for strict access from his service as a groom of the bedchamber, first for the Duke of York and then for the king.[86] Savile was also the prime mover behind an order restricting the access of foreign ambassadors to the king. In 1679 Savile, while serving as an envoy to France, wrote to the Secretary of State complaining that "ministers from hence (France) have liberty of all hours and all places in Whitehall and those from thence (England) must go fifteen miles to stay two days for an audience."[87]

---

[82] *Ordinances*, 360.

[83] Arlington sent a transcript to Henry Savile, then Vice-chamberlain. PRO SP 29/421 pt.3, 66.

[84] *Ordinances*, 365.

[85] Bennet may have been influenced by the favorable treatment he received in Madrid. Spain provided Bennet with a house, coach, and ten horses, grand courtesy for a representative of a king without a country (Violet Barbour, *Henry Bennet Earl of Arlington Secretary of State to Charles II* (Washington: AHA, 1914), 29–46).

[86] Savile served from 1673 to 1680 as a groom of the bedchamber. He did lose his position for two months in 1678 after voting in favor of Lauderdale's removal.

[87] BL Trumbull 71, 17.

Savile couched his complaint in terms of protecting the dignity of Charles II. When read at the Privy Council, Savile's letter produced applause. It also produced a declaration by the King in Council that curtailed the rights of foreign ministers to enter into the king's presence. Foreign envoys were allowed to speak to the king only if they both obtained an appointment from the Master of Ceremonies and informed one of the Secretaries of State of the business to be discussed the night before any such meeting. Savile's part in producing this order may have prompted the king to appoint him as Vice-chamberlain instead of the three lords who asked for the position.[88]

Prompted by the administrative competency of Arlington and Savile, the ushers pursued the protocol of 1679 vigilantly until the end of Charles II's reign. The warrant books during Arlington's tenure give evidence of his dedication to the restoration of order to Whitehall.[89] The Lord Chamberlain required a work schedule so that he could check the attendance of all his subordinates[90] and he quickly dismissed those who failed to perform their duties.[91] Regulation, order, and enforcement had become a priority of Charles's administration.

## Towards a Baroque monarchy:
## Winchester

The full blossoming of a Baroque monarchy, the buds of which we can see in Verrio's work at Windsor and the protocols of 1679, came only after the exclusion crisis. After 1681, the king was not only trying to create a court which echoed the desires of Royalist-Anglican stalwarts, but he also wished to use splendor, hierarchy, and distance to inspire awe in his subjects.

The extent to which the restriction of access became a paramount concern of the administration is shown by a dispute between the Lord Chamberlain Arlington and the groom of the privy stool the Earl of Bath, mentioned at the beginning of the chapter. Arlington, despite orders existing since 1678, had never in the previous four years been refused entrance to the bedchamber. In fact, the orders were enforced so rarely that Arlington could credibly claim that he had never even heard of these orders, even though they were posted in the withdrawing-room. By refusing Arlington admittance, the groom of the bedchamber insulted the Lord Chamberlain, implying that he could not be counted among the king's intimate friends. The groom's willingness to offend the still powerful Arlington indicates that the king and the groom

---

[88] *Savile Correspondence*, 89, 160–169; CSPD, vol. 21, 142 (May 11, 1679).
[89] Arlington was greatly impressed by the Spanish court which was noted for its order and decorum.
[90] LC 5/143, 175 (October 25, 1678); 412 (December 18, 1679).
[91] PRO LC 5/143, 422 (November 25, 1679).

of the stool were exerting considerable pressure upon the ushers to be especially circumspect in their decisions of whom they allowed to enter.

Arlington did not take this insult lying down. He petitioned the king for redress, demanding financial satisfaction for the injury to his reputation and asking that the king change the orders for the bedchamber which Arlington deemed an "abridgement of the best part of his [the Chamberlain's] privileges, and jurisdiction of his office and [tending] . . . to the disturbance of your service."[92] The plea was brought before a committee of the Privy Council which held hearings on the matter.

In the hearings held by the subcommittee of the Privy Council appointed to resolve this dispute, Arlington relied on custom and logic. He brought numerous septuagenarians to testify that during Charles I's reign, the Lord Chamberlain had free access to the king's chamber as symbolized by the gold treble key that the Lord Chamberlain customarily wore. The Earl of Bath, the groom of the stool, who was in charge of the bedchamber and the target of Arlington's suit, responded identically to every one of Arlington's arguments. In his introductory remarks Bath stated

> that all orders of . . . all former kings cease with their persons and are no further binding . . . and tho' they may be of use to your majesty, yet they are no rule of obedience to your servants, unless they receive a new life from your majesty.[93]

Each time Arlington invoked custom, Bath read a passage from the book of orders regulating the bedchamber. By doing so the groom of the stool underscored his assertion that the king was not bound by custom, but made customs and rules at his whim. Arlington's argument, on the other hand, suggested that the king needed to consider custom and the coherence of regulations before he acted and that custom overrode the pleasure of the king. Bath and Arlington were forced into these positions by the circumstances of their respective cases. Nevertheless, it is interesting to note that Bath – who in this instance proposed a more restrictive policy of access – inclined to a vision of the king as arbitrary in both the early modern and modern sense of that term. In Bath's view the king could issue edicts without regard to the coherence of law or custom. Although generally a proponent of closed access, Arlington, when he argued that the king should allow the Lord Chamberlain to enter the royal presence, inclined to a conception of the monarch bound by law and custom. There appears to have been an alignment in early modern minds between arbitrary government and closed access.

The privy councilors who decided this case were guided by the king's dictum that his court should be "governed by the *rules* and *practice* of the king [his] father of blessed memory."[94] The problem, of course, was that the

---

[92] PRO LC 5/201, 15–16.
[93] PRO LC 5/201, 17.
[94] PRO LC 5/201, 25; emphasis added.

rules differed from the practices. The privy councilors acted as good trimmers should.[95] Practice was on the side of Arlington, rules on the side of Bath. Theoretically they agreed with Arlington's vision that the king should adhere to custom, and that he ought to allow a certain amount of openness at court. However, they sensed which way the wind was blowing, that the king was endeavoring to create a Baroque image of monarchy, and therefore found in favor of Bath.[96]

The center of this creation of an image of Baroque grandeur was to be the king's new palace at Winchester. Contemporaries and historians have wondered at Charles II's decision to build a new palace at Winchester in 1682. Evelyn understood that the king's haste to complete the project came from a desire to replace Newmarket, which had been partially destroyed by fire in 1683, as the site of his "Autumnal diversions." But Charles, as Evelyn knew, had begun building Winchester before fire destroyed Newmarket and the scope of the new palace far exceeded the needs of a hunting lodge. When Defoe visited the uncompleted shell of the building he also saw Winchester as a replacement for Newmarket, but suggests that Charles II meant the new palace to serve as a summer home. This is unlikely because the king had just expended a huge amount of money on Windsor to equip it for that very purpose. Whig historians have seen a more sinister motivation, looking to Winchester's proximity to France as the reason for the king's choice of site.[97]

French influence certainly played a role in the construction of Winchester. Charles II wanted his hunting lodge of Winchester to resemble Louis XIV's hunting lodge of Versailles. The palace, if completed, would have played a crucial part in his assumption of a baroque and authoritarian style of rule. Wren and Charles created Winchester with a location, design, and layout meant to generate respect and awe as well as to alter significantly the patterns of communication and access between king and subject.

---

[95] Halifax, author of *Character of a Trimmer*, was a member of this committee.

[96] The Council reported to the king that they were "humbly of the opinion that the evidence produced by the Lord Chamberlain and proofs of the practice in all former times as to the point of coming into the bedchamber without leave are very material and strong in his favor, even in the house of the king your royal father, but that the books of the bedchamber produced by [Bath] in the year 1661 signed by your majesty countersigned by [Bath] and asserted by Mr. Secretary Nicholas to have been transcribed from the old books doe exclude generally all persons whatsoever except the princes of the blood, and such are sworne of the bedchamber which orders have been confirmed by subsequent orders of your majesty made in the year 1678 excluding among others [of] the great officers the Lord Chamberlain by name. We think it [our] duty at the same time to observe to your majesty that the above mentioned books of orders made in 1661 have been but rarely put in practice as to the particulars now controverted since the time of their being constituted and that they do likewise contain several paragraphs relating to the aforesaid particulars which we find to be unusual and not agreeable to constant practice" (PRO LC 5/201, 74).

[97] *Wren Society VII: The Royal Palaces of Winchester, Whitehall, Kensington and St James 1660–1715* (Oxford: 1930), 11. Summerson, 223.

The location of Winchester carried many attractions for the king. It was near the sea which allowed him to exercise his second greatest passion: sailing. It had beautiful views and scenery and it was close to horse-races.[98] The main attractions, however, lay in its historical significance and its distance from London.

Winchester's historical significance separated it from other sites in England. Besides London, Winchester was one of the few cities able to claim that it had served as a capital. It had been the capital of the kingdom of Wessex and even in the eleventh century served as the location of the royal treasury. Winchester, furthermore, was associated strongly with King Arthur. Locals claimed that Winchester was the site of Camelot. While visiting Winchester, James Yonge recorded in his diary that "under a hill . . . is King Arthur's castle and the great hall where he and his knights used to dine. In the end of the said hall hangs a round table, said to be King Arthurs."[99] Charles II seemed eager to associate his new building with that history. He made sure that the new palace would occupy the exact location as had the medieval castle. This was no easy accomplishment. The purchase of the lands which contained the ruins of the castle cost £36,000 and removing the ruins required intensive labor. Receipts record that laborers were paid for "pulling down the East Wall of the castle, for digging, and wheeling away the foundation of the castle, throwing downe the wall of the west end of the countie hall . . . pulling down the north wall of the castle, and the black Tower, the east wall joining to the chappel, digging down the south east bulwark, the crown of the arch, at the north east tower, digging and wheeling away the call house wall, and a wall at the southeast angle of the keep to make way for the middle line."[100] Such care, along with the size and grandeur of the intended palace, suggests that Charles II meant for Winchester to be much more than a hunting lodge. He meant to create a new location from which royal authority could emanate and he chose Winchester because the spot had regal associations.

Charles intended to reside in Winchester for about half of each year. The size and cost of the project as well as the haste with which he urged on Wren all indicate that Charles placed a great deal of importance on the palace.[101] While Winchester was being built the king stayed twenty-four days in the Hampshire town in 1683 and twenty-five days in 1684. One can only assume that the king planned on spending more time in the finished palace than he

---

[98] Yonge comments, "The back part [of Winchester Palace] looks towards the plains which made the king love it." 193.

[99] Yonge, 193. According to Martin Biddle's *King Arthur's Round Table: An Archaeological Investigation* (Rochester, NY: Boydell & Brewer, 2000) the Table was built by Edward I – a fan of Arthurian literature – to celebrate the betrothals of his son and two daughters. Caxton in his 1485 Preface to the works of Mallory claimed that the round table was at Winchester, testifying to a common belief that it was the genuine article.

[100] Colvin, 309–310.

[101] See p. 25 above.

did viewing its construction. Furthermore, as the years progressed, Charles's trips to Newmarket increased in length and Charles spent more and more time away from Whitehall. If, as Evelyn and others claimed, Charles expected Winchester to replace Newmarket, we can assume that he meant to reside in Winchester at the same time of the year as his Newmarket journeys and for a greater duration.[102] The fact that Charles intended to spend most of the spring and fall at Winchester supports my contention that the new palace was to serve as his primary seat of authority.

The interior design of the palace also suggests that Charles meant for it to serve as his chief residence. Wren provided for a whole network of rooms for the administration. On the king's side of the palace the architect designed a council chamber complete with anteroom,[103] closet, and stairs and offices for the Secretaries of State.[104] Windsor by contrast lacked such an apparatus. When the king resided at Windsor he had to travel once a fortnight to Hampton Court in order for the Privy Council to meet. At Winchester, however, the architectural structure was well suited for meetings of the Privy Council and other administrative functions.

Making Winchester his primary residence may have increased the prestige of the king. Unlike London, where the king was no longer the sole focal point of social life,[105] in Winchester he would be the primary attraction. Winchester was eighty miles from London; this would have seriously altered the patterns of access. Local corporations and other interest groups often employed an intermediary who resided in London to interact with the king and Parliament; these agents would not be able to operate in Winchester. It would require at the very least a day of travel and lodging which would be very dear because of the influx of suitors.[106] Only those with important business would undertake a visit to the king. Winchester's relative inaccessibility would winnow away unwanted suitors.[107] Since to many contemporaries distance bred awe, by removing from the center of London, Charles may have attempted to convey the difference between king and subject.

---

[102] Charles tended to visit Newmarket in the early fall and spring (see Appendix). Sunderland intimated to Jenkins that Charles intended to come to Winchester twice a year (Colvin, 305).

[103] Interestingly Wren specified a clerk's seat in the anteroom, which allowed the council easily to hold closed sessions. In closed sessions only Privy Council members attended and minutes were not taken.

[104] *Wren Society*, 17.

[105] The development of theater and coffee houses created a public sphere where the king was not the sole focal point. Steven Pincus, "Coffee Politicians Does Create," *JMH* (December, 1995): 807–834.

[106] Such was the case at Windsor. Yonge, 171.

[107] When Charles traveled to Newmarket, equally distant from London, no such phenomenon occurred. Since the king rarely visited the Norfolk town for longer than two weeks, suitors could wait until he returned to London.

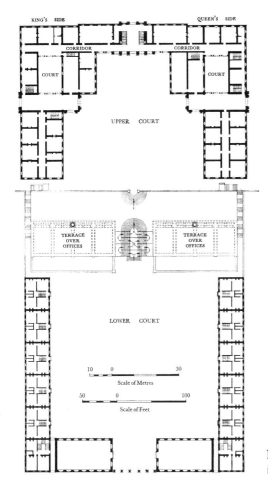

**Figure 9** Winchester interior

Once a suitor reached Winchester Palace, he would have encountered patterns of access different from other castles. Plans of the interior design of the palace survive (Figure 9), as does a description of accommodation, in Wren's hand, which lists the functions of rooms on the main floor of the castle. Unfortunately, the list does not refer to the plans, and any assignations of a certain room on the plans to a certain function on the list can be only guesswork.[108] Even from such scanty evidence, however, we can determine some of the effects the new palace would have on access. First, there appear to have been more rooms in the state and privy chambers of

---

[108] *Wren Society*, 13. Simon Thurley, however, has endeavored to assign rooms on the plan to the list. His assignations, while certainly plausible, do not seem conclusive. See Thurley, "A Country Seat Fit for a King: Charles II, Greenwich, and Winchester" in ed. *The Stuart Courts* Eveline Cruickshanks (Stroud, UK: Sutton, 2000), 233–235.

Winchester than in other palaces. In contrast to Windsor, which contained a guard chamber, presence chamber, privy chamber, withdrawing-room, great bedchamber, little bedchamber, and closet, Winchester had in addition a privy gallery, an anteroom, a lobby, a cabinet, and a dressing-room. If the staterooms in Winchester were to act as a linear filter as did those at Windsor, there were that many more stages where unwanted suitors could be detained while giving them the satisfaction of being allowed to enter the privy or even the withdrawing-room. Furthermore, Winchester featured the innovation of having the guard chamber separated from the rest of the staterooms by a grand staircase. This separation acted to differentiate clearly those allowed to enter the staterooms from those who were not. It furthermore conveyed a message of the king's superiority: to reach the sovereign a suitor had to ascend to a higher level.[109]

For the most part the palace's design enhanced distance and display at the expense of informal interaction. The one exception is the complex of rooms which Wren designed for the page of the backstairs.[110] Charles, always wishing to keeping his options open, wanted to preserve at least one way in which he could engage in informal meetings. Of course, the king had total control over who could and could not enter through the backstairs. Informal meetings were possible, but only at the king's behest; in his new palace, Charles would have controlled access to his person.

The exterior of the building was designed to project majesty (Figure 10). Wren's plans contain numerous staircases to underscore the idea of the king residing on a higher level. The idea of the loftiness of majesty was emphasized further by the altitude of the cupola which would have risen thirty feet above the roof and would have been seen from the English channel.[111] The palace was not only grandiose; it was also unified, symmetrical, and geometrical. It was constructed of right-angles and the whole complex makes up a rectangle. The main block is exactly 200 by 300 feet. It could also be viewed as inscribed in two 3–4–5 right triangles. In its geometricity and in its entire design, the palace resembles Versailles as it looked in the 1680s.

The Earl of Ailesbury in his memoirs records that Charles told him in 1685, "I shall be most happy this week for my building [Winchester] will be covered with lead." Ailesbury continues, "This was Sunday night and the Saturday following he was embalmed."[112] Charles II's program to create a baroque monarchy never reached fruition and any effects such a program would have had must be left to the realm of speculation. It is possible that by his removal to Winchester the king could have created a Versailles in England. Louis

---

[109] *Wren Society*, 17–19.

[110] Wren lists as separate rooms "The Inner roome of the Back Staires, the Waiting-roome of the Back Staire," and "Back Staires." *Wren Society*, 17.

[111] *Wren Society*, 15.

[112] HMC *Ailesbury*, 20.

**Figure 10** Winchester Palace as it would have looked if completed

XIV attracted local elites to move to Versailles and, in so doing, he severed them from their regional power base. But Charles's situation differed greatly from Louis's. He had neither the monopoly of patronage to attract potentates to Winchester nor the bureaucratic apparatus to replace local elites.[113] Furthermore, Winchester had to compete with the many attractions of London. Certainly, the rewards that the king could dole out and a desire to influence policy may have attracted many to Winchester in an attempt to influence the king or to catch his eye. But if access had been restricted to such a degree that most attempts to communicate with the king failed, then the king's adoption of a baroque style of governance could have just as easily have resulted in that bane of monarchs: an empty court.

[113] The bureaucratic apparatus such as the tax office and navy administration were still in their infancy.

# 3

## *The politics of access*

When he returned to England, Charles, moved by the experience of his exile and the promptings of his advisors, gave every indication that he would become one of England's most accessible kings. But for extended periods of his reign, Charles emulated his father's regard for distance, for to the king the regulation of access was neither a matter of preference nor an outcome of habit, but rather a political tool to be used to accomplish specific goals. As long as Charles believed that England was an organic entity, and that his realm was an inherent unity, he utilized open access to diffuse tension and to deflate factional warfare. When he recognized the depth of the political and religious divisions in his land, and began to think of the country not as a united whole but as an artificial construct, Charles opted to become a leader of one party, and therefore he allowed only those who supported his political agenda to enter into his presence, to communicate with him, and to act as conduits between center and locality, thereby hoping to bolster his supporters and dishearten his opponents.

Charles's progress from affability to severity followed a serpentine path, for many factors besides his perception of English society came into play. Chapter 4 will narrate this journey to examine the role his advisors, short-term political goals, and historical events played in Charles's developing ideas on regulating access to his person. Charles changed his policies of access primarily to accomplish political goals, and this chapter will explore further the political ramifications of Charles's experimentation with access on the central and the local level.

### The restored king

When Charles returned to England in 1660 he was confronted with a host of disparate elements in society all wanting his favor. His companions in exile, royalists who stayed in England and suffered persecution, the Presbyterians who claimed to have brought him back, the Catholics who had helped him escape after the battle of Worcester, religious radicals who could rebel at any moment, and the armed forces all wanted the king to act in accordance with their agendas, and their agendas were often mutually exclusive. Charles sought to calm this disparate array through the employment of a policy of open access. For an accessible king lowers the stakes in factional warfare; with an accessible king, failure does not mean irrevocable loss, for another chance to sway the monarch will appear.[1] It is possible, therefore, for a king who is committed to an open access policy to rule with factions at court and Parliament and a variety of religions in the country.

The degree of affability which Charles showed shocked his contemporaries. The Venetian resident, Francisco Giavarini, reported to the Senate on July 23, 1660 that "His majesty stood uncovered, a formality not observed by any crown . . . but adopted by this king with everyone, whatever his character, for he excels all other potentates in humanity and affability."[2] John Evelyn described at length the king's openness which he observed at first hand:

> It was indeed intolerable as well as unexpressible, the greedinesse of all sorts, men, women and children to see his majesty & kisse his hands in so much as he had scarce leasure to eate for some dayes, coming as they did from all parts of the Nation: and the king on the other side as willing to give them that satisfaction, would have none kept out but gave free access to all sorts of people.[3]

After years of exile, the king was no doubt happy to see such rejoicing at his presence, but he also wanted his subjects to feel included in the new government.

His policies of access followed the council of his main advisors.[4] At the king's restoration a group led by the Earl of Southampton, Sir Edward Nicholas, Edward Hyde, and the Duke of Ormonde translated their virtual monopoly of the king's ear into places of power. For the first two years of the reign these allies maintained easy, constant, and privy access to the king. Before Privy Council meetings, Southampton and Clarendon met the king in private to set the agenda. During these meetings, Charles and the Lord Chancellor passed notes to each other. This subtler version of the classic whisper in the ear demonstrated Hyde's position as premier minister. The levity of some of these notes suggests further that Hyde and Charles enjoyed a close relationship, a relationship that belies our impression of the dour and gouty chancellor. When, for example, the king planned to meet his sister at Dover, Clarendon inquired, "I suppose you will go with a light trayne," Charles replied, "I intend to take nothing but my night bag." Somewhat taken aback the chancellor wrote, "You will not go without 40 or 50 horse!" To which the king answered, "I counted that part of my night bag."[5] The closeness of the relationship was perceived by others and influenced their actions. The king's cousin, Prince Rupert, refrained from writing a letter of

---

[1] Derek Hirst, "Court, Country and Politics before 1629," in Kevin Sharpe (ed.) *Faction in Parliament* (Oxford: Oxford University Press, 1978), 111.
[2] *CSPV*, vol. 32, 74.
[3] Evelyn, vol. 3, 247 (June 4, 1660).
[4] See above, p. 18, for Hyde's and Ormonde's views on access.
[5] W.D. Macray (ed.) *Notes Which Passed at Meetings of the Privy Council* (1896), 27. See also Macray, 6 for the Chancellor's attempts at humor.

recommendation for Major Buskins because "the Lord Chancellor was not his friend."[6]

Clarendon's group held power by formal position as well as through the informal favor of the king. Nicholas, as Secretary of State, received countless petitions, Lord Treasurer Southampton gave advice on every grant dealing with finance, and most grants needed the great seal which Clarendon controlled.[7] Despite this near monopoly on the king's ear, Clarendon and his allies never used their plurality of access to create a clientage.

Greed and their political outlook combined to prevent the Clarendonians from creating a following. Impoverished by exile, Clarendon and his fellows exhibited a strong desire to cash in on their current good fortune. The example of Bulstrode Whitelocke, who lingered in jail until he could gather £250 to give to the chancellor,[8] may be extreme, but contemporary opinion did view the clique surrounding Clarendon as money-hungry. Looking back on seven years of Clarendon's ministry Evelyn reported to Pepys that Lord Arlington was a better patron than the chancellor who "never did nor will do anything but for money."[9] The Venetian ambassador claimed that his Portuguese counterpart bought access at £1000 and that Secretary Nicholas's only care was "to accumulate money to leave his children wealthy."[10] Paying a price for access quantifiable in pounds made beneficiaries feel that they had fulfilled all obligations to the access broker.[11] Clarendon and his allies therefore gained little political currency by acting as intermediaries between king and suitor.

Clarendon, however, saw no need to restrict his greed. The establishment of a party of loyal followers he deemed not only unnecessary, but inimical to proper government. Clarendon deprecated parties, cabals, and prime ministers. He claimed that "great and notorious meetings and cabals had always been odious to Parliaments and though they might produce some success in one or two particulars until they are discovered, they had always ended unluckily."[12] Clarendon not only did not feel the need to build up a party; he also thought it was dangerous to do so.

---

[6] *HMC Dartmouth*, vol. 1, 2 (April 19/29, 1661; April 24/May 4, 1661).

[7] Some minor grants could be sealed with the privy seal which was in the possession of Lord Robartes (G. E. Aylmer, *The King's Servants* (London: Routledge & Kegan Paul, 1974), 14, 16).

[8] Clarendon required the fee to affix the seal to the order for Whitelocke's release. Hutton, *Restoration*, 134.

[9] Pepys, VIII, 185 (April 26, 1667). Sir George Cartaret also felt that Clarendon did not reward his followers. Pepys, VIII, 418 (September 2, 1667).

[10] CSPV, vol. 32, 177, 224.

[11] See Sharon Kettering's "Brokerage at the Court of Louis XIV" for an analysis of the difference between patrons and access brokers in France.

[12] Quoted in Paul Seaward, *The Cavalier Parliament and the Reconstruction of the Old Regime: 1661–1667* (Cambridge: Cambridge University Press, 1989), 84–5.

Clarendon's wariness of the charge of evil counselor restrained him from attempting to monopolize access to the king. Such wariness was justified. Even before the restoration, Hyde was told that Lady Monck had heard that he "condemned all counsel but his own."[13] Soon after Charles came to England, the Lord Chancellor was characterized as another Wolsley.[14] Along with deflating charges of the evil counselor, Clarendon thought open access would help bring stability to the reign.

The Lord Chancellor's speech to Parliament in December, 1660 extolled the restored monarch's open access, highlighting how it extended beyond merely allowing propinquity. Clarendon told the Lords, "you are not only admitted to his presence, but to his conversation, and even in a degree to his friendship." He argued further that Charles's subjects chose their own conduits to the kings (the MPs) who have full warrant to convey all information to and from the king. As Hyde informed the commons,

> You came up their deputies to the king; and he returns, you know, his deputies to them, his plenipotentiaries to inform and assure them that he thinks himself the happiest and the greatest prince of the world. . . . He will not take it unkindly if you publish his defects and infirmities. You may tell them so confident in the multitude of his very good and faithful subjects can do him much harm.

At the close of his speech, the Lord Chancellor depicts the monarch as wishing to extend his friendship and conversation to as many as possible: "His majesty hath been heard to say no more but, 'what have I Done I wish that Gentleman and I were acquainted, that he knew me better.'" Clarendon believed these qualities to be particularly endearing to the Members of Parliament. He claimed, "Oh! Gentlemen you cannot be yourselves, nor you cannot make your friends too zealous . . . for such a prince's safety."[15]

Concern for the prince's safety also prompted Clarendon to advise Charles to grant access to those of diverse political opinions, hoping that it would placate former rebels. Clarendon and Ormonde encouraged the king to give key positions of access to individuals who were prominent in the governments of the interregnum. Albemarle, Sandwich, and Manchester all received household positions which guaranteed them the ability to interact with the king. Charles installed William Morrice and Lord Robartes as Secretary of State and Lord Privy Seal respectively, which offices were stops along the formal route of access for petitions and grants. Having friends in high places encouraged non-Anglicans to believe that they had a line of communication to the king.

Supporters of the previous governments used their former colleagues who now held positions around the king as intermediaries to the monarch.

---

[13] *CSP Clar.*, V, 13 (May 4, 1660).
[14] *CSP Clar.*, 175.
[15] *Journal of the House of Lords*, vol. 11, 238.

The regicide Hasselrigg and Lord Fauconberg, Cromwell's son-in-law, utilized Albemarle to reach the king.[16] Lady Francis Rich, ejected fellows at the universities, and Lord Fairfax employed Manchester for this purpose.[17] Sir Robert Harley – a major player in Herefordshire politics during the interregnum – wrote to his brother about his stay at court. Throughout his lengthy description of negotiations with the king, the Duke of York, and Clarendon, Harley showed a marked preference to speak to the king through the conduits of Albemarle or Morrice, illustrating the tendency of nonconformists to rely on those of similar opinions.[18]

The proximity of Presbyterians to the king persuaded nonconformists that the monarch was on their side. Such assurance of the monarch's support continued even when evidence existed to the contrary. Twice, Adam Martindale, a Presbyterian minister, denied the validity of royal proclamations which promoted conformity to Anglican rites. The Cheshire minister believed that the king supported religious toleration. Instead of accepting the fact that the king had changed his policy, Martindale blamed his enemies for appropriating the sovereign's name in ways Charles II did not intend.[19] During the first occasion, Martindale was saved by Richard Baxter's connection with Clarendon, which must have confirmed the Cheshire minister's assumption that the proximity of nonconformists to the king meant that Charles favored their cause. Such thinking aligned with the old tenet that the king could do no wrong which underlay the theory of the evil counselor. This mind-set allowed Charles II's subjects to remain loyal to the king, even when the monarch pursued policies opposed to their welfare.

The downside of open access, however, was that it became nearly impossible to harness the authority of the monarch to a particular agenda. Open access gave the impression that those who spoke *to* the king spoke *for* the king. Even those closer to the center than the Cheshire minister had trouble determining who represented the king's intent. In Parliament itself, ministers and courtiers argued over what the king truly desired. As the Venetian ambassador reported,

> The Chancellor proposed a clause in a bill which is all but completed, in the matter of religion, tending to the advantage of the Presbyterians, urging that the king desired it, and that it was suggested in his name. Bristol, who is a Roman Catholic, opposed. . . . He showed that the king did not at all wish such a pernicious and scandalous point to be discussed in the Parliament.[20]

[16] BL ADD 38091, *passim*.

[17] HMC *Russel*, 26. HMC 8th Report App. 2, Manchester Mss, 65b, 66a.

[18] HMC *Portland*, 254 (May 20, 1661).

[19] In the first instance, Martindale was arrested for not announcing a prohibition against unlawful assemblies. In the second instance, he did not believe the strict injunction of the king's to read the Book of Common Prayer at services because it so contradicted his previous policy. Adam Martindale, *Life of Adam Martindale* (Chetham Society, 1845, vol. 4), 144,154, 158.

[20] CSPV, vol. 33, 124–125 (March 31, 1662).

In 1663 Pepys testified that the political world believed that the king's true intentions differed from the ones he stated in his speech to Parliament. "And pretty it is to consider how the King would appear to be a stiff Protestant and son of the Church, and yet would appear willing to give a liberty to those people because of his promise at Breda. And yet all the world doth believe that the king would not have this liberty given them at all."[21] Clarendon and his allies obviously had great difficulty harnessing the king's authority to their political agenda. Open access was a two-edged sword: the king could maintain good relations with segments of the population who felt threatened by current policy, but it also rendered the king's will a much less determinate and, therefore, a much less potent force.

Without a crystal-clear indication of the king's unswerving support, Clarendon and his allies were ill equipped to maintain their predominance. Their lack of a clientage gave them little grass-roots strength in Parliament and country, and their parsimonious bestowal of the king's bounty gained them enemies at court. Charles II's open access, moreover, both encouraged Clarendon's enemies to believe that they could persuade the king to leave his "old" advisors, and gave them ample opportunity to try to do so. Three forces preserved Clarendon: his ability to maintain constant access to the king and thereby deflect criticism, his administrative skills, and the king's sense of loyalty. In 1662, however, Clarendon lost the first two of these three protective forces.

In the summer of 1662, Clarendon's group could no longer maintain constant access to the king.[22] Ormonde had left the court to govern Ireland in July. Sir Edward Nicholas suffered incapacitating illness the following month. Clarendon was constantly plagued by the gout, and Southampton had kidney stones in addition to the "rich man's disease."[23] Even had they remained healthy, these "old serious lords" were not the companions Charles sought while he pursued his pleasure, and their failure to build a clientage made it difficult for them to recruit the king's boon companions for their cause.

In fact, bad blood flowed between the Chancellor and the king's most intimate companions. Sir Charles Berkeley[24] and Hyde were enemies during the exile.[25] Before as well as after the restoration Clarendon and Bristol fought over almost every issue. Clarendon viewed Bristol as a triple threat: Catholic, rash, and a Hispanophile.[26] Realizing the danger Bristol presented, at the

---

[21] Pepys, IV, 58 (February 26, 1663).

[22] Pepys, III, 227 (October 17, 1662).

[23] Seaward, *Cavalier Parliament*, 220.

[24] Contemporaries list Sir Charles Berkeley, later Lord Falmouth, among the king's favorites, but little is known about his politics. He died in 1665 during the second Dutch War.

[25] Charles Berkeley was a member of the Queen's faction during exile. John Miller, *Charles II* (London: Weidenfeld & Nicolson), 14.

[26] Hutton, *Restoration*, 167.

beginning of 1661 Clarendon sent the Earl on a mission to negotiate a marriage between the king and one of the sisters of the Duke of Parma.[27] With Bristol out of the picture, the king, on Clarendon's advice, agreed to marry Catherine of Braganza. Forced to cut off negotiations, the Catholic Earl was humiliated, which increased his hatred of Hyde.[28] As Bristol's client, Bennet became the object of Clarendon's disfavor. After Bennet returned from his ambassadorship in Spain, Clarendon moved to block Bennet's attempt to gain control of the post office and to become ambassador to France. Castlemaine, the king's mistress, disliked the Chancellor because he failed to respect her, stopped grants in her name, and took Queen Catherine of Braganza's side when the queen opposed the appointment of Castlemaine as a lady-in-waiting.

Clarendon's policy of open access may have backfired. Clarendon had urged open access to Presbyterians, hoping to bring calm to the nation. Charles II, however, interpreted the open access policy to pertain to Clarendon's Hispanophile or Catholic rivals such as Bennet and Bristol. Charles believed further that by constantly stymieing Bennet, Clarendon was both failing to reward loyalty and concentrating too much power in his and his allies' hands. Moved by the pleas of Castlemaine, Bennet, Bristol, and the king's new favorite, Charles Berkeley – who all took advantage of Clarendon's frequent absences – Charles promoted Bennet to Secretary of State.[29]

Bennet took the place of Sir Edward Nicholas. The displacement at such a key position of Clarendon's ally with Bristol's protégé signaled to the world that Clarendon had lost his sway in the king's council. Pepys reported on October 17, 1662, "the young men, get the uppermost and the old serious lords are out of favour."[30] This damage to reputation impinged directly upon political power. When rumor suggested a minister's downfall, his carrots became sour and his sticks became soft. Clarendon, worried about his reputation, assured Ormonde that his "credit is not diminished with the king, though the late change [Bennet's replacement of Nicholas] makes a great deal of noise."[31] Bennet also posed a more practical challenge to Clarendon. A work-horse who was literate in five languages, Bennet was able to replace Clarendon as the administrative head of the government.

Bennet threatened not only Clarendon's position, but also his policy of open access. The new Secretary of State endeavored to monopolize access to the monarch for political ends. Unlike Clarendon, Bennet strove to maintain

---

[27] Hutton, *Charles II*, 158–60.

[28] CSPV, vol. 32, 243–297.

[29] Violet Barbour, *Henry Bennet, Earl of Arlington Secretary of State to Charles II* (Washington: AHA, 1914), 72.

[30] Pepys, III, 227 (October 17, 1662).

[31] CSP Clar., 277–278 (October 25, 1662).

constant, privy, and *exclusive* access to Charles. He built a private staircase from his office to the royal closet and he was constantly around the king both in pleasure and business.[32] Bennet allied himself with Charles's companions of pleasure to engross the king's attention. Pepys mentions in October, 1662 that no one had the royal ear as much as Berkeley, Lady Castlemaine, and Bennet.[33] Bennet strove to make sure that no one outside of his circle gained access to the king. In February 22, 1664 Alsopp, the king's brewer, reported to Pepys that the king was being "led away by half a dozen men, that none of his serious servants and friends can come at him. These [half-dozen men] are Lodderdale, Buckingham, Hamilton, Fitzharding, [Charles Berkeley] . . . Projers is another and Sir H. Bennet." The brewer also accused these advisors of taking away the tables in order to ensure that no one could gain access to the king.[34] Pepys heard from John Baron Crew[35] that the young courtiers capitalized on their relationship with Castlemaine to approach the king "when he is with my Lady Castlemayne and in a humour of delight and then persuade him that he ought not to hear or listen to the advice of those old dotards or counselors."[36] For the latter part of 1662 and the first half of 1663 this group appears to have successfully displaced Clarendon as the wellspring of policy and administration. The Chancellor was seen waiting at court to speak to the king "as others do."[37]

Unlike his predecessor who opposed the creation of political factions, Bennet used his control of access for political purposes, to create a faction in Parliament composed of his clients. To gain the support of MPs he obtained private audiences with the king for individual MPs. He made promises and doled out patronage as freely as was possible. Two influential and long-time court supporters Sir Courteney Pole – who proposed the hearth tax – and William Courtenay received a reward for their service only after Bennet had gained some control of the royal bounty. Bennet not only rewarded those who had been loyal to the king; he wanted to use his position of access to become the sole intermediary between king and MPs. Bennet, along with the king's favorite Charles Berkeley, thought "that the king should take his measure of the House of Commons by no other report but theirs, nor dispense

---

[32] Barbour, 72.

[33] Pepys, III, 227 (October 17, 1663).

[34] Pepys, V, 56 (February 22, 1664). For the general discontent which occurred when Charles took away the tables see *HMC Ailesbury*, 170 (August 21, 1663) and *HMC Finch*, vol. 1, 274 (September 3, 1663). In an attempt to save money Charles II reduced the number of people who had the right to eat for free at court. Contemporaries called this move "taking away the tables." For an analysis of the reforms of court see Andrew Barclay, "Charles II's Failed Restoration: Administrative Reforms Below Stairs, 1660–1664" in *The Stuart Courts* ed. Eveline Cruickshanks (Stroud, UK: Sutton, 2000), 158–170.

[35] Crew was the Earl of Sandwich's father-in-law.

[36] Pepys, IV, 137 (May 15, 1663).

[37] Ibid.

his grace through any other conduit." This policy ably created a small loyal faction. It failed, however, to control Parliament in the service of the king.[38]

Bennet's attempt created a strong backlash in Parliament in 1663. MPs who were not part of the cabal, as well as their constituents, took umbrage at attempts by the king to control Parliament.[39] As Paul Seaward perhaps over-states, "This more interventionist management, while providing occasional success, changed Parliament more fundamentally than had any of the developments of the Civil War eroding the assumption of shared interest between court and country and replacing it with mutual distrust."[40] The rumors of profligate and profane behavior at court and Bennet's and Anthony Ashley Cooper's[41] stance of tolerating Catholicism could only have reinforced a view of the court as inimical to local interests. Lewdness, Catholicism, strict access, and arbitrary government were all intertwined in the early modern English mind.[42] The king's brewer, after complaining about the monarch's restricting access to his person, immediately expressed fears about the king dissolving the militia and establishing a flying army.[43]

The rift created between "court" and "country" was echoed by a rift between Charles's personal actions and his public policy. The king, urged on by Bennet and Ashley, had been advocating a policy of religious toleration, but at the same time he had been consumed by events in his private life such as the dispute between the queen and Castlemaine and unsuccessfully wooing the young Francis Stuart. His pursuit of private pleasure cut people off from obtaining physical proximity to the king, and Bennet's attempts at mono-polizing access curtailed communication to those who were not allied with the Secretary of State. Such inaccessibility rendered impotent one of the king's tools for bringing about a more tolerant society. For when the king closes himself to his people, as Charles did in 1663, the stakes immediately become higher and factions become that more desperate to win, for failure to win the king's favor might mean perpetual exclusion.

The actions of the Earl of Bristol, that inveterate gambler, demonstrate the extremes to which this situation forced individuals. In the spring of 1663, Bristol's position at court was slipping fast. His most influential ally, Castlemaine, had lost her pre-eminent position in the king's favor to the *ingénue* Frances Stuart. To keep herself in the sight of the king, Villiers pursued

---

[38] Seaward, *Cavalier Parliament*, 84–85.

[39] One example of such umbrage is the Commons's outrage at Richard Temple's offer to manage the House of Commons.

[40] Seaward, *Cavalier Parliament*, 99.

[41] The future Earl of Shaftesbury.

[42] See Peter Lake, "Anti-popery: The Structure of a Prejudice" in *Conflict in Early Stuart England*, ed. R. Cust and D. Hughes (New York: Longman, 1989), 72–106, for the connections between lewdness, Catholicism and arbitrary government. See above, p. 22.

[43] Pepys, V, 56 (February 22, 1664). A flying army was a small, professional, and highly mobile force.

the friendship of the nubile teenager, designing frolics, such as the mock marriage between herself and the newcomer, to entertain the king's new love interest. As a result of her diminished position, Castlemaine's influence over politics lessened considerably. Bristol himself had been humiliated by the Richard Temple fiasco[44] and became convinced that his political survival was an all-or-nothing situation. The Catholic Earl, in a desperate gamble, decided to become the champion of the Commons, and lead them in a revolt against his political rival, Clarendon. Bristol, citing mostly rumors, brought impeachment charges against Clarendon in the House of Lords. Unfortunately for Bristol, his charges had neither evidence nor royal support and the Lords dismissed them. Charles II was enraged at Bristol's tactics and issued a declaration for his arrest. The Earl never fully regained his position.[45]

This event brought a quiescence of faction at court. Rid of Castlemaine's and Bristol's influence, urged on by the king, and shocked at the havoc faction could wreak, the rest of the administration came to a *modus vivendi* which enabled the crown to present a united front to Parliament. The effect of unity in the presentation of the court agenda to Parliament was magnified by Charles's restriction of access. MPs no longer felt that the king could be swayed easily to their side, that their allies in court would bring over the king. Opposition to the king's current agenda became direct opposition to the king. Such a policy increased the pressure on MPs to side with the court, but it also made a rejection of the current court policy tantamount to a rejection of the monarch.

Luckily for Charles, the Northern Plot of October 12, 1663 made both opposition to the king a scarier proposition and increased the king's willingness to adopt the proposals of the cavaliers in Parliament. Charles's pro-toleration stance had been anathema to the majority of MPs who defined their royalism more in opposition to Cromwellians and nonconformists than as unswerving obedience to Charles II. The plot convinced the king that indulgence would not appease religious radicals and therefore he abandoned the policies of toleration.[46] Charles fully adopted the policies of the cavalier Parliament, approving and lending his political support to the Conventicle Act and the Five Mile Act. The abandonment of toleration brought a coherence to his political agenda and his policies of access. An inaccessible monarch is much more capable of suppressing nonconformity, because he gives no hope to the nonconformists that they will one day attain power. For a while, at least, Parliament and crown united. This unity enabled Charles to garner support for a war against the Dutch.

---

[44] See n. 38.
[45] Hutton, *Restoration*, 200–204.
[46] Charles II abandoned his policy of toleration for nonconformists because of the rebellion. He abandoned his policy of relaxing the recusant laws because one of its most active proponents Bristol had fallen in disgrace after attacking Clarendon.

Good relations between Parliament and the king were not to last, for Charles's new policy had a problematic origin. Unlike his father, Charles II did not restrict access in order to use distance as a tool to inspire awe, nor did he restrict access to discourage nonconformists; rather he simply wished to follow his pleasure. In his pursuit of a private life he abandoned communicating with his subjects. The English did not appreciate this. Late in 1662 the Venetian ambassador reported, "Indeed the discontent is general and everyone complains of the king, that he allows himself to be governed by ministers while he cares for nothing, attending only to his hunting, his lusts and other amusements which are not well interpreted."[47] Pepys filled his diary with wishes that the king mind his business and with instances of others declaring the same.[48] The popular rumor that during the disastrous Battle of Chatham the king and Castlemaine amused themselves by chasing a butterfly demonstrates the widespread nature of the belief that the sovereign was out of touch with his subjects. During the second Dutch War, the sense of Charles's isolation could only have increased, since the plague forced Charles to separate himself physically from his subjects.

Satires and more serious works responded to the lack of access to the king.[49] Andrew Marvell, among others, tied naval defeats to the king's countenancing evil counselors while he pursued pleasure. In his "Second Advice to the Painter", Andrew Marvell attacked the rapacious courtiers surrounding the king. The poet depicted Clarendon as starting a war with Holland solely to distract the nation from his own treason. In his address to the king which concludes the poem, Marvell depicts evil intermediaries between the king and country as a plague of locusts devouring the country:

> Imperial prince king of the sea and isles
> dear object of our joys and heaven's smiles:
> what boots it that thy light does gild our days
> and we like basking in the milder rays,
> while swarms of insects, from the warmth begun
> our land devour and intercept our sun.
>
> (967–974)

Although by no means his only criticism of courtiers – lack of bravery, stupidity, incompetence, and greed have prominent cameos in all three of Marvell's "Painter" poems – the poet returns continually to the issue of communication to the king. In the "Third Advice to the Painter," the Duchess of Albemarle urges her husband to relate to the king the true state

---

[47] *CSPV*, vol. 33, 205 (November 3, 1662).
[48] Pepys, VII, 370 (November 14, 1666), *passim*.
[49] See my "The Politics and Representation of Access in Edward Howard's *The Change of Crownes*," *Restoration* (spring, 2000, vol. 24:1), 1–10.

of affairs, and the incompetence and greed of his courtiers. "Tell the King all how they countermine" (339). The "Last Instructions to the Painter" dated September 4, 1667, almost immediately after Clarendon had his seals taken away, and before he left England, highlights in its conclusion the motifs of the evil counselor and the incognito king. Marvell refers to the motif of a king learning directly from one of his subjects the problems of a nation:

> Kings in the country oft have gone astray
> Nor of a peasant scorn'd to learn the way.
> (959–960)

Marvell goes on to criticize the evil counselors for urging the king to pursue partisan politics:

> Bold and accurs'd ar they that al this while
> have strove to isle our Monarch from his isle
> and to improve themselves, on false pretence,
> about the common prince have rais'd a fence;
> The kingdom from the crown distinct would see
> and peel the bark to burn at last the tree.
> But Ceres corn, and flora is the spring
> Baccus is wine, the country is the king.
> (967–974)

The organic imagery is telling. Marvell not only decries the evil counselors for isling "the monarch from his isle" and enclosing the common ground that is the king; he attacks their philosophy of state which presumes that the kingdom is an inorganic entity that can be ruled only by force. He assails the evil advisors for convincing the king that his interests lie counter to those of the country. Marvell posits in its place an inherent unity and coherence of king and country, asserting by metonymy that their interests are one and the same and that, once Charles realizes this essential truth, the king has no need of force to govern his people. The poet's solution is simple and clear: "Give us this court and rule without a guard" (990). Get rid of the evil counselors and the standing army, Marvell tells the king, and the country will rejoice.

Charles could not have maintained the accessibility which he displayed upon his restoration, but his restriction of access was not only a function of time or his pursuit of pleasure. A change in advisors and political goals forced him towards a more restrictive policy of access. The Northern Plot had dissipated his affection for religious radicals and Charles could, for a while, countenance their persecution. But the isolation brought about by plague and war enhanced the negative connotations of inaccessible kings. Mindful and reminded of his need for the nation's support, the king turned once again to a policy of open access.

## Everybody's king: the politics of access under the Cabal (1667 to 1673)

From Henceforth, sir, be everybody's king,
And then you are yourself. Lend equal ears
To What all say, and like a skillful chemist
Draw the quick spirit off from every counsel
and from your wise breast breath it as your own.
(Sir Robert Howard, *The Duke of Lerma*, 1668)[50]

When in the fall of 1667 Baptist May, keeper of the king's privy purse, heard that Charles had dismissed Clarendon, May fell to his knees, embraced Charles and declared that he could "for the first time call him [Charles] king of England."[51] By this emotional display Baptist May intended to signify that Charles now ruled England on his own. In fact, Charles had firmly grasped the tiller of state long before Clarendon's fall from grace. Yet, in some sense, May's exclamation was correct. Upon the dismissal of the Chancellor, Charles made sure that he would steer the nation's course. He did this by showing himself more often to his subjects, being open to their grievances, and by preventing any of his ministers from gaining enough power to pursue a course independent of the king. This policy brought about chaos at court and factional warfare, but it also gave Charles a wide variety of supporters, a big tent in modern political parlance. Charles, in effect, was not satisfied with being the head of the royalist- Anglican faction; during this period he was trying to be, in Robert Howard's words, "Everybody's King."[52]

The popular reaction to the king's active role in putting out the great fire of 1666 helped sway Charles to return to open access. Henry Griffith wrote Sir Bernard Gascoigne that the Duke of York and the king "stayed the fury of the fire by . . . handing water in buckets when they stood anckels in water and playing the engines many hours together as they did at Temple and Cripplegate which people seeing fell to work with effort having so good fellow laboreres."[53] Griffith was not alone: many London residents wrote their friends in the countryside to inform them of the king's bravery and active role.[54] Such a favorable response re-educated Charles as to the power of his person and the importance of being seen by his subjects.[55]

---

[50] Robert Howard, *The Duke of Lerma* in *Dryden and Howard 1664–8*, ed. D. D. Arundell (Cambridge: Cambridge University Press, 1929), 247.

[51] Maurice Lee, *The Cabal* (Urbana: University of Illinois Press, 1965), 27.

[52] For more on Robert Howard and the dramatic display of access see my "The Politics of Access in Edward Howard's *The Change of Crownes*," *Restoration*, 24, no. 1 (spring, 2000), 1–11.

[53] HMC *Hodgkin*, 306.

[54] HMC *Hastings*, 369–373; HMC *Leeds*, 11th Report App. vii, 7; Evelyn, 454.

[55] It certainly educated him as to the benefits of being seen fighting fires. In June, 1670 Charles took part in putting out a fire in The Strand (Spurr, *1670s*, 15).

Charles's dismissal of Clarendon in August, 1667 displays both a commitment to accessibility and a wariness of one politician becoming too powerful.
The king informed Ormonde that his reason for removing the Lord
Chancellor from office was "too big for a letter."[56] Historians have speculated
over that "big" reason, claiming either that Charles suspected Clarendon of
encouraging Francis Stuart's elopement,[57] or that the king needed a scapegoat
for the mismanagement of the Dutch War.[58] Contemporaries, however,
highlighted the king's desire to foster free communication.

Ironically, the king portrayed Clarendon, who had so actively advocated
Charles's accessibility, as an obstacle to communicating with the monarch.
William Coventry reported that the king declared he was dissatisfied with
the Lord Chancellor because, "amongst other reasons . . . he took away liberty
of debate in the council."[59] Coventry told Pepys that there were many reasons
for Clarendon's dismissal but

> *instar omnium* [equal to the rest of them] he [Coventry] told me that while he
> [Clarendon] was so great at the Council-board and in the administration of matters,
> there was no room for anybody to propose any remedy to what was amiss or to
> compass anything, though never so good for the kingdom, unless approved of by
> the Chancellor, he managing all things with that greatness which now will be
> removed, that the King may have the benefit of others' advice.[60]

George Downing similarly informed Pepys that the king "doth call the
Chancellor that insolent man and says that he would not let him [the king]
speak himself in council."[61] Whether Clarendon's limiting of communication
to the ruler actually prompted his dismissal or not, Charles – by vocally
and frequently expressing the sentiment that the Chancellor had prevented
the sovereign from communicating with his subjects – was signaling that he
now valued the ability to hear advice from a variety of conduits.

Charles not only wanted the advice of his counselors and subjects to reach
him without the hindrance or filtration of a premier minister; he also desired
that his commands reach his subjects directly. By reviving the custom of
attending debates in the House of Lords, the king eliminated intermediaries
between him and the upper house. Charles had used the power of majesty

---

[56] Hutton, *Restoration*, 276.
[57] Charles was infatuated with Francis Stuart and rumors abounded that he planned to
divorce his wife to marry the court beauty. Rumor-mongers also claimed that Clarendon
acted to prevent this union to ensure that his granddaughter, Mary, would become Queen
of England.
[58] Hutton, *Charles II*, 250–251.
[59] BL Althorp C4, William Coventry to Henry Saville, September 3, 1667.
[60] Pepys, VIII, 415 (2 September 1667).
[61] Pepys, VIII, 427 (8 September 1667).

previously to influence legislation. In November, 1661, when the House of Commons was reluctant to pass a revenue bill, Charles summoned MPs to the House of Lords, where they observed king and all the Lords dressed in full regalia. The Commons quickly voted the king his revenue.[62] The king's approach in 1670 was subtler. Charles downplayed his presence in the House of Lords: he attended "without royal pomp,"[63] he never spoke in the debates, and he claimed that he observed them only because he found the debates "more amusing than a play."[64] But he substantially, albeit quietly, impacted the course of debate.

By whispering in the ears of his supporters, Charles was able to make his opinions unequivocally known, a tactic which freed the king from the worry that one of his counselors, by taking a stand against the royal interest, would co-opt or dilute the regal imprimatur. The monarch's presence, furthermore, made taking such a stand against the royal interest difficult, for opponents could not easily rationalize that they were speaking in the interest of the king, when he was present and clearly taking the other side. By attending the upper house, Charles altered the hierarchical seating arrangements as well as the course of debate. Normally, the Lords arranged themselves according to precedence of title, but when the king stood by the fireside, royal supporters crowded around the king with no regard to the established hierarchy.[65] The disruption of seating arrangements reinforced the conception of the monarch as the fount of all honor and title, which, in turn, made opposition to the king that much harder.

Charles's appearance in the upper house affected legislation. The Venetian ambassador reported that the king's presence in the house resulted in both the Roos divorce bill and the Second Conventicle Act passing the upper house drafted in the way Charles wished.[66] Arlington, in a letter to Lord Fauconberg, rejoiced at "how happily the complexion of Parliament is changed since your lordship left us, they having disposed themselves to do everything to his majesty's mind and satisfaction" The Secretary of State claimed the peers were happy that the king attended their deliberations once a day and "they solemnly, in a body, attended him in the banqueting house and gave him humble thanks for his favor therein."[67] Charles II did not exert the power of his person on the Lords alone. In 1670, after the Commons delivered thanks to the king for deciding in its favor against the House of Lords, he invited MPs

[62] Derek Hirst, "The Conciliatoriness of the Cavalier Commons Reconsidered," *Parliamentary History* (vol. 6, no. 2, 1987), 222.
[63] *CSPV*, vol. 36, 180.
[64] Andrew Swatland, *The House of Lords in the Reign of Charles II* (Cambridge: Cambridge University Press, 1996), 98.
[65] Ibid.
[66] *CSPV*, vol. 36, 175 (April 4, 1670); p. 180 (April 18, 1670). Swatland, 94–97.
[67] *HMC Var. Coll.*, vol. 2, 134 (March 31, 1670).

to drink with him in his wine-cellars.[68] But widespread joy at his presence – if it ever truly existed – did not last.

Charles's presence in the Lords occasioned strong opposition. During debates, several peers expressed their discomfort at their sovereign's attendance. Lord Brixton, for example, withdrew when the king came to the upper house, but "as soon as the king came out he returned again."[69] On March 6, 1671, John Lord Lucas and the Earl of Clare objected to debating a revenue bill in front of Charles. Lord Lucas claimed "that according to the statutes of the realm the king should withdraw from the assembly when his own affairs were discussed; and it behoved his majesty discreetly to permit a sharp debate to be held in his presence on questions of order and desert." The Earl of Clare made similar statements, expressing that "he knew not why the king should whisper to any unless it were to direct them how to give their votes, and moved that the king might be desired to withdraw out of the house, and leave them a free debate." The power of the regal presence, as these peers feared, won the day. The upper house approved of the entire sum offered by the Commons.[70]

Direct rule meant more than the ability to communicate directly to the House of Lords. It also meant not being beholden to any one minister or faction, opening access to a variety of persons and political opinions. Charles needed to ensure that no minister would have or appear to have sole control of the royal ear or administration. To this end the king delayed for years appointing new officers to the posts of Lord Chancellor, Lord Treasurer, and Captain-General.[71] These ancient posts had many rights and privileges including the ability to bestow a considerable amount of patronage. Charles was wary of any of his ministers gaining an independent platform from which to develop a loyal clientage and was also careful to prevent any of his advisors from appearing pre-eminent.[72]

Realizing that no one minister was pre-eminent, suitors used a variety of conduits to reach the king. Castlemaine, Buckingham, Bath, Lauderdale, Ashley, Arlington, William Legge, and William Coventry, among others, served as intermediaries.[73] Charles's accessibility made many wary of relying on any one individual to deliver a plea to the monarch; suitors feared that

---

[68] Ronald Hutton, "The Making of the Secret Treaty of Dover" *HJ* (vol. 29, no. 2, 1986), 316.

[69] BL Althorp B5, July 20, 1670.

[70] *CSPV*, vol. 37, 24 (March 5, 1671). Swatland, 97. Haley, 358.

[71] *CSPV*, vol. 37, 143 (January 8, 1672). The Venetian Ambassador, however, claimed that Charles delayed appointing new officers "to give them all at once and oblige several persons who rule the lords."

[72] Hutton, *Charles II*, 258.

[73] BL ADD 27447, 310 (October 30, 1667); BL ADD 28052 61, 64; BL ADD 32094, 173, 275; BL ADD 36988, 90; HMC *Ormonde*, vol. 1, 35–40; HMC *Montagu*, 418; HMC *Dartmouth*, vol. 1, 19 (September 26, 1670); MS Carte, 38, 132.

their adversaries would contact the king by another method. Those desiring a royal boon, therefore, tried to employ all available conduits to the sovereign. The Venetian ambassador, for instance, in his attempt to receive aid against the Turks, went to the king, the Duke of York, the Duchess of York, the queen, Buckingham, and Arlington.[74] Similarly, when John Birkenhead wanted a mandamus for a position at Cambridge, he spoke to Charles, both secretaries, Buckingham, and the Lord Chancellor of Cambridge.[75] Such precautions seemed necessary if petitioners did not want to be beaten to the punch. When Thomas Osborne (later Earl of Danby) wished to obtain a place in the commissions of customs for Sir John Finch, he appealed to the Duke of Buckingham; but when the Duke approached the king, he was told that the commissioners had already been chosen on the advice of Clifford and Ashley.[76]

Through openness to a variety of conduits, the king succeeded in keeping any minister from gaining too much power, but such accessibility also created a very tumultuous political environment. The king's commitment to open access allowed factions to criticize their opponents incessantly, which forced courtiers to attend the king continuously for fear that one of their rivals would bring about their downfall. The Venetian ambassador described Arlington as "always by the king's side."[77] Lauderdale also stuck close to the king, and when he was called away to Scotland, Sir Robert Murray, Lauderdale's client, looked out for the Scottish Secretary's interest.[78] Robert Paston (later Viscount and Earl of Yarmouth) wrote his wife that he would "forbear the court," but that he had to return to the court in twelve days "so as not to be out of the king's eye."[79] Attendance on the king could save political careers. The Duke of Ormonde, when attacked by Roger Boyle the Earl of Orrery, rushed to London to defend himself, which kept him in the king's good graces. Although Ormonde lost the Lieutenancy of Ireland, he remained Lord Steward of the household.[80] Arthur Annesley the Earl of Anglesey also succeeded in defeating his opponents by speaking directly to the king. In his diary Anglesey recorded that he had

> found that some had been undermining me with the king and shaken him so far that he told my Lord Arlington that it was not reasonable I should have a £3000 pension and the privy seal both. Being acquainted I went to his majesty . . . and upon reasoning matters with him set all to rights and disappointed my enemies and his majesty bid me come next morning and I should have the privy seal.[81]

---

[74] CSPV, vol. 35, 226–228 (July, 1668).
[75] HMC Hodgkin, 310 (July 3, 1671).
[76] HMC Lonsdale, 95 (October 3, 1671).
[77] CSPV, vol. 35, 14 (September 7, 1668).
[78] Hutton, Charles II, 267–268.
[79] BL ADD 27447, 324 (October 30, 1667).
[80] Hutton, Charles II, 261.
[81] BL ADD 40860, 22 (April 21, 1672).

Anglesey's diary testifies to the instability of the king's favor. Politicians could not feel secure in their posts because they knew that their opponents had ample opportunity to whisper in the king's ear.

The sense of insecurity was justified. As a result of the political chaos, many major players such as William Coventry, Clarendon, Anglesey, Ormonde, Earl Robartes, Sir Orlando Bridgeman, and Berkeley lost their positions. In 1667 the Duke of Buckingham was dismissed of all offices, only to be returned to favor the following year. Rumors of the rise and downfall of ministers flew about London. Pepys recorded hearing that Arlington was to be stripped of office and that Bristol would regain the king's ear.[82] Even when one's enemies were disgraced, the king's counselors could not feel secure, because Charles often allowed dismissed ministers to return to his good graces. Bristol and Anglesey were allowed back to court. William Coventry never returned to office, but well-wishers constantly visited him while he was in the Tower, which suggests that many believed Coventry's downfall to be temporary.[83] The uncertainty of tenure reinforced the ministers' dependence on the good graces of the king.

Although the rapid rise and fall of ministers may have underscored their dependence upon the king, open access created a very chaotic administration, as one faction constantly tried to up-end the other.[84] In some cases, policy took a back seat to politics. Buckingham, for instance, adopted a pro-French policy solely because Arlington favored the Dutch.[85] When Robert Howard, a client of Buckingham, proposed in the House of Commons that he farm all the new taxes, Clifford and Downing immediately objected, only to discover that Charles had already agreed with Howard's proposal.[86] Except for a brief period in 1670, Charles's policy of openness to all resulted in a very unsatisfactory relationship with Parliament.

The parliamentary session of 1670, however, demonstrated some of the benefits of open access. Open access prevented suspicion of the king's actions which, considering his ongoing negotiations with France, was quite fortuitous. Most importantly, open access allowed the king to be considered as above the political fray. Since he had representatives from so many political factions in his court, the king was not seen as supporting any one group. The king's position outside of faction may explain why many former critics of the court comfortably became supporters of the administration. Sir Robert Howard, Edward Seymour, Sir Robert Carr, Sir Richard Temple, and Sir

---

[82] Pepys, VIII, 505–507, 530 (October 28, 1667, November 15, 1667).

[83] Pepys, IX, 470 (March 5, 1669).

[84] This intense factional warfare may have led Charles to chose two Lord Lieutenants of Ireland whose main distinguishing characteristic was that they had no factional ties (Hutton, *Charles II*, 261–262).

[85] *CSPV*, vol. 37, 117 (November 6, 1671); 114 (November 18 1672).

[86] Hutton, *Charles II*, 276.

Frescheville Holles became famous as the five recanters who "openly took leave of their former party to head the king's business."[87] They were not alone. Many of the administration's most prominent critics became court pensioners. William Garraway became a customs commissioner with an annual salary of £2000. Thomas Littleton was appointed Treasurer of the Navy and then given a victualing contract. Sir Richard Temple received a position on the Board of Customs with a salary of £2000. The chief speaker of the opposition, John Vaughn, was bestowed with a judgeship. Certainly Richard Temple, who had tried to make himself a nuisance, may have been brought over because of the promise of royal goodies. But Vaughn, Garraway, and Littleton were men of principle who would have resisted switching allegiance if it meant abandonment of their political tenets. Gaining them to the king's side was not a matter simply of offering the proper incentives. However, since the king was not identified with any one minister or faction, it became possible to support the king without severely modifying political principles. Indeed, except for revenue bills, Vaughn, Garraway, and Littleton rarely followed the "court interest."[88] These MPs could see themselves as simply joining the discordant choir of advisors surrounding the king.

Charles's religious policy coincided with his desire to broaden his support base. He filled sees with bishops who had a variety of opinions on the problem of dissent. Such a policy enabled most groups to believe that the king was sympathetic. Charles's sympathy with nonconformists was articulated most clearly in his issuance of the Declaration of Indulgence in 1672. His attitude towards those who took advantage of the Declaration of Indulgence also sheds light on Charles's desire to court all segments of opinion. Charles wanted dissenters to see their freedom as a gift of grace, not of right, and to be aware that the free exercise of their religion relied solely on keeping in the good graces of the king.[89] The king encouraged grateful addresses from nonconformists to be "driven high as possible" in order to emphasize their dependence upon his grace.[90] Charles was also wary of alienating the Anglicans: while the Declaration of Indulgence was in effect, Charles appointed bishops who strongly opposed toleration.

Despite such overtures, many in Parliament, especially irked by the relaxation of the anti-Catholic recusancy laws, did not share Charles's desire to create a big tent and in 1673 Charles desperately needed Parliament's support, for Charles in alliance with France declared war on the United Provinces. The administration tried to wage the war with the money obtained

---

[87] B.D. Henning (ed.), *The House of Commons 1660–90* (London: Secker & Warburg), vol. iii, 539.

[88] Henning, *Commons*, vol. ii, 373–380, 748–751; vol. III, 628–630. Ronald Hutton, "The Secret Treaty."

[89] Hutton, *Charles II*, 266–267.

[90] Foreign Affairs Committee SP 104/177, f. 19ᵛ, quoted in Hutton, *Charles II*, 293.

by the Stop of the Exchequer,[91] but soon ran out of cash. In the beginning of 1673 only a parliamentary grant could finance the military effort. This fiscal crisis increased Parliament's bargaining power, but Charles's issuance of the Declaration of Indulgence, the culmination of his attempts to create a society of toleration, had incensed many members. These members decried the indulgence as both encouraging Catholicism and an unlawful extension of the king's prerogative. The alliance with France only strengthened many MPs' predilection to associate Catholicism with arbitrary government, and they were hesitant to vote further supplies to the king. Forced by financial difficulty, Charles bowed to the uproar in the Commons. He did so, however, in a way which highlighted his personal involvement, tearing up the Declaration with his own hands.

This action mollified Parliament somewhat, but MPs still feared Catholic machinations at court. To ensure that Papists did not worm their way into the king's confidence, Parliament proposed a Test Act which forced all office holders to take an oath that they did not believe in transubstantiation. This act removed all crypto- Catholics who would not take a false oath from office. Strapped for finances, and unaware of the repercussions, Charles assented to the bill.

The Test Act created the most important political event of Charles II's reign, the admission on the part of James, Duke of York and heir presumptive to the throne, that he adhered to the Catholic Church. This admission led to the removal of all non- Anglican advisors to the king. The Test Act forced Clifford, a secret Catholic, and James to resign all offices in June, 1673. Ashley (now Earl of Shaftesbury), who had nonconformist sympathies and a strong anti-Catholic mind-set, led, or at least was perceived to have led, an attack on James and was consequently dismissed as Lord Chancellor in November, 1673. Buckingham repeated Bristol's mistake, abandoning the king to seek support among the Commons. This tactic proved doubly unsuccessful. Buckingham alienated the king by going to the House without Charles's permission and by attacking his fellow ministers in the House. He further did little in his speech to gain the House of Commons's support. Charles dismissed him from all his offices in January, 1674. The only advisors left from the Cabal were Arlington and Lauderdale, both of whom also faced sharp criticism in the house in January, 1674, but because they kept on the good side of the king they remained in office.[92] The Test Act had removed all the representatives of toleration from the king. Few in his presence now urged the king to con-sider the needs and power of alienated segments of society. The lack of such advisors around the king opened up the door for Thomas Osborne and his policy of one-party government and restricted access.

---

[91] For more on the Stop see Andrew Browning, "The Stop of the Exchequer," *History* (June, 1930), 333–337.

[92] Lee, *The Cabal*, 202ff.

## King of the ultra-royalists: the politics of access
## (1674 to 1685)

Following the failure of the Declaration of Indulgence to gain acceptance
in Parliament (1673), Charles never again strove to be everybody's king.
Although he had to tread carefully, Charles had resigned himself to garner-
ing support from only one segment of society, called variously by historians
the ultra-royalists, royalist-Anglicans, or Tories.[93] In line with this decision,
Charles, urged by Osborne, began a policy of strictly guarding access to his
person, so that he could bestow access as a reward for the loyal and deny access
to punish his political opponents.

Financial crisis and a political vacuum occasioned Thomas Osborne's
meteoric rise. Unable to raise funds from a Parliament irate at James's
Catholicism and facing a huge debt from the third Dutch War, Charles had no
answers to his lack of money. Thomas Osborne, who had risen to the rank of
Lord Treasurer in 1674 due largely to his financial acumen, endeavored to
convince Charles that the only way out of his fiscal dilemma was to embrace
a high-church ideology and thereby gain unqualified royalist-Anglican
support. To achieve this purpose Charles adopted political policies which
included a public anti-French stance, persecution of dissenters, and the
"observance of rigid honesty and economy in financial matters."[94] Danby also
persuaded his sovereign to change his policies of access, showing his face to
those who sided with him and denying access to those who opposed him.
Osborne convinced the king to cease trying to please all his people, to stop
being accessible to every segment of his society, and, instead, to befriend his
true allies, those who adhered to church and king and who, incidentally,
appeared to make up a majority of Parliament.

Osborne's plan to regulate access was neither new nor unique.[95] Arlington
had urged the king to adopt a similar policy in 1662, but Charles had refrained
from setting himself up as the leader of any one party, since doing so was
divisive in the extreme and the restored king was all too well aware of
the dangers of a polarized state. While he had previously restricted access
(1662–1664) and the plague and war had separated Charles from his subjects,
such restriction was neither systematic nor political in motivation. Indeed,
even in the mid-1670s, Charles may have been uncomfortable with restricting
access, for he appears to have needed constant encouragement from Danby

---

[93] The party when they referred to themselves as a group called themselves the loyal
party. Mark Knights discusses the issue of party names and identity at length in his *Politics
and Opinions in Crisis: 1678–1681* (Cambridge: Cambridge University Press, 1994),
108–112, *passim*.

[94] Browning, "The Stop," 117.

[95] See J. Miller, *James II: A Study in Kingship* (Hove: Wayland, 1977), 66 for one similar
opinion.

and his allies.[96] A group of bishops[97] recommended that the king ensure the enforcement of laws against papists and recusants by giving "*countenance* [to] those who shall conscientiously endeavor that the laws may have their due and regular course and to *discountenance* those who shall endeavor to obstruct such proceedings."[98] Danby told his colleagues "that nothing is more necessary then to let the world see he [the king] will reward and punish . . . that nothing can spoil his affairs at home but unsteadiness of resolution in those steps he has begun & want of vigor to *discountance* all such as pretend to others."[99] Perhaps the most important piece of persuasion Danby engaged in was the Compton Census. The Census, by showing that dissenters comprised less than 5 percent of the population, reassured the king that he could implement a political regime which alienated nonconformists.[100]

Although Charles may have been reluctant at first to alienate nonconformists, a number of factors persuaded him to support Danby's agenda. The failure of previous attempts to promote toleration indicated to the king that the nation, or at least the elected representatives of the nation, had no desire to create a society which encouraged difference. Furthermore, those elements in court which had previously argued the benefits of toleration no longer existed. Sandwich, Albemarle, Manchester, and Robartes had died; Buckingham and Ashley were out of favor; the nonconformists had lost their conduits to the king. But perhaps the most important force behind the plan to restrict access was the Earl of Danby's personal commitment to the ultra-royalist cause.

While Charles may have had misgivings over implementing a restrictive access policy, this reluctance did not dilute the meaningful actions he took to restrict access to his person. He forbade Catholics from entering the court in November, 1674. The king abolished the council of trade and changed household regulations. He also restricted access to the Privy Council. In November, 1675 he ordered "That no person whatsoever be permitted to stay in the council chamber when any three of the lords of his majesty's Privy Council are there present and that no person whatsoever not being a Privy Councillor do presume to come into the council chamber to the Privy

---

[96] Charles momentarily considered relaxing his strict access policy. In June, 1675, urged by James Duke of York, Charles toyed with letting Shaftesbury back into favor, and allowed him to kiss his hand. On June 24, however, Shaftesbury was ordered to stay away from the court (Haley, 385; *HMC Laing*, vol. i, 403–404).

[97] For the alliance of Danby with the bishops see Mark Goldie, "Danby, the Bishops, and the Whigs" in *The Politics of Religion in Restoration England*, ed. T. Harris *et al.* (Cambridge, MA: Blackwell, 1990). Goldie also stresses the fear Anglicans had of the king turning Presbyterian.

[98] *CSPD 1673–1675*, vol. 16, 548–549; emphasis added.

[99] BL ADD 28042, 11; emphasis added.

[100] BL EG 3329, 119. George Withton to Danby. See A. Whiteman (ed.), *The Compton Census of 1676: A Critical Study* (London: British Academy Oxford University Press, 1986).

Council."[101] The denial of access came not only in the issuance of general rules but also in the specific banishment from court of those who opposed Danby's agenda. Charles banished Buckingham from the court in September, 1674,[102] and removed Robert Carr from the Privy Council for "misbehaving himself in the Commons."[103] Even Arlington was ignored for a month after his clients led an impeachment of Danby.[104] Such restriction of access not only indicated who had lost the king's favor, but also rendered access more desirable by making it rare.

Sir John Reresby, a Yorkshire MP, records extensively how Danby and the king used access to reward those who supported them. By his own account Reresby had tended to side with the country party,[105] but he took the middle course on a revenue bill and voted in favor of a £600,000 sum for the building of ships. The Lord Treasurer

> took it so well that I went not to the height of those men that did all they could to weaken the crown that he would needs carry me to kiss his majesty's hand, which ceremony I had not then performed since my arrival in town . . . [he] presented me in the lobby of the house of lords and being nobody present but the king, his lordship, and myself. My lord told the king a great many good things of me, more than I deserved, but last that as my family had been loyal he knew my disposition was to follow the steps of it. . . . The king said that he had known me long, and hoped I knew him so well that I should not believe those reports of him. I know, says he, it is said that I intend the subversion of the religion and government, that I intend to govern by an army and by arbitrary power, to lay aside Parliaments, and to raise money by other ways. But every man, nay those that say it the most, know it is false. There is noe subject that lives under me whose safety and well being I desire less than my own, and should be sorry to invade his property and liberty as that another should invade mine. Those members of Parliament, said the king, that pretend this great zeal for the publique good, are of two kinds, either such as would subvert the government themselves and bring it to a commonwealth again, or such as seem to join with that party and talk loud against the court, hoping to have their mouths stopped by places or preferments. . . . I replied that it was true that the pretenses were many and plausible, I believed to some, that those people made to oppose that which others understood to be his majesty's interest, but it had gained little upon me, that had the honour of being so long known to his majesty, and had been so lately confirmed in my belief by those assurances I received from my lord treasurer; that I should never to the best of my knowledge do anything but what became a true and faithful subject, and what should be consistent with the prosperity of his majesty's royal person and government. The

---

[101] E.R. Turner, *Privy Council*, 393.
[102] Bod. Lib. Carte, 38 (September 5 1675).
[103] *HMC Beaufort*, 69 (June 13, 1678).
[104] Hutton, *Charles II*, 328; BL ADD 32095 (September 19, 1675).
[105] Reresby, 97.

king told me that he was very well pleased that he had seen me, commanded me to wait upon him sometimes, and said *I should have access to him when and wherever I desired it.*[106]

This incident presents the distilled version of Danby's plan. Charles used the power of his person to convince an MP to support his agenda. Charles presented Reresby with a choice of either contradicting the king to his face or admitting that Reresby did not believe that the king aimed at creating arbitrary government. Reresby, of course, could simply have lied to the king, but stating out loud that he did not believe the king aimed at arbitrary government may have been the first step towards the internalization of that concept. Just as important as this social pressure was the promise of access. By assuring Reresby of the ability to talk to the monarch, Charles allayed fears of arbitrary government, for arbitrary government was associated with closed access. As Reresby himself said, "This condescension in the King to give soe mean a person this satisfaction [the meeting and the promise of access] did much convince me of the reality of what he said."[107] The offer of access was also a considerable bribe, for in this period of restricted access a meeting with the king could prove valuable.

Reresby took the king up on his promise of access. He records, "I very often visited and dined with my lord treasurer, and often waited upon the king, and when he saw me would ask what passed."[108] Reresby employed these opportunities to promote his own and his constituents' interests. For his constituents he obtained a special dispensation from the Hearth Tax for the cutlers of Hallamshire, a £10 bounty on highwaymen, and a plea-bargain agreement for an informer which led to the capture of other highwaymen. He personally gained the king's aid in a lengthy election dispute, cleared his name in the death of an African servant, and received the command of the garrison at the fort at Burlinton with a salary of £200 p.a.[109] Reresby was not alone in having the king use access to sway him to his side. In the fall of 1675 Charles spoke with over a hundred MPs (in groups of twenty) to convince them to support the court's measures.[110]

Part and parcel of Danby's plan for restriction of access was that he himself should serve as the bottleneck, as the sole conduit to the king. To ensure that he controlled access to the king even during private moments, Danby obtained a post in the bedchamber for his son and maintained a close alliance with the Duchess of Portsmouth, the king's mistress.[111] Portsmouth benefitted from this alliance; Danby made sure that the king had enough money to pay

---

[106] Reresby, 111–112, emphasis added.
[107] Ibid., 112.
[108] Ibid., 114.
[109] Ibid., 116, 119, 120, 122, 131–133, 140, 145.
[110] Hutton, *Charles II*, 331.
[111] Browning, "The Stop," 137, 129.

for her gifts.[112] Furthermore, she gained the reputation of wielding powerful influence in the administration. She wrote a letter to Ormonde in favor of a suitor which expressed that the Lord Lieutenant "would look on my letter as a thing of course."[113] Sir Robert Southwell believed Portsmouth's mediation meant that Harry Barkley would soon be free of the Tower.[114] Portsmouth's aid proved valuable to the Treasurer. Rumor had it that while "the king was at Newmarket there was great falling out between the duke and the treasurer, whose friend, Portsmouth ('tho she had but newly miscarried) went down immediately to keep the staff where 'twas."[115]

The way contemporaries approached Danby testifies to his desire to control access to the king. The Duchess of Portsmouth wrote her political ally in favor of one Skelton Buck, who was angling for a position as Don Carlos's tutor.[116] Portsmouth emphasized that Buck relied solely on Danby's patronage, believing that such an admission was a prerequisite to gaining the Lord Treasurer's support.[117] John Munson, similarly, thought that expressing his gratitude in the terms "to become so absolutely your creature" would carry weight with Danby.[118] Danby's emphasis on being the sole conduit aided his attempts at monopolization of access to the king. In 1675 the French ambassador believed that Danby had a virtual monopoly of the king's favor.[119]

His near monopoly of access made the Lord Treasurer quite sought after. The Earl of Stratford claimed that he had been seeking an appointment with the Lord Treasurer from March 25 until June 20, 1675 but had not been successful. Even powerful courtiers had to go through Danby to get what they wanted from the king. The Lord Treasurer served as a conduit for Lord Ogle, Buckingham, Plymouth, Progers, and Ormonde as well as for less notable suitors.[120] Danby aimed at monopolization of access not only for self-aggrandizement or to keep rivals away from the king. The Treasurer rationalized his control of access as necessary both to assure that no one thought nonconformists were reaching the king, and to control finances. Danby insisted that no one plead directly to the king to lighten their tax load or to increase the expenditure of a branch of government.[121] Through his near-

---

[112] Hutton, 335.
[113] HMC Ormonde, vol. 4, 35–40, Duchess of Portsmouth to Ormonde, 1678.
[114] Bod. Lib. Carte 38, 252 (February 6 1674/5).
[115] HMC Verney, 467 (April 13, 1676).
[116] Don Carlos was one of Charles II's illegitimate sons.
[117] BL EG 3330, 51.
[118] BL EG 3329, 130 (June 23, 1676).
[119] Browning, "The Stop," 164.
[120] HMC Portland, vol. 2, 152 (December 27, 1676), Danby to Ogle; BL EG 3331, 51,117–128; BL EG 3328, 107.
[121] Arlington had to communicate through Danby about the retrenchment of expenses of the household above stairs: see PRO LC 5/141, 329. Reresby had considerable difficulty obtaining his tax break for the cutlers of Hallamshire: Reresby, 104–105, 119, 125.

monopolization of access Danby was able to mitigate the financial hazards of a king with an alarming propensity of saying "yes."[122]

Yet Danby's monopolization of access had deleterious effects, for closed access generated suspicions. There were rumors that the king aimed at arbitrary government and that the preparations for the war with France were a hoax designed to generate revenue. Danby's close alliance with Portsmouth, the king's French mistress, only fanned the flames. Danby noticed such fears in his memoranda for his meetings with the king.[123] The old fears of evil counselors emerged as well. Edward Dering received a letter which stated: "I do humbly conceive that there is nothing of greater moment than the placing of honest men about the king and the duke for if these gentlemen get them to themselves God have mercy upon such as are not their favorites."[124] Even Danby's financial improvements were looked at cynically. The king, opponents said, was saving £10,000 a week and would use the money to cause a fall of rents, thereby rendering the landed classes totally dependent upon the monarch.[125]

Danby's use of access as a political weapon solidified the opposition. Since the king used access to delineate whom he favored and whom he disdained, those who were shunned knew that they would have no opportunity to sway the king to their side. Now, to change public policy politicians turned to Parliament, for private channels no longer existed for those out of favor. The presence of an, albeit nascent and unorganized, opposition combined with the climate of suspicion, rendered the ground very fertile for the insinuations of Tongue and Oates, the informers who announced the existence of a popish plot to kill the king.

The king was amazed at the credulity with which the Commons accepted the ravings of this curious pair, but the prevailing climate of suspicion explains the danger the Parliament saw in the proposed plot. The fear of evil counselors (a fear spurred on by closed access) was interconnected with the terror of papacy; and at first the former received more attention. On December 2, 1678 the commons voted "to represent [to the king] the dangers of his adhering to private counsel and not taking the counsel of Parliament."[126] In fact, it was

---

[122] According to C. D. Chandamon, Danby was more successful at increasing revenue than decreasing expenditure. For one short period of time, however, the Lord Treasurer did implement a significant retrenchment of expenses (C. D. Chandamon, *The English Public Revenue* (Oxford: Clarendon Press, 1975), 230–240).

[123] Danby, however, blamed the "fears . . . grown both so general and so great" on the "success of France" (BL ADD 28042, 3–11 (April 4, 1677)).

[124] BL Stowe 746, 14. Internal evidence in the letter suggests that it was written before September 1677. The author, Sir Allen Ashley, requests Dering's aid in securing a position in the bedchamber for the Earl of Oxford. The Earl was sworn in as gentleman of the bedchamber in September, 1677 (Sainty and Bucholz, 149).

[125] Browning, "The Stop," 132.

[126] CJ, vol. ix, 551, quoted in Browning, "The Stop," 302.

an attack on Danby as an evil counselor, not calls for the exclusion of James, which brought about the end of the cavalier Parliament.

The revelations of Ralph Montagu gave substance to the fears of Danby as an evil counselor. Montagu had served as ambassador to France and had been a loyal supporter of the court. The ambassador was also a notorious lecher (no mean accomplishment in Restoration England). In France, Montagu had engaged simultaneously in an affair with the Duchess of Castlemaine and the Duchess's daughter Anne Countess of Sussex. When the king's former mistress found out that her lover was sleeping with her daughter, she became incensed and complained to the king, Anne's father. Montagu rushed off to London, without leave, to plead his case personally in front of his monarch, but at this point in his reign Charles was strictly guarding access. He had no desire to hear Montagu's explanations. In a meeting arranged by Danby – who, by arranging the interview, demonstrated his control over access to the king – Charles refused to hear any explanations from Montagu and stripped him of all employments.

Ambitious and vengeful, Montagu sought election in Parliament and joined the opposition in an attempt to bring down Danby, his former patron. After much political maneuvering Montagu revealed letters in his possession which substantiated one of the rumors that had poisoned Parliament against Danby in 1677. The letter that Montagu produced gave credence to the suspicion that the proposed war with France was a sham designed to get money out of Parliament and to raise a standing army. In the letter the French promised Danby a subsidy for Charles II in return for peace. In calmer times, Danby's explanation, that he had lacked the finances to wage war on France and was trying to get money from them to do what he had to do anyway, may have worked. But the rife suspicion of the evil counselor drained the credibility from any explanation which presupposed the honesty of the king's chief minister. Articles were passed for Danby's impeachment. In the ensuing debate, as in previous moves against Danby, it is striking to see the degree to which Parliament stuck to the familiar trope of the evil counselor. Lord Herbert reported to his father that Stephen Fox told the king "that if he had voted for my lord treasurer, knowing so much as he did, he had voted against the king."[127]

In order to salvage his reign Charles returned to his old policy of open access. The taint of the evil counselor had grown to such an extent that he realized he could not simply replace one prime minister with another. He reached out to the Presbyterians and Denzil Holles and made a secret deal whereby, in return for Danby's resignation and a dissolution of Parliament, they would refrain from impeaching the Lord Treasurer. In January, 1679 Charles dissolved Parliament and, for the first time since the beginning of his reign, called for a general election.

---

[127] *HMC Beaufort*, 80 (December 24, 1678).

The outcome of that election demonstrated the effects that Danby's policy of closed access had on popular opinion. Despite the uproar caused by the popish plot, anti-courtier sentiment, not anti-Catholicism nor the desire to exclude the Catholic Duke of York from the line of succession, dominated both pamphlets and voter sentiment. John Aubrey recorded that John Birkenhead, a Master of Request, was mocked and scorned at Wildon as a pensioner.[128] In his study of the succession crisis, Mark Knights demonstrates that, in the first election of 1679, the "dominant issue was not exclusion, but the undesirability of choosing courtiers and pensioners of the court."[129] The king himself claimed that a dog had a better chance of being elected than a courtier.[130]

The intense anti-courtier sentiment, both in elections and among the opposition, sprang forth from the perception that Danby's policies of closed access had perverted the role of the MP as a conduit between the king and the MP's constituents. Members of Parliament saw themselves as the antithesis of the evil counselor; they proclaimed that they truly represented the people and that they were the proper intermediary between king and subjects.[131] Parliament's advocates claimed that the House of Commons could petition the king on behalf of the people.[132] The borough corporations saw their members as their agents to the central authority, whose responsibility was to push the local agenda in Parliament. MPs were also seen as having responsibilities to their constituents outside of Parliament. Many local corporations had few resources with which to contact the crown. The members they elected, however, generally resided in London and could obtain audiences with the king. If a corporation requested a member to act as their agent they need not feel obliged to that member. Unlike asking a favor from a local nobleman, requesting a member to act on the corporation's behalf seemed to the corporation as only instructing him how to perform his duty. Hence, during the restoration, local corporations, even large ones such as Exeter, often requested their members to present the king with petitions.[133]

Expectations that a Member of Parliament would intercede with the king on behalf of the local corporation explains, in part, why Sir John Neale found no anti-courtier sentiment in his study of Elizabethan elections.[134] Local

---

[128] John Aubrey, *Brief Lives*, ed. A. Clark (Oxford: Clarendon Press, 1898), 104.

[129] Knights, 209.

[130] Hutton, *Charles II*, 367.

[131] Such views went against monarchical theorists who believed that "the king as head of the body politic, filled the position of representative" (Derek Hirst, *The Representative of the People?* (Cambridge: Cambridge University Press, 1975), 157).

[132] Ronald Butt, *A History of Parliament: The Middle Ages* (London: Constable, 1989), 268–269, quoted in Annabel Patterson, *Reading Between the Lines* (Madison: University of Wisconsin Press, 1993), 64.

[133] Exeter Letter Book RO, Cape, Q/60/f, 423–442.

[134] Sir John Neale, *The Elizabethan House of Commons* (London: Cape, 1949).

corporations would desire courtiers, who had more influence with the king, to be their agents. Only when a courtier was deemed incapable of acting as an agent – when he was too inaccessible, or thought to be too powerful or busy to take care of a borough's needs – anti-courtier sentiment prevailed. Such anti-courtier sentiment emerged in 1640, when the long isolation of the court rendered all courtiers virtually inaccessible.

Danby's policy of gathering all courtiers and pensioners into one monolithic unit appeared a perversion of the ideals of MPs and their constituents. The constituents were comfortable with an MP having simultaneous obligations to the king and to his electors. Such comfort, however, lasted only as long as support of the king could be seen as a hazy loyalty, not a strict adherence to the administration's agenda; for when an MP loses his ability to dissent from the administration, he becomes unable to relay grievances about current policy to the king. Danby's advancing of an arguably pro-French and pro-Catholic agenda only amplified the apprehension that MPs were bound to the whim of an evil counselor, one who with the help of the king's French and Catholic mistress was monopolizing access to the king. When courtiers were seen as relying totally on the favor of an evil counselor they were no longer seen as intermediaries or conduits, but abettors to those who tried to lead the king away from his people. As Reresby emphasized, it was the "*treasurer's friends*" who lost every election which was tried.[135]

The power of the motif of the evil counselor was such that after the election of 1679, many continued to believe that the succession crisis could be solved by changing the king's advisors.[136] A document preserved among the Shaftesbury Papers, entitled "The present state of the Kingdom at the opening of Parliament," assumes that "if the king could be separated from the influence of his brother, his ministers and his mistress, he could be brought to comply with the wishes of the nation."[137] Rumor had it that Edward Seymour was impeached to keep him from the king's ear.[138] Reresby and the Duke of Albemarle claimed that Shaftesbury and his party believed that George Savile Marquis of Halifax had taken the place of Danby as the evil advisor.[139] Parliament put off the debate on exclusion in order to pursue Danby's impeachment.[140]

Charles II understood the importance his subjects placed on who surrounded the king and changed his advisors to allay their fears. He sent his

---

[135] Reresby, 175; emphasis added.

[136] North, *Examen* (London: printed for F. Gyles, 1740), 78.

[137] Haley, 502–503.

[138] The official charge was maladversions of naval funds. Henning, *Commons*, vol. iii, 417. The rumor is repeated by Seymour's brother (*HMC Somerset*, 107 (December 18, 1680)).

[139] Reresby, 213 (January 26 1680/1).

[140] Haley, 508–509.

brother to Brussels[141] and encouraged Danby to resign, and then let him linger in prison. To remove apprehensions further he allowed his chief critics back in court. Essex became Commissioner of the Treasury. Cavendish and Shaftesbury strolled the corridors of Whitehall once again. On the advice of Sir William Temple, Charles also created a new Privy Council with a substantially reduced membership. In the proclamation which established the new Council, Charles trumpeted his decision to reduce the size of the Council as a measure to prevent evil counselors, claiming that the unwieldiness of the previous Council had forced him to seek advice from a "single ministry or private advices or foreign committees."[142] Charles promised to avoid such devices and govern by the advice of the new Council. To please his opponents further, he appointed many of the administration's chief critics to the Council including Holles, Russell, Halifax, Cavendish, Powel, and Essex.[143] Those who had opposed the king made up a majority of the new group and Shaftesbury became Lord President of the Council. The policy worked better than Charles could have anticipated. The king not only bought himself time, but he destroyed the opposition by bringing them close to him.

Charles's embrace of the opposition destroyed their unity. Mark Knights has shown that members of the parliamentary opposition had very different ideas about how to deal with the problem of the succession. Some wanted Monmouth to be the next king, others were champions of William of Orange, and a large group wanted to place limits on the prerogative of a Catholic king, such as James II. When they had a common goal, such as impeaching Danby, they could unite, but when the court ceased to be monolithic, when no clear target to oppose existed, the opposition lost its unity.[144]

By entering into the Privy Council the leaders of the opposition also lost their credibility. Shaftesbury, Halifax, and Essex were victims of their strong belief in the myth of the evil counselor, that by controlling access to the king they could control policy. They had wagered that the king would follow the advice of the new Privy Council which they dominated, but they could not sway Charles to exclude James. Furthermore, by associating with the king they lost their patriotic credentials. Reresby recorded that "most of the other lords and gentlemen of the Privy Council, though very great patriots before in the esteem of both houses, began to lose their credit with them in some measure, soe true it is that the court and country livery can never be worn together."[145] Although the language of evil counselor was much in use, changing the king's advisors was no longer an option: Danby had so tarnished the word *courtier* that anyone joining the administration was immediately suspected of selling

---

[141] Ibid. 500–503.
[142] Turner, "Privy Council of 1679", 254–255.
[143] Ibid., 260.
[144] Knights, *passim.*, 105.
[145] Reresby, 177–178, (April 27, 1679).

out. As E. R. Turner aptly put it, "In a moment of necessity Charles II defeated his opponents by associating themselves with him."[146]

It is unlikely that Charles anticipated that he would destroy the credibility of his opponents by associating himself with them, but he clearly believed that giving access to his opponents would work as a stop-gap measure. The Earl of Ailesbury recorded the reason why Charles allowed exclusionists near his person and in his Privy Council in April of 1679. This policy, Charles told Ailesbury, was a ruse to confuse the opposition while he followed his own agenda.

> your father looked out of humour when in my presence . . . I am sure he would die at my feet I know him so well. Doth he imagine I left him out because I did not love him. He was to be left out because I do love him. God's fish they have put a set of men about me but they shall know nothing; this keep to yourself.[147]

Although Charles admonished the future Earl of Ailesbury to keep his plans secret, the king's actions soon made it abundantly clear that he meant to rule without consulting the Privy Council. He prorogued Parliament on May 27, 1679 without consulting the Privy Council and on July 3 he dissolved Parliament against the advice of the Council.[148] Such disregard for the Council's advice, along with his refusal to allow Parliament to meet for any substantive length of time, made it abundantly clear that Charles had abandoned all pretense of living up to the image of the accessible king. He abandoned the image of accessibility because such an image was irreconcilable with his decision to maintain the legitimate succession. Charles could not proclaim his accessibility when he had no intention of addressing his subjects' primary grievance, his brother's adherence to Rome. Allowing access only to Anglicans would further command the diligence and bolster the authority of those who supported James's right to the throne.

The king turned decisively towards a policy of unilateral communication: issuing commands and refusing to hear grievances or advice from his subordinates. It is no mere coincidence that Halifax, who was near the king during this period of unilateral communication, was one of the few contemporaries to qualify Charles's reputation of accessibility. The minister described the king as "being galed with importunities, pursued from one Room to another with asking faces; the dismal sound of unreasonable complaints, and ill-grounded pretenses; the deformity of fraud ill-disguised; all these would make any man run away from them; and I used to think it was the motive for making him walk so fast."[149] Halifax's description was well founded. Captain

---

[146] Turner, *Privy*, vol. II, 2.
[147] HMC *Ailesbury*, 33.
[148] Hutton, *Charles II*, 374–376. See also Haley, 535.
[149] As quoted in Bunny Paine Jones, "The Cully of Britain" (University of Houston Ph.D., 1980), 75.

John Graham reported from Newmarket to the Marquis of Queensbury that "It is hard to get any business done here. I walked but nine miles this morning with the king besides cock-fighting and courses."[150] The most affable king had now became difficult to reach.

Charles changed more than his walking pace; he began a systematic alteration of the structures of access. He cut off his subjects' ability to enter into physical proximity to his person by remodeling his palaces and the ordinances which governed access to them. He further made sure that only his political allies would benefit from positions close to the king. He removed from the court many officers who supported exclusion.[151] He suspended Shaftesbury from the Privy Council and brought Essex, Russell, Cavendish, Powel, and Sir Henry Capel to resign by his refusal to call Parliament.[152] He refused to allow Parliament to meet. Most substantially, however, the king, unlike Clarendon's speech of 1660,[153] tried to determine who could represent the localities to him. He endeavored to make sure that only royalist-Anglicans would serve as conduits between subject and monarch and that all communication between king and locality should flow through only hierarchically established conduits . To accomplish this goal he purged the JPs and Deputy Lieutenants of anyone who signed a petition calling for Parliament and he issued quo warrantos to alter the government of local corporations.[154]

Perhaps the best example of Charles's new policy of access is his attitude in 1679 towards two groups of petitioners. Both petitioners asked for the same thing: a new Parliament. The petitioners from Berkshire conformed to the Act against Tumults and Disorders by obtaining the approval of the Grand Jury of their county. The king expressed distress that his neighbors would meddle in affairs which did not concern them, but he warmly told them, "wee shall agree better over a cup of ale when we meet at Windsor than we are like to do here." On the other hand, the petitioners from Essex violated the provision of the Act against Tumults. The king took their petition and answered that

> he was supremely surprised to hear them meddle with matters that so immediately concerned the crown and him, and that against the leave of the best and chief men of the county. That he believed that some of those who subscribed to the petition might mean well, but they were abused by those that did not. And his majesty was pleased to add that he was not willing to call to mind things past. That he did remember the act of oblivion, though he did not remember it as they did. That he saw sundry who stood in need of that act of oblivion, and that they would do well to take such courses as might not need another. That he very well remembered

---

[150] *HMC Drumlanring* (March 9, 1683).
[151] Reresby, 214 (January 30, 1681).
[152] Haley, 565.
[153] See above, p. 57.
[154] See below, pp. 111, 117, 118ff.

forty. And he turned away saying 'Mr. Mildmay I would you remember forty'. To which he very insolently replied sir I remember sixty.[155]

The harsh rebuke that the Essex petitioners received underscores the importance the king placed on all communication coming to him through the "proper" channels, on controlling who had the right to complain to the king.

Charles's harsh rebuke also illuminates the king's motivation behind his strictly controlling access. By his clear reference to the events of 1640 Charles made it clear that he no longer wished for an act of oblivion, that he no longer wanted to plaster over the differences in society. To ensure the legitimate succession which so much of his country feared, Charles needed to become a leader of a party and he was doing everything in his power to convince the Anglican-Tories that he was on their side. He engaged in personal reassurances; both Ailesbury and Reresby record that the king assured them that he "would stick by his old friends."[156] Reresby also records many instances when the king deprecated his opponents by characterizing them as over-holy hypocrites.[157] Similarly on March 12, 1681 Charles dropped in on a group of loyalist MPs who were drinking at Chiffinch's apartments at Whitehall. He told those gathered there that "'he would go as far as any man for the preservation of the protestant religion as law establish'd, and the utter extirpation of popery,' whereupon Sir Thomas Vernon said 'amen and Presbytery too,' to which the king rejoin'd 'with all my heart, for I have smarted from those people already."[158] To convince the Tories further, Charles gave to them the control of all conduits of access to his person.

Handing over control to the conduits of access to royalist-Anglicans was done to allay apprehensions that the king would once more alter his policy to favor the Whig interest. Both Halifax and the Duke of Newcastle thought that such a change was likely. Both told Reresby that "the king's changableness and silence in affairs . . . made people in fear to serve them."[159] By giving access exclusively to Tories, Charles tried to demonstrate that he would not and could not be persuaded to switch sides.

Such an attitude, however, forced the opposition to adopt increasingly desperate measures. From the traditional presentation of grievances to Council and in Parliament, the king's opponents turned to demonstrations of public opinion such as monster petitions and pope burnings. When even these measures seemed increasingly unlikely to effect change, some of the more radical exclusionists came to the realization that the only way to change

---

[155] *HMC Fleming*, 165 (January 24, 1679/80).
[156] Reresby, 182, 202 (May 23, 1679, November 7, 1680). See also his assurance to Robert Paston Earl of Yarmouth, BL ADD 36988, 165.
[157] Reresby, 208, 224 (December 24, 1680, April 20, 1681).
[158] Knights, 290.
[159] Reresby, 210–211 (January 11, 1680/1). For similar sentiments see Reresby, 299 (March 23, 1682/3).

the king's policy was to change the king. Hence they hatched the Rye House Plot to kill the king and his brother. Charles, however, welcomed this new divisiveness that his strict policy of access fostered. By bringing his opponents to the edge of rebellion he forced those less committed than the Rye House plotters to confront the choice of a possible Catholic successor or a Civil War. When taken to the brink, few were willing to cross over to rebellion

The effect of this policy may best be seen in the person of Roger Whitley, who throughout Charles's reign represented the middle road. Whitley was a court pensioner who had voted against the court during the succession crisis, and was declared suitable for election by Smith's Protestant Intelligencer.[160] However, when confronted with the possibility of outright rebellion, this exclusionist rejected overthrowing the government and came to espouse full-fledged support of Charles.[161] By forcing many like Whitley to realize that the alternative of a Catholic successor was civil war, Charles ensured that his brother would have enough support to become the next king.

[160] Knights, 283.
[161] Bod Lib. Eng. Hist, c712, Roger Whitley's Diary April 27, 1684, April 30, 1684.

# 4

## Local politics and access
### Rifts, reconciliations, and purges: access and local politics, 1660 to 1667

When Charles II landed at Dover on May 25, 1660 the elders of the city anxiously expressed their loyalty to the returned king, presenting him with a gilded Bible and saluting him with cannon fire. In the next few months the representatives of many civic corporations and counties jumped on the loyalist bandwagon. The mayor and town chamber of Exeter, for instance, ordered three hogsheads of wine to be poured into the city conduits to enable the whole town to toast the king. They followed this celebration with a petition to Charles which expressed the corporation's loyalty and offered their monarch a gift of plate valued at £500.[1] Exeter was far from alone. The corporations of Chester, Coventry, Lyme Regis, and Totnes as well as the nobility and gentry of Warwickshire, Lancashire, and Cheshire, to name but a few, sent addresses to the king proclaiming their loyalty.[2] Even minor manorial boroughs such as Clitheroe acclaimed the king's return with pomp and celebration.[3] The universality of such representations of joy, however, merely covered up the deep rifts that existed within English society that the Civil War had exposed, created, and deepened.

Upon his return, Charles manipulated the conduits of access between localities and the king in order to heal those deep rifts. The king used himself as a model of clemency, and his advisors stressed that forgiveness could heal the country's wounds. When addressing the corporation of Kingston upon Thames, three Privy Councilors urged the town council to learn from the example of their monarch's compassionate nature and to desist from suing their fellow officers.[4] But the Civil War created wounds too deep to heal and often, as in Kingston upon Thames, Charles's appeal for mercy fell on deaf ears. Charles's attempts to unite his people had only limited success. He was stymied both by his need for security and a reluctance on the part of many Englishmen to forget the past.

[1] DRO, Exeter Act Book X (1651–1663), 133–136.
[2] *CSPD*, vol. I, 4–6.
[3] M. A. Mullett, "'Men of Known Loyalty': The Politics of the Lancashire Borough of Clitheroe, 1660–1689," *Northern History*, 21 (1985), 100–111.
[4] Paul Halliday, *Dismembering the Body Politic* (Cambridge: Cambridge University Press, 1998), 57–58.

To analyze the patterns of communication between the restored king and localities this chapter will focus on four counties: Cheshire, Devon, Norfolk, and Warwickshire. These counties were chosen because they each had large urban corporations which needed to communicate with central government.[5] They were also selected because they varied geographically, topographically, and in their pattern of loyalty to the crown during the English Civil War.[6] While this chapter will concentrate on these four counties, corroborating evidence will occasionally be brought from other parts of England.[7]

Analysis of corporations within the four counties reveals three main patterns of communication between the king and local elites in the first years of the reign. Cities known for loyalty benefitted from a multiplicity of conduits to the monarch which, in turn, engendered a slightly more tolerant society. Towns noted for rebellion, on the other hand, generally had only one avenue of access to the ruler. If these previously disloyal communities obtained a reliable patron with access to the king's person, they could still reach the king. Such ability to interact with the monarch persuaded nonconformists to work within the political system. Cities which could not rely on a patron – and these were often the most radical corporations in England – failed to obtain any aid from the court. These cities consequently lost their ties to the central authority which greatly diminished their power and led them to become ineffectual as governing bodies.

Although Charles occasionally denied access to individual corporations, he generally endeavored to promote bilateral communication in relation to entire counties. The restored king's commitment to listening to his subjects contrasts greatly with historians' depictions of Charles I's reign. Charles I never encouraged his subjects to address the crown with grievances. Upon his restoration, Charles II made sure not to recommit his father's mistakes and endeavored to create paths for his subjects to convey their opinions to him.[8]

Partly to open up avenues of access, Charles diminished the power of the Lord Lieutenants. A county's Lord Lieutenant headed its militia and often served as a primary conduit between center and locality. The Militia Bill of

---

[5] Cheshire – Chester; Devon – Exeter and Plymouth; Norfolk – Yarmouth, King's Lynn, Norfolk; Warwickshire – Coventry.

[6] For some excellent studies of these counties during the English Civil War see John Morrill, *Cheshire 1630–1660; County Government and Society During the Puritan Revolution* (Oxford: Oxford University Press, 1974); Anne Hughes, *Politics, Society, and Civil War in Warwickshire, 1620–1660* (Cambridge: Cambridge University Press, 1987).

[7] This chapter analyzes localities only in England because in Ireland and Scotland (and Wales to a lesser degree) a totally different dynamic of access existed.

[8] Derek Hirst, "The Privy Council and Problems of Enforcement in the 1620s," *Journal of British Studies* 18(1) (1978), 58. Kevin Sharpe, "Crown, Parliament and Locality: Government and Communication in Early Stuart England," *English Historical Review* 101 (399) (1986): 345–347.

1661 empowered the king to approve Deputy Lieutenants which gave the monarch some control over the patronage of Lord Lieutenants. Charles welcomed further communication from the Deputy Lieutenants which bypassed the Lord Lieutenants.[9] Victor Stater argues that such a reduction in authority in tandem with Charles's predilection for appointing only the most loyal peers to lead county militias rendered the Lord Lieutenancy more willing to perform the drudge work, and more concerned with the "needs of the crown," than local concerns.[10]

By allowing open access, Charles did diminish the independency of the Lord Lieutenants, but that independency was diminished in two directions: from the king and from the residents of the county. While Charles wanted the Lord Lieutenants to carry out his dictates, he also wanted them to be aware of and responsive to local concerns. For this reason, Deputy Lieutenants could easily circumvent the Lord Lieutenants and directly address the central administration. Far from Charles I's obsession with hierarchy, his son encouraged information to flow to the center through a multitude of conduits.

The pattern of appointments to the Lord Lieutenancy reflects such a concern with fostering communication between county and king. Charles appointed individuals with local ties to head the county militias; of the thirty-seven Lord Lieutenants appointed in 1660 at least twenty-nine had strong associations with the counties they led.[11] Residents of the county could approach a Lord Lieutenant who was a fellow resident or had other significant ties to the county more easily than one who was a stranger. Charles may have sacrificed social standing to approachability. The king, furthermore, wanted the Lord Lieutenants to have ample time and opportunity to converse with their countrymen. Unlike his father and grandfather, Charles tried to keep the purvey of any one Lord Lieutenant to a single county.[12] In December, 1660, only four Lieutenants led the militia of two counties and one had the responsibility for three counties. Except for the Earl of Northumberland (who led Northumberland and Sussex) the other four Lieutenants led counties, such as Cheshire and Lancashire, which generally had been treated as one administrative unit. Charles's Lord Lieutenants had few obligations which kept them from visiting their counties. In 1660, only twelve of the Lord

---

[9] Victor Stater, *Noble Government* (Athens, GA: University of Georgia Press, 1994), 75–77.

[10] Stater, 68.

[11] Weiser, "Reconstruction of Monarchy," Appendix E.

[12] Under Charles I, Lord Lieutenants often had multiple counties under their aegis. In 1629, for example, the Earls of Salisbury, Huntingdon, Sackville, and Montgomery were responsible for two counties, the Earl of Pembroke had three counties to administer, the Earl of Suffolk four, and the Earl of Northampton a whopping seven counties. In Warwick, Anne Hughes explains, the Deputy Lieutenants preferred to correspond with the Earl of Conway, a resident of their county, rather than with the elusive Northampton. In 1627, the Deputies asked Conway how to deal with some residents who refused to pay the charges

Lieutenants were Privy Councilors and two had other administrative or court posts which kept them in London, but the other twenty-four Lieutenants had no governmental duties to keep them from visiting and corresponding with their counties. Nine of the thirty-four Lord Lieutenants had some relations with the governments of the interregnum. In his appointments to the Lieutenancy Charles promoted open access by increasing the number of conduits to the king, making those conduits more open to people in the localities, and by eschewing any political bias in his choice of Lord Lieutenants and Deputy Lieutenants.[13]

The example of Cheshire shows the benefits of open access. In Cheshire, Charles split the posts of Lord Lieutenant and Custos Rotulorum between an Anglican and a Presbyterian.[14] The former royalist officer Derby became Lord

of raising men, a matter directly touching the militia. Yet even when Lord Lieutenants had a smaller dossier than the first Earl of Northampton, they failed to serve their counties. Northampton's son, the second earl Spencer Compton, was Lord Lieutenant of only Gloucestershire and Warwickshire, yet he never entered the county of Warwickshire, leaving the Deputy Lieutenants to their own devices, and, after Conway died, leaving Warwickshire with virtually no ties to the court (J. C. Sainty, ed., *Lists of Lieutenants of Counties 1660–1974* (London: List and Index Society Special Series, vol. 12, 1979); Hughes, *Warwickshire*, 60; Sharpe, "Government and Communication," 344).

[13] Here, I disagree with Victor Stater who sees Charles as sacrificing social standing at the altar of loyalty. Stater claims that if Charles had been concerned solely with appointing the most powerful and respected individual in a county, then Bolingbroke and Pembroke would have received the commissions for the county. Stater's assumption, however, fails to take into account how the English Civil War had overturned the social hierarchy of a county. Pembroke, rumored to be a Quaker and insane, clearly could not win the necessary respect to command the county and individuals such as Albemarle and Sandwich, who – while perhaps not having the most lofty title in their county – were certainly the most powerful. Furthermore, although Stater sees a preponderance of Anglicans among the Deputy Lieutenants, such a preponderance may not have come from a conscious policy of the king. Instructive parallels may be drawn from Ian Green's *The Re-establishment of the Church of England 1660–1663* (Oxford: Oxford University Press, 1978). Green asserts that the king appointed Anglicans to cathedral posts before the church settlement was complete not from any desire to establish a Laudian church, but because he was pressed by petitioners for these posts and was anxious to gratify them. A similar bottom-up dynamic probably occurred among Anglicans – seeking to become Deputy Lieutenants – who used their connections to obtain these posts. Over 25 percent of the Lord Lieutenants who Charles installed represented Presbyterian interests. Considering the small percentage of the peers who joined with Parliament against Charles I, Charles's appointment to the Lord Lieutenancy reflects the political sentiment of the upper echelons more than any desire to secure an Anglican preponderance in the Lieutenancy. (According to J. P. Kenyon, twenty-five peers supported the Parliament in 1643, twelve in 1645 (*Stuart England* (New York: Penguin, 1975), 165).).

[14] The Custos Rotulorum was the keeper of the counties judicial roles and head of the county commission. According to Norma Landau, in the late seventeenth and early eighteenth centuries the same person did not "always hold both offices" (Norma Landau, *The Justices of the Peace 1679–1760* [Berkeley: University of California Press, 1984], 14, 100 n.7.

Lieutenant and the Presbyterian who led a royalist revolt in 1659, George Booth, became the head of the JPs. Such a policy of appointment gave both Presbyterians and Anglicans conduits to the monarch. The residents of Cheshire, furthermore, could bypass these official conduits. To obtain his release from jail, Adam Martindale approached the king through Richard Baxter and Clarendon.[15] Richard Legh, a Deputy Lieutenant of Cheshire, could write Henry Bennet in 1662 asking for the removal of Derby and his replacement by Lord Gerard.[16] Sir Roger Bradshaigh and Colonel Kirkby of the adjoining county of Lancashire, of which Derby was also Lord Lieutenant, had sufficient access to the court that they managed to effect both the removal of two of Derby's appointments for Deputy Lieutenants in Lancashire and the appointment of Lord Brereton to be Derby's co-Lieutenant in Cheshire. Their success, in some measure, came from the king's dislike for the tactless Derby, but Charles's open access enabled this pair to easily bypass Derby when corresponding with the king.[17]

Lord Brereton figured prominently in another incident which demonstrated Charles's commitment to open access in Cheshire. Upon hearing that Thomas Stanley had a commission for a baronetcy, Brereton led a group of prominent Cheshire gentry to twice petition the king against Stanley's receiving the dignity. Brereton and his allies claimed that Stanley had "continually withstood the royal interest and had indicted Sir George Booth and others to high treason."[18] Stanley replied with two petitions of his own.[19] The king gave the four petitions enough credence to commission Denzil Holles and Charles Berkeley to investigate.[20] The monarch's appointment of this pair is telling. Holles was a former Presbyterian while Berkeley went into exile with the king. Charles clearly wanted both sides to feel that their case was properly represented.[21]

In Cheshire, the home of a Presbyterian-led royalist revolt, one could expect a multiplicity of conduits of access to the king. But Cheshire was not unique. King's Lynn, in Norfolk, had so few connections upon the Restoration that they had to ask their MPs (Sir Ralph Hare and Edward Walpole) how to address the king.[22] When they petitioned Charles to renew their charter in 1661 they asked Hare (Now MP for Norfolk) and Walpole along with Sir William Hovell (MP for King's Lynn in 1661) and the Lord Lieutenant

---

[15] See above, p. 58.
[16] Stater, 77.
[17] P. J. Challinor, "Restoration and Exclusion in the County of Cheshire," *Bulletin of the John Rylands Library*, vol. 64, No. 2 (1981–1982), 365–366.
[18] Ibid.
[19] *CSPD* vol. I, 132, 364.
[20] P. J. Challinor, "The Structure of Politics in Cheshire, 1660–1715" (Wolverhampton Polytechnic Ph.D., 1982), 26.
[21] Stanley was vindicated and received the baronetcy.
[22] NRO, King's Lynn, MFRO 430/4, 147.

Horatio Townshend to present their petition.[23] Even with such minor players serving them, King's Lynn interacted successfully with the king.[24]

Charles's commitment to open access bore some fruit. The diary of Thomas Mainwaring suggests that gentry in Cheshire from opposing sides in the Civil War interacted socially and even intermarried. Cheshire JPs appear less vindictive than most in prosecuting nonconformity.[25] The city of Chester elected one Anglican and one Presbyterian to Parliament in 1661,[26] which suggests that the burghers of Chester echoed Charles's sentiments that members of both denominations should have a conduit to the central government. In the election of 1661, King's Lynn in Norfolk, like Chester, elected one staunch royalist, Sir William Hovell, along with Edward Walpole who had held local office during the interregnum.[27] Open access appears to have fostered political stability in Hampshire as well. "During much of the first decade of Charles II's reign," Andrew Coleby contends, "a degree of political stability was ensured by the fact that no religious group within local society could be entirely confident of, or totally despair of, royal favour."[28] While disappointing to ultra-royalists, the policy of non-partisanship fostered security.

Corporations noted for radical dissent had fewer options in approaching the king, but they could still reach him. In Devon, for instance, the city of Exeter called on Sir William Morrice to present petitions to the king.[29] Exeter's town council relied primarily on their countrymen Morrice and George Monck, Duke of Albemarle, and showed their appreciation by giving Morrice a gift of plate and electing Albemarle their High Steward.[30] Exeter's

---

[23] NRO, KC 7/11 (May 3, 1661).

[24] Andrew Coleby found a similar ease of access in Hampshire. In the 1660s residents of Hampshire called upon the Earl of Portland, Thomas Culpepper (governor of the Isle of Wight), Southampton their Lord Lieutenant, and Joseph Williamson to communicate with the king. They could employ other resources when necessary: in 1665 the residents of Hampshire asserted that Culpepper had mishandled the government of the Isle of Wight and they petitioned the king for his removal. To save Culpepper face, the petition was officially rebuffed, but the Earl of Clarendon privately reassured the Hampshire residents that their grievances would receive redress and that "the Lord Treasurer, the Lord Ashley, and I myself, we are friends to the country."(Andrew Coleby, *Central Government and the Localities* (Cambridge: Cambridge University Press, 1987), 142–145).

[25] Challinor, "Restoration," 362, 367–368. The diary exists in manuscript form in the Cheshire Record Office. CRO, DDX/384/2.

[26] Henning, *Commons*, vol. i, 152–153.

[27] Ibid., 327.

[28] Coleby, 148. Warmington echoes Coleby's sentiments at least with regard to the gentry of Gloucestershire. The residents of Gloucester, however, could not effectively access the king. A. M. Warmington, *Civil War, Interregnum, and Restoration in Gloucestershire 1640–72* (Rochester, NY: Royal Historical Society, The Boydell Press, 1997), 208, 174ff.

[29] DRO, Act Book X, 135.

[30] DRO, Act Book X, 334.

avenues, however, consisted solely of Albemarle's clientage. Morrice and Exeter's two MPs were Monck's kin. Yarmouth, more notoriously non-conformist than Exeter,[31] had to rely solely on their High Steward Clarendon to interact with the king, but Clarendon strongly defended their interests, most notably by removing clauses from their new charter which impinged on Yarmouth's right to choose its own officers.[32] While neither of these towns benefitted from a multiplicity of avenues to the king, the open access of the first years of Charles's reign made it very easy for them to express their concerns to the central government.

The central government reaped some rewards from its policy of openness to areas of previous dissent. The most crucial reward was political stability. In Yarmouth, for instance, twenty-three independent corporators resigned in July, 1660 which suggests that they were willing to abide by the new power structure.[33] Furthermore, the mass resignation did not mean the complete disenfranchisement of all non-Anglicans. As Perry Gauci establishes, the central government understood that "the administration of the provinces was heavily dependent on local initiative and knowledge."[34] The government therefore needed to contain representatives from all prominent sections of society. Four former supporters of Cromwell continued to serve as aldermen of Yarmouth[35] which encouraged nonconformists to work to change the laws from within the system, to restrict their protests to normal political channels.

The city of Coventry, however, did not benefit from a prominent inter-mediary to the king. One of the most radically religious and anti-monarchical cities in England, Coventry shut its gates to Charles I during the Civil War and appears to have warmed little to royalty after the Restoration.[36] Charles II ordered the city walls to be torn down to prevent them from rebelling. Coventry did congratulate the king on his return and resigned their fee farm rents to him, but they waited until late June to do so.[37] To add injury to insult, stockpiles of arms were found in former rebels' houses in Coventry.[38] Soon afterwards they elected Thomas Hobson as their mayor. In the words of the Lord Lieutenant of Warwickshire, The Earl of Northampton, Hobson was "an actor against the king in the late rebellion under Lambert, enlisting

[31] The Lord Lieutenant of Norfolk, Horatio Townshend, reported to Clarendon about Yarmouth in September, 1661. "I could not have imagined," Townshend declared, "there had been such a nest of schismatical rogues within his majesty's kingdom." Perry Gauci, *Politics and Society in Great Yarmouth 1660–1772* (Oxford: Clarendon Press, 1996), 105.

[32] Gauci, 109.

[33] Ibid., 102.

[34] Ibid., 104.

[35] Ibid., 103.

[36] For the extent of Coventry's nonconformity see Judith Hurwich, "A Fanatick Town," *Midland History*, vol. 4, no. 1 (1977), 15–44.

[37] CRO, ba/h/c/17/2 (June 19, 1660) (hereafter referred to as Coventry Record Book).

[38] *CSPD*, vol. I, 59 (June 13, 1660).

soldiers, concealed arms, is an Anabaptist [and] called the last Parliament mad for passing the bill for corporations."[39] Even after Hobson's election was quashed, Coventry was known for the absence of royalism. P.C. Heap found in Coventry one of the highest non-compliance rates to the Hearth Tax.[40]

The Earl of Northampton did occasionally aid the citizens of Coventry, and the town recompensed him by giving him the position of recorder and by granting the freedom of the city to various of his clients.[41] But the relationship was always uneasy. Perhaps the need for another conduit to the king explains the lavish reception the Duke of Ormonde received when he passed through Coventry in July, 1662.[42] But Charles, uneasy about the loyalty of Coventry, had some trepidation undercutting Northampton's authority. For the rest of Northampton's life the city record books never register Coventry employing any other noble patron.[43]

The king saw this town as so infected with the rot of rebellion that amputation seemed the best medicine, but Charles could afford to be strict with this town and risk alienating its inhabitants precisely because it was the exception. As his attitude towards Exeter and Yarmouth shows, there were few such places which he deemed beyond redemption. For most of the corporations in the country, Charles wanted to employ the milder physic of clemency and oblivion to cure the body politic.

While the king saw conciliation as a salve for the nation's wounds, many Members of Parliament and local corporations thought the nation so diseased that only purgation and amputation could rid England of its ill-tempered humors. As Paul Halliday asserts, urban governments were torn between the ideal of the corporation as a united body politic and the reality of warring factions who denied their opponents a right to a role in government. In many

---

[39] *CSPD*, vol. II, 90 (September 15, 1661).

[40] P. C. Heap, "The Politics of Stuart Warwickshire" (Yale University. Ph.D., 1975), 68.

[41] Coventry Record Book, 138–140 (November 13, 1660, November 21, 1660).

[42] Coventry Record Book, 139–145 (July 12, 1662).

[43] A. R. Warmington's depiction of Gloucester reveals similarities with Coventry. Like Coventry, Gloucester was a seed-bed of dissent and Charles ordered its walls destroyed. Gloucester was even less lucky than Coventry, for, unlike the Warwickshire city, Gloucester had virtually no representative to the king. Its recorder was not a noted courtier or a peer, but only a judge, William Morton. This lack of paths to the king proved fatal for the corporation. Unrestrained by any alternative access to the king, the Lord Lieutenant Herbert led a particularly savage purge of the corporation. Three-quarters of the corporate body was purged, mostly at the commissioners' discretion. This stood the town in poor stead, because, unlike Yarmouth, Gloucester could not rely on local knowledge and initiative to govern the town; many of the replacements were gentry, not town members. The result was that the Gloucester town council met infrequently and willingly received a charter in 1664 which gave the king the right to veto all appointments, choose the recorder and town clerk, and severely limited the council's control of the suburbs (Warmington, 174–185).

cities internal strife over who constituted the benign humors and who constituted the ill humors, over who should be purged and who should remain, dominated civic life.[44]

The representatives of the nation did not trust the urban corporations to settle their own affairs. The Corporation Act of 1661 prompted a savage purge of municipal officers. An examination of the legislative history of this act affirms that this purge originated in Westminster, not Whitehall, which confirms my assertion that Charles desired to create broad-bottomed support for his reign.[45] The first proposed bill in the Commons selected commissioners for each county who, using their own judgement, would vet corporate officers, thereby removing all whom the House deemed unfit for government. The House of Lords responded with a vastly different piece of legislation which proposed curtailing the rights of corporations to select their own officers and allowing county JPs to enforce law within city limits.[46] This bill provides an interesting glimpse into the House of Lords' hierarchical views of access. The Lords' bill gave the king the power to select all town officials who communicated to the central government. Such a proposal would have integrated urban corporations into the hierarchical system of government. Municipal officers would be virtual agents of the king, not representatives of the town. By giving county JPs jurisdiction within city limits the proposed bill would have rendered the corporation subservient to their "betters." The imposition of this hierarchy, however, would not have purged the urban corporations. The Lords saw the problem in the country as one of a disruption of social hierarchy, not a rift in the body politic of corporations.

A bill very different from both proposals emerged from the conference of Lords and Commons. Like the house bill, the final act empowered commissioners to dismiss ill-affected corporate officials and to appoint new ones if necessary. The king, it appears, lobbied that he, not the House of Commons, should appoint the commissioners, but alterations to the Act drastically changed the function of these commissioners. The commissioners could still remove objectionable persons from local office and appoint others in their place at their discretion, but the Act stipulated that to remain in office all officials had to swear oaths of allegiance, supremacy, and against taking arms against the king, and declare against the league and covenant. Those who refused were removed as if dead.[47]

Charles appears to have tried to mitigate the effect of this act. When he and Clarendon chose commissioners he made sure that they represented a broad political spectrum. In Shropshire and Staffordshire Charles favored commissioners who had local knowledge and standing over those who had

---

[44] Halliday, xii, *passim*.
[45] This argument coincides with that of Ian Green.
[46] Halliday, 87.
[47] Ibid., 90–91.

solely royalist zeal.[48] In Exeter this also appears to have been the case.[49] The commissioners whom Charles selected generally removed only the officials who were the most noxious and whose removal the law required. According to Halliday's study of thirty-six corporations, 33.74 percent of corporate officers were dismissed. Of these at least 75 percent did not swear oaths and many of the other 25 percent did not declare against the solemn league and covenant. Thus only a minority of officers lost their positions because of the commissioners' judgement. In Plymouth, Warwick, and Barnstaple commissioners only removed officers who failed to swear oaths or take the declaration. Only one corporate official in King's Lynn and Chester suffered from the discretionary powers of the commissioners.[50]

Some perceived Charles's general lack of a desire to purge as a sign of royal reluctance to prosecute loyal nonconformists. According to P. J. Norrey, the central government emitted conflicting signals to local magistrates. The Privy Council summoned one magistrate to London where they reprimanded him for "his efforts to suppress faction."[51] Another magistrate, George Pley, faced investigation for allowing nonconformist meetings to occur in Weymouth. Pley responded that he "understood that nonconformists met in London, unsuppressed by king, council or city officers." His examiner's only reply was "If they be rogues, must we be rogues too."[52] The dissenting minister Adam Martindale of Cheshire and his allies perceived such mixed signals as tacit approval to continue ministering to a nonconformist flock. After the Act of Uniformity came into effect, Martindale records in his diary that "there came a post letter from a trusty friend at London signifying that the Lord Chancellor Hyde and the Lord Chief Justice Bridgeman had been with the king in order to [obtain an] indulgence for non-conformers and had so farre prevailed that the king sent Dr. Sheldon then Bishop of London about it. . . . Upon this I was advised to go home and to preach to my old parisioners [as] if there were none other sent to that purpose."[53] Charles tried, to some degree, to remain everybody's king. By not being the agent behind the purges, he could still be thought of as the defender of a multiplicity of interests.

In some areas, Charles's mitigation of the purge encouraged unity. Exeter corporation exhibited little desire to prosecute nonconformists. Seth Ward, the Bishop of Exeter, complained to Sheldon about the lack of Anglican zeal and the widespread desire to prohibit such Anglican zeal as divisive. On December 19, 1663, Ward wrote, "the only persons in this city who have the

[48] Ibid., 93–94.
[49] DRO, Act Book X, 247.
[50] Halliday, 95–96. In Gloucester and Coventry, however, Charles's clemency was nowhere to be found.
[51] P. J. Norrey, "The Restoration Regime in Action: Relations between Central and Local Government in Somerset, Dorset and Wiltshire, 1660–1678," HJ, vol. xxxi (1988), 805.
[52] Norrey, 805.
[53] Martindale, 167.

heart and courage to endeavor an obedience to the laws, have been checked and discouraged for their labor and some put out of employment as being too pragmaticall and forward to draw the people to obedience."[54] In Chester as well, prosecutions for nonconformity were very few.[55] But these areas were the home of loyal Presbyterian sympathizers such as Albemarle and Booth. In Coventry, the Anglican minority sought to purge and Charles encouraged them. They obtained a new charter in 1663 which allowed less leeway for occasional conformity than the Corporation Act.[56]

Some of the success of the ultra-royalists after 1663 came from the fact that the monarch had begun to adopt their opinions. Charles began a flirtation with the idea, expressed in the Lords' proposals for the corporations act, that the country should be organized on hierarchical lines. In a series of charters the king tried to gain the right of approbation for the recorders, stewards, and town clerks of cities, officers whose primary duty was to interact with the crown on the city's behalf. Those corporations which effectively communicated through the hierarchical structure and thereby showed their willingness to do so, such as Chester and Yarmouth, dissuaded the king of the need to reduce the liberties of the town. Those unable to employ hierarchical means of communication, such as Gloucester, lost their ability to effectively govern themselves. Charles, albeit haphazardly and piecemeal, was mooring the autonomous corporations more firmly to the governing structure of the nation.

This plan, however, required effort and time, and the Dutch War, the plague, and the fire deprived the king of those commodities. From 1664 to 1667 the king left the localities largely to their own devices. Communications with the counties were inevitably unidirectional and dealt with taxes or preparing the militia.[57] Perhaps the situation can best be summed up by Norwich's town clerk Thomas Corie's attempt to get aid from the Privy Council for the relief of those infected by the plague. The Privy Council replied that Corie should exhort and prevail with the gentry of the county for aid.[58] After a brief flirtation with gaining more control over corporations, the king and Council were, in effect, relinquishing their responsibility for local concerns.

---

[54] Allan Brockket, *Nonconformity in Exeter 1675–1875* (Manchester: Manchester University Press, 1962), 21.

[55] P. J. Challinor, "Restoration," 367–368.

[56] Hurwich, "A Fanatick Town," 19. Despite the new charter four dissenters remained on the council (Halliday, 100).

[57] *HMC Var. Coll.* vol. 2, 386 (March, 1665); *HMC Kenyon*, 243 (November 30, 1665); Chester Mayors Letter Books, CRO, ml3/386u, 397–406; NRO, King's Lynn MFRO 430/4, 203 (March 10, 1665/6), 204 (March 30, 1666).

[58] Walter Rye (ed.), *Extracts from City of Norwich* (Norwich: Norwich and Norfolk Archeological Society, 1905), 117.

## The king meets his subjects: access and local politics during the Cabal (1667 to 1673)

As the Dutch War drew to a close, Charles returned his attention to the localities. Now, however, he did not aim to bring municipal corporations into an integrated hierarchical structure of government. Rather, he wanted to rectify the lack of communication of the previous few years. The appointment of the Cabal signified openness to the countryside as well as at court; by surrounding himself with individuals of diverse religio-political tenets, Charles signaled his returned commitment to accessibility and, by co-opting the local ties of his new advisors, established conduits to the localities. For the next six years, Charles would welcome communication from the localities that did not adhere to the strictures of hierarchy and would meet his subjects without intermediaries.

Charles took concrete steps to signify his openness. He encouraged diversity in the militia. The king countenanced Horatio Townshend's appointment of nonconformists to posts in the Norfolk militia[59] and commanded the Marquess of Worcester to give Edward Harley the command of a regiment of foot in the Herefordshire militia, in the face of Worcester's quite valid accusations of Harley's Presbyterian leanings. Edward Harley's ability to circumvent the Lord Lieutenant and approach the king through Sir Robert Harley and Arlington testifies to Charles's willingness to circumvent the normal hierarchical structures and communicate directly with his subjects.[60]

Charles's most visible attempt to reconnect with his people were two progresses that he undertook in 1671. For a king noted for his accessibility, Charles had taken surprisingly few progresses. He had vacationed in Bath and Tunbridge Wells, fled from the plague to Salisbury, Isleworth, and Oxford, and traveled from one royal residence to another, but the only progresses Charles had undertaken were by yacht to visit naval installations (see Appendix).

Charles's progress to Devon began as just such an expedition. The king sailed to Portsmouth and then to Plymouth, but contrary winds prevented the yacht from sailing back to London and forced it to stop in Dartmouth. From Dartmouth, Charles made a land progress back to his capital city, stopping at Exeter and Salisbury on the way.[61]

The informal nature of this progress shocks historians accustomed to the near scripted progresses of most baroque monarchs. Charles popped up in Portsmouth three or four hours before anyone expected him. He then

---

[59] James Rosenheim, *The Townshends of Raynham* (Middletown, CT: Wesleyan University Press, 1989), 36.
[60] *HMC Portland*, vol. 3, 306 (January 4, 1668).
[61] *HMC Fleming*, 81 (July 18, 1671); *CSPD* (1671), 384–385, 391–392, 395; *HMC Var. Coll.* vol. 4, 137 (July 23, 1671).

suddenly decided to go to Plymouth. The Earl of Bath, hearing of the king's impending arrival late Saturday night, rode fifty miles in the dark to meet the king in Plymouth. Once the king arrived, he abandoned any pretense of a fixed schedule. One correspondent reported that

> on a sudden while the mayor and magistrates were together consulting how they might further treat him, and were going to wait on him to understand his remove, he came into the town as far as the new quay, and went presently down to the barbican stairs, where he landed and went into his pinnace. The mayor and magistrates being so surprised, not having time to kiss his hands at his departure, went after him in a wherry to Mount Edgcombe.[62]

The same correspondent details how when his majesty came to Plymouth, it alarmed the gentry of Devon and Cornwall who all rushed to Plymouth to kiss the king's hands. The king's sudden appearance also alarmed Exeter corporation. Exeter, which had recently received a favorable ruling from the king regarding their rights over the river Exe,[63] strove to show their appreciation. Hearing the king was nearby, the council quickly assembled a delegation and a gift of a gold ball worth £500. However, the king's sudden movements prevented the council from reaching Charles before he embarked once again. Luckily for them, after being stopped by contrary winds the king went to Exeter in person, where he received the golden gift.

The casualness of this progress, while no doubt worrying in the extreme to those responsible for the king's entertainment, lent an air of spontaneity and genuineness to the proceedings. Because the response was not scripted, support for the king seemed more sincere. The hurried nature of the southwest gentry, the Earl of Bath, and the town of Exeter all testify to the eagerness of the leaders of Devon and Cornwall counties to see the king, be seen by the king, and be seen with the king, all of which publicly demonstrated their support for the monarch and the monarch's approval of the gentry.

Charles, not content to simply see the support of the people, acted as much the politician as the monarch, campaigning actively to endear his subjects to him. Besides touching for the king's evil, Charles praised the city of Plymouth, remarking upon the "excellency of that most excellent harbour beyond any other in his dominions, of the prospect of the royal citadel, town, and the rivers." The king, furthermore, promised that his interaction with the citizens of Plymouth would continue. He "told the mayor that he should be no stranger to this place, for he should visit it again in some short time." The king specifically mentioned local concerns such as the preservation and cleaning of the harbor and promised the city that they could always relay any proposal to him through the Earl of Bath. Thus, Charles, in person, used the promise of access and communication to gain public support.

---

[62] CSPD, 384–385.
[63] See below, p. 103.

By mentioning the Earl of Bath by name, Charles signified two reasons for his progress: gaining the loyalty of his subjects, and bestowing upon local governors the mantle of royal favor.[64] Charles demonstrated further his support of local governors and the governors' reliance on the king in a ceremony surrounding the bestowal of the key to the city. When the king approached the gates of Plymouth, Bath presented him with the key to the city, Charles returned it to him, saying "he could place it in no better hands." When he reached Exeter, Charles performed the same ceremony, demonstrating the approval of the king for the town council. By such ceremonies Charles not only strengthened the authority of local officials by tying them closely to the royal person, but also underscored the notion that their authority came from the monarch.[65]

The trip to Devon was such a success that Charles immediately began plans to visit Norfolk and Suffolk.[66] This trip lacked the spontaneity of the visit to Devon, but it was still far from scripted,[67] and Charles carefully demonstrated his accessibility to the citizens of Norfolk and his concern for their interests. Again he acted like a campaigning politician, feeding heartily on Yarmouth's famous herrings. Like his progress before the coronation, Charles's trip to Norfolk was more in the medieval than the baroque mode; more a dialogue between ruler and ruled than an assertion of absolute power.[68] The city of Yarmouth used the opportunity of the king's presence to push their agenda; in particular support for the fishing industry, they presented the king with a golden chain of interlocking herrings worth £300.

Richard Bower, an avid royalist, reported to Arlington the details of the king's visit to Yarmouth. Bower disliked his tolerationist Lord Lieutenant Horatio Townshend's countenance of former rebels and used the opportunity of the king's visit to disparage Townshend. Bower, interestingly, shows Townshend as trying to limit access to the king during his visit.[69] Ironically, Bower employed the literary device of the evil counselor to disparage the king's open access policy.

---

[64] The Earl of Bath was Governor of Plymouth as well as Groom of the Stool. With Albemarle's death on January 3, 1669/70, his cousin Bath became the acting Lord Lieutenant and the chief noble of the counties of Devon and Cornwall.

[65] The previous description of the king's progress to Devon drew upon the following sources: Exeter Act Books in DRO, Act Book XI, 216; *CSPD*, vol. 11, 385–386 (July 16, 1671), 391–392 (July 21, 1671);. HMC *Fleming*, 81 (July 18, 1671; July 25, 1671).

[66] A newsletter writer reported, only ten days after Charles left Exeter, that the king was considering going to Norwich and Yarmouth in September. *CSPD*, vol. 11, 400.

[67] For the confusion of the king's reception see Thomas Corie's report of the king's progress to Norwich: BL ADD 27967, 88.

[68] See below, p. 121.

[69] Townshend did have a tendency to be protective of his position as intermediary between county and center. In 1664 he had become upset at John Gladman because Gladman had corresponded with Albemarle without first obtaining Townshend's approbation (*HMC Townshend*, 26).

The avid royalist Bower could not countenance the fact that the king honored nonconformists during the progress. Charles received and knighted James Johnson and George England, both former council men ejected for Presbyterianism. Instead of deprecating Charles II's policy of open access which encouraged Presbyterians, Bower blamed Townshend as the classic evil counselor who prevented good advice and loyal subjects from reaching the king. Bower described Townshend pushing Sir James Meddowes in order to prevent Meddowes from presenting the king with a petition.[70] The fact that Bower related all this to the king's chief minister Arlington, however, belies the fact that the king was reliant solely on Townshend to see how matters stood in Norfolk. Indeed, the king was probably happy to see that his policy of open access resulted in a situation where to use Bower's words "all parties and factions were unanimous as to the kings reception, striving to outvie one the other."[71]

This period of open access led to parties striving to outvie one another because all factions felt confident that they could reach the king. In Coventry this situation of open access led to considerable disorder. The Coventry city record book records a number of instances where citizens circumvented the town council and directly approached the king against the interest of the governing body. In August, 1671 Abel Brooksby refused the chargeable position of mayor because he had obtained a royal letter exempting himself from any local office in return for the good service he had done Charles II's and the late king's soldiers as a physician. The city of Coventry reacted against this reprieve, both because they thought it impinged upon their rights under their charter and because Brooksby had not performed any such services. They approached their Lord Lieutenant and recorder Northampton with evidence that Brooksby was an apothecary, not a physician, and at Worcester had aided the rebels, not Charles II's forces. Furthermore, the Coventry city council argued that allowing subjects to petition the king directly for exemption from city office would create wide disruption in local government, a notion which Northampton echoed to Arlington.[72] In a letter addressed to Coventry, Charles wrote, "wee having made further reflection upon that matter and considering the partiality of such indulgences and the inconvenience they may be of in their examples in other places, have thought fit therby to revoke our said letters in favor of the said Abel Brokesby and to leave you the freedom

---

[70] Meddowes had recently resigned his commission in protest at Townshend's appointment of Presbyterians as officers.

[71] *CSPD*, 517 (October 9, 1671).

[72] Although Northampton agreed with Coventry in this case, he did not want to be seen as coming to the lists in favor of the radical city. In his letter to Arlington he stressed that his position of recorder obliged him to "serve them in all just affaires to my utmost power," and he asked only that a delegation from Coventry be allowed to meet Arlington to argue their case.

of your choice in the succeeding election."[73] By gaining Northampton's aid, the city of Coventry succeeded in changing the king's mind.

Coventry, however, did not resolve the problem of citizens approaching the king directly without council consent. In October, 1672, the Record Book noted that "some persons of this house have lately and *unduly* preferred a petition to his majesty in the name of the mayor, bailiff and commonality of this city."[74] Coventry had enough influence to coerce this group to desist from their petitioning. In Gloucester, however, the city had lost control over its own town council and was unable to control who approached the king. In a disputed local election of 1670 the gentry sponsored Henry Fowler while most of the citizens supported William Bubb. Due to the savage purges of local officials in 1662 and 1664, the citizens had lost all means of access to the king and could not take their case to the monarch. All communication to the center went through Fowler, the recorder Henry Morton, another avid royalist, and the Lord Lieutenant. As such, these gentry leaders convinced the king to issue a new charter to Gloucester which named the entire town council. Most of this new council were gentry, not city dwellers, and the new council had little desire to deal with the day-to-day running of city government. Gloucester, for all purposes, was left without any functioning municipal authority.[75]

The relative failure of the Gloucester in relation to Coventry shows the importance of having a competent access broker. In a period of open access, the need for an access broker remained vital because established institutions had to be especially vigilant against their opponents who could now reach the king with relative ease. Established institutions needed someone at court to defend their interests. Exeter, for instance, had to battle against one Mr. Browning who wanted to cut from the River Exe a passage of water for his fulling mill. Browning went to court and presented his petition to the Privy Council. Exeter solicited the aid of its MP Sir James Smith as well as Bath, Secretary Coventry, and Speaker Edward Seymour, and defeated Browning's petition.[76] Coventry could rely on Northampton at least against the likes of Brooksby. But not every city adapted well to this period of open access.

Chester, for instance, battled local gentry ineffectually. From 1669 to 1672 the city and the local landed elite contended assessment rates.[77] In 1671 Thomas Cholmendely on behalf of the county had the city bakers patent, which extended their authority outside the city walls, stopped in Chancery.[78]

---

[73] Coventry Record Book, 206–208.
[74] Ibid., 218.
[75] Warmington, 189–190.
[76] DRO, Exeter Letter Book Q/60/f, 437–438.
[77] Chester CRO, ML4, 435 (December 2, 1669, June, 1670, February 2, 1670/1, February 4, 1670/1, 15 March, 1670/1); Challinor, "Restoration," 367.
[78] Cheshire CRO, DSS 1/1/14.

Chester's recorder William Williams could not curry favor at court in either dispute. The events surrounding Chester's parliamentary by-election of 1672 reinforced the perception of Williams's inability to cultivate a court interest. His opponent Robert Werden received a letter of recommendation from the Duke of York; Williams received a letter from Shaftesbury asking him to stand down. The freeholders of Chester appear to have blamed Williams for their losses at court. Despite numerous electoral shenanigans such as issuing new patents for freemen, abruptly changing the time and place of the election, and promising to pay off the city's debts and lend it £500, Williams, the recorder of the city, lost by fifty votes even after securing the support of the teller.[79] Aware of the lack of court interest at Williams's disposal, many voters probably did not want him occupying two offices that served as intermediaries between king and city.[80]

Disputes between gentry and city often had a religious tinge because Charles's open access policy revived the belief among nonconformists that he supported a tolerationist agenda. In Coventry, dissenters who believed in an impending indulgence met frequently and openly.[81] In June, 1669 when the governor of Chester Castle, Sir Geoffrey Shakerly, went to Bosley Chapel to arrest the dissenting minister Garside, he was surprised at the "insolence" of "some of the chief of the female disciples [who] said openly that the king tolerated their meeting, and that they therefore wondered I disturbed them."[82] Shakerly should not have been overly surprised. According to P. J. Challinor, the translation of the moderate Widkins to the Chester see, the appointment of Sir Orlando Bridgeman as Lord Keeper, and the lapse of the first Conventicle Act all seemed to indicate that the king was "condoning their disregard of the conventicle laws."[83]

Contemporaries commented on the connection between open access and the widespread belief of immanent toleration. Richard Bower claimed that the king's being seen conversing with Dr. Owen both brought Anglicans to believe that his majesty did not fully support the prosecution of nonconformists and convinced all segments of society to predict rightly that the kings would soon formally declare toleration.[84] The recorder of Leeds directly

---

[79] BL ADD 33579. *Henning, Commons*, vol. I, 152–153. The election was the bloodiest in the restoration. Three people were trampled to death by the crowds when the place of election was moved.

[80] At this period there was little political disagreement between Williams and Werden. *Henning, Commons*, vol. I, 152–153.

[81] Hurwich, "A Fanatick Town," 21.

[82] *CSPD*, vol. 9, 354 (June 5, 1669).

[83] The seeming approbation of the king was important not only because people thought they were not being prosecuted, but also because it blurred the lines of schisms and rebellion (P. J. Challinor, "The Structure of Politics in Cheshire, 1660–1715" (Wolverhampton Polytechnic Ph.D. dissertation, 1982), 56).

[84] *CSPD*, vol. 11, 464–465 (September 1, 1671).

connected dissenter confidence with the perception that the king had appointed those who favored nonconformity to the Privy Council. "Many good people in this place thought that more liberty might be used and taken in their meetings to worship god, then had heretofore been attempted, seeing in all or most parts of the kingdom it was allowed or connived at by the magistrates, and the present disposition in the counsell seemed or was so reported to looke that way."[85] Even after the king personally tore up the Declaration of Indulgence, Nonconformists claimed his support. The minister of the Presbyterian meeting at Coventry claimed in December, 1673 that "his majesty's license under seal was the security of his person and his justification for the place."[86]

Anglicans did not take this lying down. For while they did not have the monopoly of the king's ear that they wished, they still had access to his person and, consequently, they believed that they could convince the king that his security was dependent on strictly enforcing the anti-dissent laws. The Anglican reaction was, unsurprisingly, most evident among churchmen. Some Anglican zealots may have gone too far in their attempt to bring the administration to their side. The recorder of Leeds reported to Dering that the dissenters in his city held two relatively open meetings which attracted "many spies." These spies found nothing faulty in the services. But the vicar and another minister

> pick up all information and tales they would meete true or false and send them away to the bishop now at London, and the better to spirit him to their business and to enrage the counsel, tells the bishop a most vile forgery [vith] that Mr. Jylpin in one of these meetings did sing a psalm . . . that god would put a [synod] into the hands of the saints to execute his judgement upon the king and burne the nobles in . . . fire.

This blatant lie worked. Hearing of this from the bishop, the king wrote "to the mayor to suppress such factions and put the laws in execution against offenders." The efforts of the bishop and vicar caused the nonconformists to meet "more private and in less numbers." But the mayor seems to have persecuted nonconformists only reluctantly. The recorder of Leeds reported that the mayor arrested only twelve of the numerous congregants and imposed only minor fines on them.[87]

The bishops and archbishops, despairing of temporal support, tried to take matters into their own hands. In a letter to Edward Bayntun dated 7 September, 1670, Seth Ward, Bishop of Salisbury, used the king's name like a mantra in order to convince the Wiltshire JP that – despite royal support of Bridgeman, Ashley, and Buckingham – Charles had authorized and called

---

[85] BL Stowe, 745, 31.
[86] Coventry City Record Book, 230 (December 19, 1673).
[87] BL Stowe, 745, 31.

for the suppression of conventicles.[88] The Archbishop of Canterbury began collecting data to make his case to the king about the danger of non-conformists and the relative ease of suppressing them. In June, 1669 he commanded his bishops to ask four questions throughout their sees:

1) Where and how many conventicles are held in every town or parish and at whose house or in what places they are usually held?
2) What are the numbers that usually meet at them, and of what condition or sort of people they consist?
3) Who are their ministers, teachers, heads or governors, and who are the principal persons frequenting and abetting those meetings?
4) What authority they pretend and from whom and on what grounds they look for impunity?[89]

What Sheldon asked indicates how he wished to use the information. The first three questions gathered intelligence about the size and power of the enemy: information which would be helpful in their apprehension when the Conventicle and Five Mile Acts were renewed. It is unclear if the Archbishop intended to employ these data to convince the king that dissenters comprised only a small minority and could therefore be prosecuted without causing a large segment of the population to rebel. Anglicans certainly employed such a strategy following the Compton Census of 1676. However, although the number of nonconformists that the 1669 inquiry discovered was within the same order of magnitude as the Compton Census, the 1669 inquiry had an air of uncertainty about it. Unlike the Compton Census which presented nonconformists as a percentage of all parishioners, the 1669 inquiry simply listed conventicles and numbers without any context. Furthermore, respondents often reported that conventicles were "numerous" without giving a specific number. The inexactitude of the response rendered the inquiry an inadequate tool to convince the king to change his policy.[90]

The fourth question aimed at more than an estimation of nonconformist numbers; it seems to have been directed at the very problem which Bower, Dering, and Shakerly perceived, namely that the nonconformists believed the king was on their side. By inquiring about their pretended authority, the Archbishop signaled his desire to confront the king with the proposition that royal openness to Presbyterians and their sympathizers spurred on dissenters.[91] Indeed, several of the dioceses reported back that the conventiclers believed the king supported their right to worship, although just as many conventiclers

---

[88] *The Commonplace Book of Sir Edward Bayntun of Bromham*, ed. Jane Freeman (Devizes: Wiltshire Record Society, vol. 43, 1988), 22–23. The words "His Majesty" appear nine times in a short letter.

[89] *Bayntun*, 21–22.

[90] See Lyon Thomas, *Original Records* for the returns of the 1669 inquiry.

[91] Norrey, 807.

**Table 2** Censuses of nonconformists[92]

| Diocese | Number of nonconformists in the 1669 Census | Number of nonconformists in the Compton Census (1676) |
|---|---|---|
| St Asaph | 300 | 643 |
| Bangor | 0 | 247 |
| Bath and Wells | 11050 | 5856 |
| Canterbury | unclear but numerous | 6297 |
| Chichester | 2760 + numerous | 2453 |
| Devon | 1500 | 5375 |
| Llandaff | 460 | 905 |
| Glamorgan | 700 | |
| Monmouth | 800 | |
| Lichfield and Coventry | 5450 | 4014 |
| Lincoln | 870 | 10297 |
| Leicester | 2190 | |
| Norwich | 11860 | 12785 |
| Sarum | 3700 | 2401 |

claimed they were following London's example. The king's open access, while generally discouraging to royalist Anglican clergy, nevertheless encouraged them to believe that they could bring him into their camp.

The laity appear to have been less interested in prosecuting nonconformists than the clergy. Some, such as Bower and Shakerly, tried to take matters into their own hands. Lord Herbert resolutely prosecuted nonconformists and purged the bench of anyone who appears to have supported them. But more often, the Justices of the Peace – whom the bishops needed to rely on to arrest nonconformists – balked at prosecuting their neighbors. Edward Bayntun and many of his fellow JPs replied to Seth Ward's call for a more diligent execution of the Nonconformity Act with a letter meant to give the impression that there was little need for the execution of that Act. The group of JPs related to the bishop "we have met and made diligent inquiry into the grounds of the informations therin mentioned and cannot find that there hath been any such great and outrageous meetings as were represented."[93] In Coventry the issuance of a royal decree against conventicles drove the great meeting out of Leather Hall, but private meetings continued to abound unprosecuted.[94] The mayor of Leeds also seemed unconcerned with prosecuting the dissenters since he allowed most of the members of a dissenting congregation to leave unarrested.[95] The opaqueness of royal policy

---

[92] This table was assembled with data taken from Thomas, *Original Records*, and Whiteman, *Compton Census*.

[93] *Bayntun*, 23.

[94] Hurwich, 22.

[95] BL Stowe, 725, 31.

had much to do with JPs' reluctance to prosecute nonconformists; when they suspected the king would soon change his mind, JPs hesitated to alienate their neighbors.

In Wiltshire and Exeter a clear annunciation of royal policy led to a more rigorous performance by JPs. Once the crown took a personal interest in the performance of Wiltshire JPs even sympathizers of dissent, such as Sir Edward Bayntun and Sir Edward Hungerford, took part in prosecuting dissenters.[96] According to Bishop Anthony Sparrow of Exeter, nonconformists had been claiming that the assize justice Vaughn carried royal instructions to favor them. Sparrow claimed that the rumor made "the justices . . . spirit faln & no man almost durst appear against the factions who had overrun us."[97] When Vaughn arrived, to Sparrow's delight, the Justice fully declared the laws against the conventicles which encouraged the JPs to perform their duties. When a clear indication of the king's will was lacking, however, Justices of the Peace were left to their own interpretations, and they often opted for the safe course of inaction.

If a clear annunciation of royal will could obtain the co-operation of the JPs to control dissent, why did the king not pursue such a policy throughout his reign? A number of factors explain his hesitation. First and foremost, he consistently feared that too harsh a religious policy would bring about open rebellion. Furthermore, he had little zest for ousting religious, as opposed to political, dissenters. But the king's need for cash may have contributed the most to his reluctance to pursue a strict religious policy.

Quite simply, during this period, much of the revenue was collected by a locally resident volunteer force.[98] To gain revenue, Charles needed the support of these volunteers, because if they and the taxpayers were not fully supportive of the regime, they would use every loophole possible to diminish the amount of taxes their locality paid. The essential ineffectiveness of this system, especially after the collapse of the Hearth Tax in 1669, led to the collection of taxes by salaried officials. These salaried officials filled only managerial positions such as the Agents of Taxes, but they closely supervised local tax collection, thereby influencing local officials to refrain from issuing undue exemptions.[99] It is significant that during these years of open access and communication, the collection of the revenue was a relative success. However, more importantly, the creation of a bureaucracy, albeit a very limited one, designed to oversee the collection of revenue made the political program that Thomas Osborne was about to introduce more palatable to the king.

[96] Norrey, 806–807.
[97] Brockett, 20.
[98] JPs did receive some remuneration, but the amounts were so small as to be negligible. Lionel K. J. Glassey, *Politics and the Appointment of Justices of the Peace* (Oxford: Oxford University Press, 1979), 3–7.
[99] Chandamon, 96–98. Norrey, 802–803.

## One party throughout the land: access and
## local politics, 1673 to 1685

Danby's political program stressed the need to convince royalist Anglicans that Charles would not abandon them. To give those wary of the king's steadfastness a double assurance, Danby persuaded the king to allow access to only those of an Anglican stripe: the eradication of royal advisors advocating accommodation with dissent both stripped from nonconformists their belief in the king's support and severely reduced the chance of the king hearing the arguments of the Anglicans' opponents. Danby was not content to displace sympathizers of dissent from the king's immediate presence. To ensure that all orders and communication between county and crown would be interpreted on an Anglican bias, the Lord Treasurer attempted to install only true sons of the church in every office that served as a conduit between king and country.

Convincing Charles of the necessity of becoming the leader of one party and excluding all nonconformists was no easy task. As late as 1675, George Scott could report that "some thought that my Lord Shaftsbery and the Marquiss of Winchester, who have not been at court this twelve month, will again come in favour, seing upon Sabath last they were speaking with the king. If this be, it's supposed there may be some alteration in affairs."[100] Robert Paston wanted to convince the king that numbers were on the side of the royalist Anglicans. He claimed that "My Lord Chief Baron will let . . . the king and my lord treasurer know that those that love the crown here are more numerous by far than those that observe their own method and think to serve the king by new wayes which he desires not to be served by."[101] As Mark Goldie remarks, "Cavaliers and churchmen could never afford the luxury of taking Stuart kings for granted, and the appalling spectre of a 'presbyterian' monarchy never left them."[102] Only after the Compton Census of 1676 ascertained that less than 5 percent of the population dissented, did Danby fully convince the king that they could safely purge nonconformists and their sympathizers from the rolls of local officialdom.[103]

Due to the king's caution, the purge of local officials was necessarily piecemeal. Danby still needed to avoid both rampant suspicion and the disruption of the normal functioning of local government that any wholesale eradication might incur. The most blatant alterations occurred in the Assizes. The Justices

---

[100] *HMC Laing*, vol. 1, 403.

[101] BL ADD 36988, 117.

[102] Goldie, "Danby, the Bishops, and the Whigs," in Tim Harris *et al.*, *The Politics of Religion in Restoration England* (Cambridge, MA: Blackwell, 1990), 76.

[103] The results of the Compton Census are printed in Whiteman, *Compton Census*, cxxii–cxxiii. There are many statistical problems with the results of the Census, such as the fact that it did not account for occasional conformists. But it still probably convinced Charles that he could safely alienate dissenters.

of the Assizes were the most effective means to convey the king's will to the countryside, for, unlike the JPs, the Judges of the Assize saw themselves as agents of the crown.[104] In 1676 Charles appears to have desired to make more use of this body. In June of that year he dismissed Justice Ellis which began "a series of arbitrary replacements of judges holding office during pleasure by men who could be relied upon to support Charles's dynastic policy."[105] In Ellis's place Charles appointed the infamous William Scroggs who, interestingly, was later to deny subjects the right to petition the king. There was also a minor attempt to regulate officials in town councils,[106] but Danby concentrated on countywide officers, specifically upon the Lieutenancy and the Justices of the Peace.

Two Lord Lieutenants, Oliver St. John of Hampshire and Horatio Townshend of Norfolk, were removed because they had opposed the king in Parliament and had "patronized men of embarrassing political pasts."[107] Danby's kin took their place.[108] Replacements of living Lord Lieutenants had occurred before in Charles's reign. Shaftesbury, Buckingham, and Clarendon lost their Lieutenancies for political offenses. But the nature of the deprival of office of Townshend and St. John differed qualitatively. The political power of Shaftesbury, Buckingham, and Clarendon which enabled them to effectively command obedience derived from their official capacity as advisors to the king. Losing the king's favor meant a significant loss of authority which seriously hampered their ability to lead the county. Townshend and St. John, however, were local magnates whose position came from their social prestige and personal power within the county. Dismissing them was a much more powerful statement. By doing so, Charles claimed that all power and honor in a county derived not from the personal power of a Lord Lieutenant but from the crown and that displeasing the crown would result in a loss of political power. The absolutist connotations of this statement were not lost on the localities.

[104] Bacon viewed the judges as intermediaries between center and locality, advising them "to represent to the people the graces and cares of the king; and again upon your return to the king the distastes and griefs of the people." In their charges to the bench and through more informal means the judges did relay royal orders to the counties, but they almost never conveyed the griefs of the people back to the crown. Sharpe, *Personal Rule*, 422–430. Morrill, *Cheshire*, 10.

[105] J. S. Cockburn, *A History of the English Assizes, 1558–1714* (Cambridge, Cambridge University Press, 1972), 249.

[106] See Halliday, 184.

[107] Coleby, 98.

[108] Yarmouth was a distant cousin and old friend of the Earl of Danby. Edward Noel, heir to Viscount Campden, was Danby's wife's brother-in-law. Noel had some ties to Hampshire, having married Southampton's daughter, but these ties were recent (Gauci, 133–135; Coleby, 98–99).

The remodeling of the Justices of the Peace was more widespread than that of the Lieutenancy. According to Lionel Glassey, from 1675 to 1679 at least one living JP was ousted in twenty-six of the fifty-seven English and Welsh counties. Most of these dismissals, Glassey reminds us, were routine. In some counties, such as Herefordshire and Warwickshire, there is little evidence that Danby tried to purge the bench.[109] Glassey, however, found considerable evidence of a purge in three counties. In Middlesex – on Sir John Robinson's urging – Sir Robert Peyton and his cohorts, all allies of Shaftesbury, were dismissed. In Norfolk, the Earl of Yarmouth left out a trio of very influential Presbyterian sympathizers.[110] In Kent as well, prominent MPs and a Knight of the Bath were left out of the commission. These three counties were not unique. Glassey notes that the ever-vigilant Marquess of Worcester dismissed twelve MPs in Monmouthshire, Breconshire, and Glamorgan, and that the Earl of Bath dismissed four JPs from Devon's bench, although there is no evidence that these dismissals were politically motivated. Furthermore, there are a number of instances of political removal that escaped Glassey's eye. Sir Edward Bayntun was removed from the Wiltshire bench in 1677 because he was an inveterate opponent of court.[111] In Hampshire, the dismissal of Lord St. John from the Lieutenancy and the bench coincided with a purge of JPs with questionable pasts. Thomas Jervoise, Sir Robert Hengly, and Henry Whitehead were all left out of the Commission of the Peace. All three had some political power, since they served as MPs in the next Parliament.[112] The purging of these local officials was just one step in a general tightening of access, undertaken to convince Anglicans that they need not fear that the king would once again abandon their cause.[113]

Local elites and town corporations reacted to this change in the patterns of access to the king in two ways: some looked for new pathways to reach the king, others saw the lack of access as a sign of absolutism and Catholicism. The case of Great Yarmouth is extremely interesting. Since the appointment of High Steward was for life, Yarmouth had to wait until Clarendon's death to replace the fallen minister as its chief representative to the crown. For seven years it lacked a viable conduit to the crown. When the time came to pick a new High Steward after Clarendon's death, Yarmouth city turned to Robert Paston the Earl of Yarmouth. This choice was curious in the extreme, since the Earl and the corporation of Yarmouth had been engaged in a serious and protracted legal dispute over the Earl's plan to develop the southwark of Yarmouth. However, the town of Yarmouth needed a representative with

---

[109] Key, 307. Glassey, 36.
[110] Sir John Hobart, Sir Robert Kemp, and John Holand.
[111] *Bayntun*, 17.
[112] Coleby, 149–152.
[113] See Goldie, "Danby, the Bishops, and the Whigs" for Anglicans' apprehension of a Presbyterian king.

access to the king, and Paston had familial and political ties to the king's chief minister Danby. Desperate for an avenue to the administration, Yarmouth willingly placed its well-being in the hands of a former legal adversary.[114]

Quite often, local elites and town corporations reacted adversely to Danby's policy of limiting access. While the dismissal of local officials was piecemeal, nevertheless, his policies gave off the impression that the Lord Treasurer was trying to alter the composition of the Justices of the Peace. The importance of such an impression emerged when John Arnold and Henry Porbert of Monmouthshire claimed in Parliament that the Marquess of Worcester had removed them from the Commission of Peace because of their Protestant ardor and that four Justices of the Peace in their county were Catholics. Their claims were tenuous, and certainly not the fault of the central administration, but in the atmosphere of closed access and dealings with the French, they sufficiently raised fears of Catholicism and absolutism.

Such fears were expressed in the counties. Lord St. John, commenting on the number of troops in the pay of the monarch, claimed that the king's advisors wanted to create an absolutist state by force.[115] When Paston replaced Townshend as Lord Lieutenant of Norfolk, one correspondent wrote Paston's wife claiming that the "discontents of the other party . . . say 'Popery is to be introduced that's why Townshend's lay aside'."[116] But the most vocal way of protesting the king's closed access policy was the wave of anti-courtier sentiment which swept the country. Commentators on all sides remarked on how difficult it was for a courtier to be elected.

Oates's and Tongue's revelations of a popish plot brought anti-courtier sentiment to fever pitch. In all three general elections of the succession crisis, courtiers fared poorly. Fears of absolutism and Catholicism played a major role in anti-courtier sentiment, but corporations often worded their reluctance to elect courtiers as a preference for local men. Certainly, telling courtiers that a corporation would choose one of its own may have been a euphemism to dissuade courtiers from standing without insulting them. Still, the insistence on having a member of the borough represent them suggests a desire for a true representative of the borough to the Parliament and to the king, and a distrust of the ability of courtiers to promote or even express local interest when that interest clashed with current administrative policy.[117]

Even loyalist strongholds such as King's Lynn employed the language of local preference. When the placeman Robert Wright informed the corporation that he would be willing to stand for them, King's Lynn replied, "to acquaint him that this house taking notice of the general averseness of this

---

[114] Gauci, 112–128.
[115] Coleby, 150.
[116] BL ADD 36988, 109.
[117] This argument echoes that of Knights, 282–283.

corporation to chose any other than an inhabitant of this town and free of this society . . . this house cannot with any assurance encourage his coming downe for that purpose."[118] In the wake of the revelations of Danby's relations with France and suspicions of his tampering with the Justices of the Peace, corporations hesitated to place the means of expressing their grievances into the hands of courtiers, and consequently turned to local men.

Charles reacted to the uproar over the popish plot, the exclusion crisis, and the general anti-courtier sentiment by returning to open access. The king placed Whigs around him, in his Privy Council, and among his personal attendants,[119] but such a move was merely a ploy to buy himself time. The Whigs, realizing the inconstancy of this king, wanted to consolidate their gains by placing the instruments of enforcement of law, the representatives of the king to their counties, in the hands of their supporters. Shaftesbury and his allies proposed a systematic purge of the JPs and went to great lengths to determine who should stay and who should go. Charles, however, wanted neither to alienate his allies on the ground nor to hand over the lines of communication with the localities to perceived enemies. When the Whig-dominated Privy Council presented him with a list of those they wished removed from the Justices of the Peace, the king reacted to each name by claiming that the Justice in question "had good chines of beef, kept good fox hounds or some such indifferent matter which it was ridiculous to contradict or dispute upon."[120] Charles could change the constituency of his Privy Council without any major repercussions, but, since he was planning to switch back to an Anglican agenda, he needed to avoid the disruption in government and authority that upheavals in the membership of the county benches would incur.

Charles's intention was not clear to most loyalists.[121] In Hampshire, the second Earl of Clarendon knew of several local gentry who were waiting for some clear demonstration of crown policy before they acted. The Earl of Yarmouth, staunch Anglican though he was, hesitated from meddling in Yarmouth city politics before the crown issued an unambiguous directive.[122] Some historians have seen this lack of a clear directive from the crown as reason for the enormous failure of the court interest in three successive general elections.[123] But Charles could not take a directly partisan stand. Until he was sure of his support, he wanted to rest his throne on a broader bottom than ultra-royalists.

---

[118] NRO, MFRO 430/4, January 29, 1678/9.

[119] Richard Newdigate, who was later taken off the Commission of the Peace of Warwickshire, became a gentleman of the privy chamber in 1678.

[120] Glassey, quoting Roger North, 39–43.

[121] Ailesbury, who claimed that Charles informed him of his plan to return to an Anglican agenda, was ordered by the king to keep such plans secret.

[122] Coleby, 212. Gauci, 149.

[123] See e.g. Stater, 136–137.

The events of the three exclusion Parliaments, however, made it clear to Charles that he had to choose either to ensure the "legitimate succession" or political maneuverability. Charles opted for his brother, and in doing so strove to become the leader of the cavalier interest. But he moved towards the Anglican interest haltingly, and the cavaliers – wary of the king whom they had reason to believe might turn back to the Presbyterians – were distrustful. The ensuing relationship resembled a troubled and envious courtship. The Anglicans tried to woo the king with testimonies of their devotion and power, and jealously guarded other suitors from approaching him. The king also needed to court the Anglicans so that they would sacrifice their time, money, effort, and influence. He courted them by offering exclusive access and adopting their agenda.

The king began to convince the Anglicans that he was truly on their side in the winter and spring of 1680. He had already dismissed Shaftesbury from the Privy Council in the summer of 1679, but Anglicans were still unsure of the king's commitment. Charles used declarations, private and public, to re-energize the Anglican forces. In March, 1680 the Privy Council issued a circular letter to the magistrates of each town to enquire as to their compliance with the Corporations Act.[124] The fact that people excluded in 1662 or who had not taken the oaths had slipped into municipal government had long been a complaint of fiery Anglicans who welcomed the letter and the substantive actions taken to see to its enforcement.[125] Charles also began to talk like a royalist Anglican. In February, 1680, the king stated that the nonconformists' "carriage this last year has been such that they have not reason to expect any favour from him, and that he will take all advantage against them the law will give him."[126] The Earl of Yarmouth told one Norfolk correspondent that the king "saith he will stick to his friends and fear no enemies."[127] The most important declaration of the king to the localities was issued after the dissolution of the Oxford Parliament.

Ordered to be read in every church and chapel in the country, *His Majesties Declaration to all his Loving Subjects touching the Causes and Reasons that moved him to dissolve the last two Parliaments* placed the blame for the late crisis squarely on the shoulders of the Whigs in Parliament.[128] The declaration condemned the Whigs as "ill men who are labouring to poison our people, some out of the fondness of their old beloved commonwealth principles and some out of anger at being disappointed in the particular designs they had for the accomplishment of their own ambition and greatness."[129] Despite

---

[124] For one example, see Chester CRO ML4/512.
[125] Knights, 261.
[126] Ibid., 262.
[127] BL ADD MSS 36988, 165.
[128] A copy of the declaration appears in *English Historical Documents Volume 8 1660–1714*, ed. Andrew Browning (London: Eyre & Spottiswoode, 1953), 185.
[129] *English Historical Documents*, 187.

such rhetoric, Mark Knights is correct in seeing this document as relatively moderate and conciliatory in tone. The king's testimony to his willingness to accept the advice of Parliament – even concerning limiting the powers of a popish successor – along with the royal promise "to have frequent Parliaments, and both in and out of Parliament to use our utmost endeavours to extirpate popery, and to redress all the grievances of our good subjects, and in all things to govern according to the laws of the kingdom," gained widespread support.[130] Yet the importance of the monarch's clearly placing himself opposite the Whigs and vilifying them as forcing a return to "the late troubles and confusion" raised the spirits of the grass-roots cavalier party.[131]

Taken purely on their own, such words from this mercurial king would have only slightly encouraged the court party, but Charles preceded and accompanied these words with meaningful actions. Most notably, the king purged the bench of some of the most virulent exclusionists. In late 1679 Richard Newdigate and Thomas Mariet were excluded from the Warwickshire commission. In April, 1680 six leading Whigs found themselves no longer part of the Cheshire bench. In Wiltshire and Kent, anyone who signed a tumultuous petition calling for a Parliament lost his office as a Justice of the Peace. In Hampshire eleven Tories took the place of ten Whigs.[132] According to Lionel Glassey forty-five to fifty MPs who voted for exclusion were purged from the rolls of the JPs in 1679 and 1680.[133] Charles was clearly demonstrating to the countryside that he knew who his friends and enemies were.

Yet, as Glassey notes, such purges while demonstrative and enormous were still incomplete. Sixty MPs who voted for exclusion remained in the commission.[134] Why did Charles refrain, especially at first, from instituting a thorough reformation of the JPs? Some historians have lighted upon the idea that the king was trying to bring moderates over to his opinion, but few scholars have been satisfied with this explanation because so few moderates switched sides.[135] Others have seen problems with a lack of co- ordination between center and locality. For each county, the king relied on the testimony

---

[130] Indeed, some "loyal addresses" singled out these three clauses to be thanked and failed to mention Charles's statement that he would uphold the legitimate succession, thereby making these addresses more a sign of protest (Knights, 323–324).

[131] Coleby, 212–213. Royalist Anglicans had long solicited the king to declare his support for their agenda. From 1670 to the dissolution of the Oxford Parliament Danby, Sir Thomas Thynne, the second Earl of Clarendon, the Bishop of Exeter, and the Archbishop of Canterbury all asked the king to make his true opinions known (Knights, 317–318).

[132] Heap, 82. Challinor, "Restoration," 373. Knights, 260. Glassey, 51. Coleby, 162.

[133] Glassey, 49.

[134] Many of these were removed in a second purge which followed the dissolution of the Oxford Parliament, but even after the second purge Whigs remained dominant on the benches of Westmoreland, Northumberland, and Lincolnshire. Glassey, 50, 54–545.

[135] Coleby, 163. Glassey, 50. Challinor, 373.

of one or two key magnates. Some magnates dismissed loyal JPs for personal animosities. Others trod gently, wishing to prevent a permanent rift within county society.[136] But the lack of co-ordination between center and locality does not explain why MPs whose disloyalty was proven by their voting records remained on the *Liber Pacis*. A more convincing explanation may be obtained from P.C. Heap's close study of the county bench of Warwickshire.

Heap traced the careers of the forty-two local men who were on the Warwick Commission of 1681. Seventeen of them appeared on every *Liber Pacis* through 1690.[137] The ability to stay in office through the topsy-turvy alterations of the Justices during those years suggests more than an ability to trim. Rather, governments had a need of men who could perform the many duties required of Justices, and therefore kept in place those who were willing to perform the drudgery of local governance and who could command the respect necessary to obtain obedience. In the tumultuous atmosphere of the succession crisis, Charles could ill afford to sacrifice his ability to govern in the countryside and therefore may have refrained from replacing too many JPs at once in order that the local governing body could retain members with the requisite authority and knowledge to run the county.

When royalist Anglicans saw such hesitancy they realized that they had to reinforce the king's commitment to their agenda. They endeavored to convince Charles that they could raise revenue and govern effectively without the aid of dissenters. The gatherers of loyal addresses and abhorrences of petitioners no doubt meant to show the strength of the loyal party to the entire country, as their publication in *Vox Angliae* testifies. But the organizers of these testimonies of loyalty addressed them to the king, which suggests that they were meant primarily for his eyes.

Christopher Monck the second Earl of Albemarle, Justice Jeffries, and the Earl of Yarmouth designed the first addresses primarily to persuade the king that he should continue to pursue a strictly Anglican agenda. Paston not only wanted to assure the king of his county's loyalty and thereby win for it the king's favor, he also wanted to impress upon the king the loyalty of the entire nation. In a letter to a Norfolk correspondent Paston juxtaposed Charles's favorable reception of the Norwich address with the king's plan for "a thorough reformation of deputy lieutenants, justices, constables and militia

---

[136] For examples of JPs being dismissed for personal animosity see the case of George Fletcher (HMC Fleming, June 20, 1680 to July 15, 1680). See also the case of James Oxinden (BL Stowe 746, 48).

[137] There were seventy-six names on the commission, but twenty-nine of them were Privy Councilors, two were Assize judges, and three had died. Eleven of the forty-two local men were placed on the 1681 Commission for the first time. Of these only three survived as Justices under William and Mary (two died). Of the thirty-one local men who had been on the Commission before 1681, by 1690, ten had died, seven were not appointed to the Commission, and fourteen were on every commission from 1681 to 1690.

men." Paston saw one as leading to the other.[138] Even more significantly, Paston continually desired the people of Norwich to tangibly show the king the depth of their support. He urged his fellow Norfolkians to "turn our words into coin," suggesting a gift of 1000 guineas.[139] Other addresses tried to assure the king that he need not fear if dissenters revolted. Hereford promised to "defend Charles and the succession 'with the last drop of our blood and penny of our fortune.'" The county of Northampton and the city of Colchester made similar pledges.[140] Such addresses strengthened the king's resolve to continue pursuing an Anglican agenda.

Charles showed his resolve by dramatically purging local officials. Soon after the dissolution of the Oxford Parliament, Charles ousted sixty MPs who voted for exclusion from the rolls of the Commission of the Peace. After the purge one contemporary asserted justifiably that there was no one left on the Commission who did not "run to court."[141] Charles did not restrict himself to remodeling the JPs. Suffolk, Essex, and Manchester lost their appointments as Lord Lieutenants and the Privy Council ordered anyone purged from the lists of JPs also removed from the Deputy Lieutenancy.[142] The administration also endeavored to appoint only loyal sons of the church as sheriffs and judges.[143] Such a commitment to thoroughly purging local offices of their enemies reassured ultra-royalists that the king would not abandon them, for he could not. He had handed over the conduits of communication to members of one party.

Whigs could no longer serve as official conduits to the king. They, and anyone who failed to communicate through acceptable hierarchical structures, were also denied informal access. In a letter to Halifax, Cavendish expressed concern that his loyal address to Charles would meet with an unfavorable response because it did not come from the proper authorities of the Lieutenancy and jury.[144] People with Whig sympathies, even the powerful, had little success when they tried to contact the king. A letter from the Whiggishly inclined Arthur Annesly Earl of Anglesey who had served as Lord Privy Seal (1672 to 1682) testifies to such difficulty. Anglesey wrote Secretary of State Middleton pleading for a chance to speak to the king. "My lord," Anglesey implored, "I choose the way w$^{ch}$ may give your lord least trouble to move you againe for his ma$^{ties}$ being reminded of appointing his owne time for my attending him; and the rather because I understand by a noble person

---

[138] BL ADD 36988, 165.

[139] BL ADD 36988, 165 (May 12, 1681; July 5, 1681).

[140] Knights, 322, HMC Verulam, 84 (July 13, 1683).

[141] Glassey, 54.

[142] Challinor, "Structure," 90. See Chart of Lord Lieutenants. Mulgrave was also dismissed as Governor of Hull in 1682.

[143] Challinor, "Restoration," 373. Coleby, 162.

[144] BL Althorp (March 31, 1684).

I can fully trust that his ma^tie expressed lately that he would make such an appointment."[145] Tories did not have as much trouble communicating with the king. The Assize judges, firmly in the king's pocket, now became powerful links between county and center.

The commitment to a strict policy of access came not only from a desire on the part of the king to placate his Anglican supporters; Charles also intended to take the advice which Newcastle have given him over twenty years before and pursue a politics and imagery of distance. As such even Tories had some difficulty reaching the king. Shakerly, the governor of Cheshire Castle, had to consider carefully how to approach the king in order to obtain gunpowder and other supplies to secure his fort.[146] Bernard Howard, albeit a Catholic, could not circumvent Gainsborough his Lord Lieutenant. Howard got no further than Sunderland in his attempt to convince the king that a further purge of the JPs was necessary in Hampshire.[147] This limitation of access appears to have reduced significantly the amount of communication between county and king. The Chester City Record Office, for instance, has no correspondence between the center and the city from 1683 to the end of the reign.

In this milieu of restricted access those who had an avenue to the king could reap benefits. The Earl of Yarmouth's position appears to have been greatly enhanced. He wrote to his wife that when he entered Norwich, he was greeted as if he were a king.[148]

The events surrounding the Quo Warranto[149] proceedings exemplify the king's desire to turn over all conduits of communication between town and crown into the hands of Anglican stalwarts. At first the king forced the surrender of charters primarily to control the appointment of recorders, high stewards, and town clerks, officials whose main duty was to serve as intermediaries between local corporations and the royal administration. In 1682 Sir Leoline Jenkins told Samuel Thomas, who was petitioning for a new charter on behalf of "the loyal party" of his town, "that his majesty intends in future to reserve to himself in all charters the power of approving and confirming the recorders and town clerks and consequently will do it in your case, if he grant your petition, and 'tis to be supposed that nobody that loves the king will repine at such a reservation, since he has sufficient experience of it being absolutely necessary."[150] The first charters granted following the

---

[145] BL ADD 41803, 45.
[146] Cheshire CRO, DSS 1/1/9, Jeffrey Shakerly to Sir George Shakerly.
[147] Coleby, 163.
[148] Gauci, 1–2.
[149] A Quo Warranto was a legal device whereby the king investigated by what warrant a corporation existed. Generally the king's investigators would examine the charter of a town to see if the town council had violated any of its provisions. Since such violations were ubiquitous the issuance of a Quo Warranto generally meant the end of a corporation's existence.
[150] CSPD, vol. XXII, 6 (January 3, 1682).

dissolution of the Oxford Parliament were in accord with Jenkins's statement. Their only significant innovation was the king's right to approve all recorders, mayors, high stewards, and town clerks; in other words, anyone who acted as a representative of the corporation to other entities. But Charles's concern with controlling the flow of information between corporation and administration soon grew into a desire to totally integrate local corporations into a hierarchical system headed by the king.

His attitude changed because the Quo Warranto proceedings, like so much else in the last four years of the reign, emerged from a combination of royal and royal-Anglian desires.[151] Local initiative, as Colin Lee and Paul Halliday stress,[152] spurred on the Quo Warranto proceedings. Local Tories, demanding from the king the right to be the sole interpreters and enforcers of law, pleaded for invasion. Since with the issuance of a new charter the "loyal party" could institute a one-time purge of their political foes – a purge which could last for decades since town councils were often self-perpetuating oligarchies – they endeavored in the face of considerable resistance to force the town council to surrender the charter. Once the king committed himself to an ultra-royalist agenda, local Tories could feel secure that the new charter would leave out their enemies and therefore risked legal costs and creating further rifts in municipal society to gain the surrender of their charters. Soon, however, the charter surrenders took on a life of their own as noblemen – seeking to show the king their influence over their localities – brought in surrenders from local corporations. Under the influence of these surrenders and bolstered by the apparent power of the loyal Tories, Charles moved towards creating a governing apparatus similar to the one proposed in the Lords' version of the corporations act of 1661. By 1683 almost every new charter gave Charles the right to remove at will every officer in the local corporation, from high steward to common council men. Local officers no longer served the interest of the towns; they were now serving at the pleasure of the king.

The new hierarchical system was a success, but a qualified one. Two major problems existed. First, the creation of a strict hierarchy amplified the power and independency of local Tory magnates who now, by controlling "the information running between town and crown . . . dictated how decisions by each were made."[153] Over-mighty lords once more ruled the country. In Hampshire, for instance, Edward Noel consolidated virtually every prominent local office into his hands.[154] Not only did he serve as Lord Lieutenant and Custos Rotulorum, the Earl of Gainsborough also became Governor of Portsmouth. The king's subjects, even loyal subjects such as Sir George

---

[151] I owe much of the following discussion to Halliday, 194–200.
[152] For Lee's study of Dover see Colin Lee, "'Fanatic Magistrates': Religious and political conflict in three Kent boroughs, 1680–1684," *HJ*, vol. 35, no. 1 (March, 1992), 43–61.
[153] Halliday, 234.
[154] Coleby, 160.

Fletcher,[155] were at the mercy of these over-mighty lords, and the king had to carefully cultivate noble support.

The government from top to bottom was in the hands of one party. Charles sacrificed his maneuverability at the altar of the legitimate succession. As long as his policies coincided with that of the ultra-royalists, he could count on their loyalty. But he was locked in. Charles never got the chance to see what would happen if he deserted the Anglicans once again, but his brother's abandonment of them cost him his crown.

---

[155] See p. 116 n. 136. After considerable ado and a three-year span Fletcher was able to regain his commission as a deputy lieutenant (HMC Fleming, 75, 76 (April 21, 1683)).

# Monopolizing the king's ear

## Trade revived: access and economics at the dawn of the restoration (1660 to 1662)

King Charles, King Charles, Great Neptune of the Main
The royal Navy Rig
And We'll not care a Fig
For France, For France For Netherlands or Spain
The Turk who looks so big
We'll whip him like a Gig
About the Meditterain
His Gallies all sunk or taken
We'll seize on their Goods and Monies.[1]

A group of singers costumed as sailors greeted Charles II with these verses during his cavalcade through the streets of London the day before his Coronation. This ditty clashed with the rest of the entertainment; the casual tone does not conflict with the obscure classical references and the Latin epigrams that fill Ogilby's *The Entertainment of Charles II*. The discord is not only of style, but of substance. The progress which featured four arches was set as an imperial triumph. According to Roy Strong, when entries began to be staged as triumphs, "the entry ceased to be a dialogue between ruler and ruled and developed instead into an assertion of absolute power with a corresponding expression of subservience by the urban bourgeois class."[2] Yet here, in the midst of a triumph, the citizens of London voice a blunt request for a blue water policy made directly, if somewhat inelegantly, to the king. This episode represented the rule, not an exception, of the interaction between the monarch and the merchant community during the first few years of his reign. Charles II established a policy of open access allowing merchants to convey their concerns directly to him. This open access helped instill confidence that the king would not sacrifice economic well-being to the whims and pockets of his courtiers. Such confidence restored the legitimatory force inherent

---

[1] John Ogilby, *The Entertainment of Charles II*, ed. Ronald Knowles (Binghamton: Medieval and Renaissance Texts and Studies, 1988), 107.
[2] Roy Strong, *Art and Power: Renaissance Festivals 1450–1650* (Los Angeles: University of California Press, 1973, 1984), 45.

in the patrimonial economic system,[3] and this, in turn, gave Charles the authority to grant monopolies.

The restored royal administration intimated almost immediately that it would establish open access; nevertheless, guilds, trading companies, and local corporations realized that they might encounter considerable difficulty retaining or regaining their privileges. Many of these economic entities had received new charters during the interregnum and counted avid supporters of the previous government among their chief officers. Furthermore, merchants knew all too well that Parliament – composed mostly of landowners – tended to view merchants as engrossers whose interests were inimical to their own.

The trading companies, however, benefitted from a conservative reaction against the lack of order and economic depression of the closing days of the interregnum. When John Bland published *Trade Revived*[4] the government was in such throes that the author of the Epistle Dedicatory could refer to the rulers of England only with the generality "those grandees who sit at the head of the government."[5] Bland responded to the chaos that surrounded him by calling for a flurry of laws to restore the hierarchy and order of the patrimonial system. His argument focused on the need to restore companies which would regulate trade. This theorist viewed the market as so complex and the demand for goods as so inelastic that only strict regulation of merchants could avoid "overcloying" (glutting) the market. The author ranted against those who left "commerce open to all people whose ignorance hath not only suffered our native commodities to lose their value abroad, but also at home."[6] Bland argued further for each person having a well-defined position in economic society, singling out for censure individuals who participate in two trades.[7]

---

[3] Joyce Appleby describes the patrimonial economic system which flourished during the Tudors' reigns as focused upon ensuring that grain and other essential products would reach the starving, thus placing the maintenance of social order over economic growth. Laws ensured that grain would be sold to those who most needed it, not to those who could most afford it. Within this system, monopolies, in particular guilds, were seen as staving off the anarchy that everyone thought would follow from individual competition. As Appleby states, "restrictions drawn up by companies of craftsman and honored by the law supplied the direction sure to be lost if everyone looked out for himself." In this hierarchical system, which Appleby terms patrimonial, it was crucial that everyone knew his or her place. The sovereign's position was at the top of the pyramid and he or she served as a focal point (Joyce Oldham Appleby, *Economic Thought and Ideology in Seventeenth Century England* (Princeton: Princeton University Press, 1978), 27–30).

[4] Thomason did not buy this tract so we cannot be sure of the date. Internal evidence suggests that it may have reached the press in February or March, 1660 (n.s.).

[5] John Bland, *Trade Revived* (1660), 1.

[6] Ibid., 2.

[7] For instance, retailing and wholesaling. Bland, 5.

Bland's was not a lone reactionary voice in the wilderness. Even religious radicals such as the Quaker Ralph Hide,[8] who claimed he was neither a member nor could expect to be a member of any company, called for the restoration of corporations.[9] Despair at the "sad markets" for wool abroad convinced Hide that "we have been pulling down and destroying that fabric which our forefathers have been so many ages in bringing to perfection."[10] Soon after the restoration Hide called for one grand remedy.

> The restoring or our several companies of merchants to their former rights. . . . Certainly nothing hath been more to our ruin, than our want of due correspondence with each other in our trades; whereas in a well ordered company the publick good of trade is sought after, and advised by grave and most experienced merchants as well as home and abroad. . . . Nothing in the world can . . . so perfectly recover us . . . as well as constituted companies can do. . . . I was once of another minde; as to this particular but I have seen my errour fully in the disorder and decay of trade.[11]

Bland and Hide present a new justification for the crown's regulation of commerce. As Richard Conquest notes, "in the middle decades of the century . . . the English economy was not threatened with instability and crisis requiring the 'paternalistic' responses of the Tudor and early Stuart governments."[12] Dearth and famine had ceased to plague the nation. Now, the English were troubled by a previously incomprehensible idea: too much stuff.[13] Instead of needing to ensure that engrossers did not artificially raise the price of grain, the government gave groups of merchants the authority to engross products, namely the right to limit the supply of exports or imports in order to create order in an otherwise chaotic market.

This system relied on the premise that the king would intervene if engrossers abused their privileges. The system worked in 1660 when the mayor and jurats of Rye claimed that engrossers were preventing grain from entering

---

[8] Hide is identified as a Quaker by Prof. Seligman who was the owner of the copy of the pamphlet examined. Columbia University Rare Books Library Seligman Collection 1660 E H53. Seligman Collection hereafter referred to as Sel.

[9] Ralph Hide, *A State of Discourse in Honor and for the Advance of Trade for Woolen Manufacturers* (1660), 1.

[10] Ibid.

[11] Ibid., 8–9.

[12] R. Conquest, "The State and Commercial Expansion," *Journal of European Economic History*, vol. 14, no. 1 (spring 1985), 159. Appleby, following Max Weber, makes an interesting distinction between patrimonial and paternal. Conquest, however, appears to use the two interchangeably.

[13] In 1668 and 1669, the House of Lords' investigation of the decay of rents revealed that enclosures, drainage, and other projects had created a glut in the market (J. Thirsk and J.P. Cooper, *Seventeenth Century Economic Documents* (Oxford: Oxford University Press, 1972), 68–88).

their town. They asked Sir John Robinson to procure them a royal warrant to allow them to stockpile grain and thereby avoid the prevailing exorbitant prices.[14] The mayor and jurats of Rye did not desire the destruction of the patrimonial system which controlled the grain trade; they merely wanted the king to perform his duty by keeping the engrossers in line. In the first two years of the reign, all of the groups striving for the king's ear supported regulation and some limitation of imports and exports.[15] Later on, some would challenge that tenet, but from the spring of 1660 to the fall of 1662 those struggling for access battled over who would design and enforce the regulations of and limitations on trade.[16]

The major trading companies and the guilds recognized that they could not rely solely on contemporary economic wisdom to restore or preserve their privileges; past experience taught them that kings often disregarded the advice of financial *cognoscenti*. To regain their privileges the guilds and companies demonstrated their loyalty to Charles II; they attempted to assuage him of any fear that granting them privileges would only strengthen secret enemies. Civic ritual provided the most public way for mercantile associations to demonstrate their loyalty.

Just before the restoration, the twelve major guilds hosted General Monck at a series of dinners, to distance themselves from their support for the governments of the interregnum and tie their fortunes to the dominant figure.[17] When Charles II returned, the livery companies, the formal constituents of the city, played a major role in welcoming the king. The Clothworkers received a missive from the city fathers instructing them how best to portray their joy and loyalty in order

> that he [the king] be received and entertained with the greatest demonstration and manifestation of our and all our fellow citizens most bounden duty, hartie assertions and joy for his Majestie happie returne . . . have ready twenty-four persons of the most gracefull, tall and comely personages of your said company every of them to be well horsed and in their best array of velvett . . . or satin and chaines of gold and . . . and also that you have in readiness the . . . banners, streamers, and other ornaments of triumph belonging to your company and that as by a former precept . . . to take the commonwealth armes out of all things used by your company and provide speedily that his majesty's armes may be put in their stead.[18]

---

[14] HMC *Rye*, 13th Rep. App. 4, 244.

[15] There was some sentiment against domestic engrossers. See *Reasons for the Bill for the Improvement of Woolen Manufacturers and Preventing the Exportation of Wool* (1660) Sel. 1660 E R 23. *The Vindication of The Clothiers of the Old and New Draperies* (1660) Sel. 1660 E V 74.

[16] See, for instance, the framework knitters, below pp. 128–129.

[17] Clothworkers Guildhall, Orders of Courts 1649–1665, February 28, 1659/60.

[18] Clothworkers, 141 (May 21, 1660).

The officers of the company along with the twenty-four comely personages rode in the king's cavalcade. The rest of the livery – literally showing their colors – assembled *en masse* to meet Charles II in front of their hall. The other eleven great companies replicated this scene.[19] Soon afterwards, the Grocers, who traditionally granted the king honorary membership, made Charles II free of the company.[20] In June the guilds hosted the monarch at a lavish entertainment. (The Clothworkers had to borrow £165 to defray the cost.)[21] The companies also footed the £6000 bill for the pre-Coronation triumph through London.

Gifts provided a tangible means to demonstrate the depth of loyalty. The guilds of London bestowed £10,000 on the king to gain his favor. Silver plate – necessary because the governments of the interregnum had melted down much of Charles I's service – had the benefit of being in constant use around the monarch and was a particularly popular gift. Andrew Riccard, simultaneously governor of the Levant Company and the East India Company, urged the East India Company to give 10,000 oz. of plate to Charles II. The language Riccard used when making his suggestion and the way the clerk recorded the event reveal that the attitude of the givers had almost as much importance as the monetary value of the present. Riccard told the company

> It would well befit this company and much improve their interest to address themselves to his majesty with some convenient present to *congratulate* his happy restoration to the crown and government and show *a sense of their loyal affection* to him as well as the Merchant Adventurers have done and the Turkey Company was resolved to do.

The journals of the company uncharacteristically made sure to note that this "mention was so readily embraced by the generality that immediately it became more the care how to perform it than to make any scruple over doing it."[22] The presentation of a gift also enabled the officers of the company to meet the king.

Andrew Riccard's ubiquity suggests another method which the companies used to ensure that their officers would have access to the sovereign: promoting those among its own members who had royal ties and purging their ranks of those whom the king would deem offensive.[23] Riccard, for instance, had had some association with the governments of the interregnum. He had

---

[19] Clothworkers, 142 (May 27, 1660).
[20] London Guildhall Lib., Grocers LC/1.
[21] Clothworkers, 144 (June 28, 1660).
[22] Brit. Lib. Ind. Office, East India Co. Records, Court Book Minutes, b126, 270; emphasis added.
[23] Sir John Banks may have withdrawn from the East India Co. because he was an associate of important supporters of the Cromwellian regime (D. C. Coleman, *Sir John Banks: Baronet and Businessman* (Oxford: Clarendon University Press, 1963), 21, 70).

served as an alderman (1651 to 1653) and as an MP for London (1654). This wealthy merchant, however, had compensating connections with the courtier Berkeley clan. Riccard's daughter Christina married Lord John Berkeley of Stratton, who had commanded troops for Charles I and who advised Henrietta Maria. Riccard's ties explain why he simultaneously led the two largest trading companies.[24] Even after he finished his two-year tenure at the East India Company,[25] Riccard always took part in any delegation sent to the king.[26]

Sir Richard Ford also took part in virtually every delegation sent from the East India Company to the administration. Ford had arranged loans for Charles II during his exile and actively advocated the Restoration when he served as a common councillor of London (1659 to 1661).[27] Ford acted as the main point of access between the company and the court; various passages in Pepys's diary and the company records suggest that Ford frequently wandered the corridors of Whitehall seeking information. Ford's efforts paid off. Once, for instance, the banker learned from "casual discourse with the chancellor" of a plan to fortify Bombay.[28] The companies who had Ford as a member immediately realized his value. In 1660 the Mercers appointed him Master.[29]

The trading companies and guilds not only tried to place their agents at court, but also sought to recruit those at court to become their agents. George Lord Berkeley, for instance, delivered several petitions for the East India Company to the king. It is unclear who else acted in the interest of the various companies at this time, but it is worth noting that the East India Company's governor was given discretionary powers to present gifts to encourage "diverse persons that will deserve well for the company . . . in the several businesses for which the company are suitors before his majesty."[30]

Prompted by professions of loyalty, contemporary economic wisdom, and whispers in his ear, Charles acted to restore and strengthen the privileged mercantile structure that had existed before the Civil Wars. Charles II encouraged the companies' attempts to gain access, particularly when such attempts were accompanied by gifts. The East India Company was "told that what they had presented his majesty with [the 10,000 oz. of plate] had found so fine an acceptance that they doubt not but to find his majesty favor in so

---

[24] Before the Restoration, Riccard was Deputy Lieutenant of the East India Co. and was in line for the top job. He had no such prominent post with the Levant company.

[25] Governors of the East India Company served for two years and could not be re-elected. The Levant company had no such rule and Riccard served as its governor until his death. At each election, Riccard would ask to be excused. Yet he was inevitably re-elected.

[26] Latham, *Pepys Companion*, 354, 27–28. *East India Company Calendar, passim.*

[27] CSP Clar., 209 (April 29, 1662).

[28] Sainsbury, 131 (September 11, 1661).

[29] J. R. Woodhead, *The Rulers of London, 1660–1689* (London: London and Middlesex Archaeological Society, 1965).

[30] BLIO East India Company Court Book, b126, 298.

just things as they are [engaged in]."[31] The East India Company (EIC) seized on this indication of favor and inundated the monarch with petitions. It delivered at least four petitions in the summer of 1660 and three more in October. The EIC successfully shaped government policy. In a petition of October 8, 1660 the EIC requested permission to export bullion and soon after the king commanded the Council of Trade to advise on the matter. The Council replied with a favorable report which drew upon Thomas Mun's theory that the export of bullion did not diminish a nation's wealth.[32]

The Levant Company also received encouragement from Charles II. He sent Lord Bellasis to inform the Turkey traders that he was pleased with their choice for consul, making sure "not only [to] express his just approbation but to command [Bellasis] to intimate as much unto the Company." He also conveyed his strong support of the company's monopoly by appointing Michael Evans, an employee of the Levant Company, to check bills of lading to prevent interloping, trafficking in goods without a proper license. To justify this appointment Charles II echoed the merchants' claims: "interloping will endanger the overthrow of that trade which is of so great consequence to this kingdom."[33]

The king's actions corresponded to his words. He signaled his support of the guild structure when he allowed the London livery companies to feast him in June of 1660, soon after his return.[34] More importantly, he granted charters to most of the major trading concerns. The East India Company regained its sole right to trade with the Far East in early 1661. The Levant Company received a new charter on April 2, 1661 which awarded it more power to control employees abroad. In February, 1661 the king granted the Eastland Company the sole trade to the Baltic states. Even the often maligned Merchant Adventurers received a new charter, although they did not retain their privileges for long.[35]

The framework of open access legitimized this new patrimonialism. According to Bland and Hide, empowering companies to control who had the right to trade would jumpstart an economic revival. But producers, as opposed to "meer merchants", were somewhat apprehensive that companies would abuse their patents, that traders would sharply reduce the amount of exports

---

[31] Ibid., 287.

[32] BL ADD 25115, 43–50. The report quotes Mun at length.

[33] PRO SP 105/152 f 49, 105/109 f 116. *CSPD*, vol. 1, 195 (August 18 ,1660). BL ADD MSS 25115 f 46–52.

[34] He also consented to be entertained by London's guilds before his coronation. William Herbert, *The History of the Twelve Great Livery Companies of London* (New York: A. M. Kelly, 1968), 183.

[35] Rudolph Robert, *Chartered Companies* (London: G. Bell, 1969), 43, 54. R. W. K. Hinton, *The Eastland Trade and the Commonweal in the Seventeenth Century* (Cambridge: Cambridge University Press, 1959), 138.

in order to buy cheaply at home and sell dearly abroad.[36] The open access of Charles's reign reassured landowners and manufacturers. If companies abused their patents, those with grievances could appeal directly to the king or at least to his Council of Trade.

The Council of Trade was more than a blue ribbon commission of experts whose recommendations were graciously accepted and then deftly ignored. The king almost always followed the advice of the Council.[37] Furthermore, any economic matters presented directly to the king duly came to the Council for consideration. In the letter patent which called for the existence of the Council, the king emphasized his personal interest in the Council's work and his desire that the Council should take into account every interest.

> We have taken into our princely consideration the present state of affairs in relation to the trade and commerce of our . . . kingdom as well as of other nations & governments well weighing how considerable a part of our crown and government doth arise from foreign and domestic trade, in that they are the chief employment and maintenance of our people . . . and to these good ends and purposes *we should not only bend our earnest affections & consultations of our own royal person*, we having had many exceeding opportunities to inform our self in matters of this nature but shall very effectually recommend them to our counsel & all our ministers of state that [commerce should be considered in all treaties with foreign princes] . . . and because our mystery or difficulty may be the more easily discerned & encountered & *that every interest may bee righted* we have thought fit to erect & establish a counsel of trade consisting of the persons hereafter named who being diversely qualified and fitted thereunto will, we doubt not, consult & propose such things as may tend to the rectifying those errors which the corruption of late times have introduced.[38]

The case of the silk-stocking framework knitters demonstrates how the council "righted every interest" by rendering its deliberations accessible to all concerned parties. William Lee of Calverton had invented the framework knitting machine during the reign of Elizabeth, but its use remained unregulated until 1654, when a group of knitters received a patent of corporation from Cromwell. The Restoration rendered the charter worthless, so the corporation petitioned the king for a new one. In its plea, the corporation of knitters claimed it had obtained the Cromwellian charter only to prevent

---

[36] *Reasons for the Bill for the Improvement of Woolen Manufacturers and Preventing the Exportation of Wool* (1660) Sel. 1660 E R 23. *The Vindication of The Clothiers of the Old and New Draperies* (1660) Sel. 1660 E V 74. "Meer merchants," a term much in parlance in the 1660s, referred to businessmen who dealt solely in wholesale goods, neither producing nor retailing them.

[37] In the minutes of the Council of Trade (1660–1662) I did not find any instances where the king did not follow their advice. BL ADD 25115, *passim*.

[38] PRO, CO 389–1, 2; emphasis added.

poor work and to stop the emigration of those who knew the art and mystery. Soon after their charter lost its force, the knitters claimed, mischief re-appeared and ill-wrought goods began to destroy their reputation. The Council, to whom the petition was referred, sought out other framework knitters, who placed the blame for the ill-wrought goods at the feet of the company itself. These outsiders claimed that the corporation both cheated customers and forced loyal men to emigrate by preventing them from employing apprentices and in some cases from practicing the trade. The opponents brought as a witness the oldest living framework knitter. The old knitter disparaged the corporation as "Oliverian" and claimed that they produced substandard frames. The attempt to paint the corporation as enemies of the state failed, but the opponents convinced the council that the corporation did not fully represent the trade. The Council therefore allowed the knitters to incorporate, but gave them virtually no power over those not free of the corporation. Anyone outside of London could also form a co-operative, and anyone in London was allowed to practice the trade whether they belonged to the organization or not. The only significant power the corporation had was to prevent the export of framework knitting machines, a clause all the knitters supported.[39]

Perhaps the condemnation of the knitters as Oliverian failed to sway the Council of Trade because many of its members had themselves collaborated with Cromwell. As the king made clear in his letter patents, he meant to fill the Council with diverse individuals, so that every interest would be righted. Charles II sent missives to each of the major trading companies telling them to nominate members for a position on the Council.[40] Examination of the members of the Council of Trade reveals a truly diverse group.[41] The Council comprised nobles, bureaucrats, and merchants. The noble presence added luster and importance to the committee, as well as easing access to the king. Since peers had automatic access to the court, the Council called on its active noble members, especially the Earl of Pembroke and Lord Berkeley, to act as conduits to the king and his Secretaries of State.[42] The commoners on the Council were widely representative of English commercial interests. All of the major trading companies had members on the Council and the Council included persons with interests in the unregulated trades as well.[43] At least nine of the twelve major guilds had representatives on the board.[44] And at

---

[39] BL ADD 25115, 144. Cooper and Thirsk, *Documents*, 259–264, 267.

[40] Each trading concern nominated four members of whom the king picked two.

[41] For a Prosopography of the Councils of Trade see my dissertation, "Reconstruction of Monarchy," Appendix E.

[42] BL ADD 25115, 38.

[43] Members of the Council had interests in the Carolinas, the Italian trade, the Spanish trade, the French trade, the Caribbean, Tangiers, and New England.

[44] The Fishmongers, the Vintners, and the Goldsmiths did not have any noticeable presence on the Council, but, since I have been unable to determine the guild membership

least fourteen of the sixty-eight members had collaborated in some way with the Oliverian regime.

The existence of the Council allowed easy access to the corridors of power even to those business concerns which had no representative among the Council's members. Since it often met in Mercers Hall, suitors need not have been intimidated by the presence of the court and the rules of entrance into Whitehall. The Council received suits from the major trading companies, but also from some minor concerns such as the Dover merchants who wanted to make their city a composition port,[45] and from Sackville Crow who wished to establish a corporation to encourage arras and tapestry making.[46] Responses were not instantaneous, but most suitors received a hearing. Shopkeepers, for instance, were upset at the number of foreigners in London and the importation of what they saw as unnecessary luxuries, and therefore petitioned the Council in November, 1660 to impose high tariffs and prevent foreigners from practicing their trade. The council took up the issue in March, 1661 (n.s.). and showed its Munite[47] and low-church tendencies by deciding that while the grievance had merit, the proposed remedies would backfire. The mostly Huguenot foreigners amounted to thousands of people, and the Council could not recommend depriving them of their livelihoods. Furthermore, the Council claimed that the foreigners kept their money in England and that skilled workmen increase a country's wealth.[48] Like Mun, the Council asserted that frivolous imports hurt a nation's balance of trade, but thought that high tariffs would result in smuggling, not a reduction in imports. Instead, the Council tendered advice that would be repeated throughout the king's reign. The king, the Council suggested humbly, should "by example encourage the wearing of English manufactures and discountenance the wearing and wearers of foreign manufacturers, as it would take off the opinion of the foreign, so it would bring into fashion and esteem the home-made manufacture."[49]

Although Charles's policy of open access allowed merchants to express their concerns to the king, traders realized there was a downside: their eco-

---

of eighteen of the commoners on the Council, it is probable that all twelve of the major guilds had representatives.

[45] BL ADD 25115, 116. A composition port allows the re-export of commodities at a substantial discount.

[46] BL ADD 25115, 280.

[47] Although Mun's *England's Treasure by Forraign Trade* was not printed until 1664, this tract was distributed widely in manuscript form. In October, 1660 the Council of Trade quoted large sections of Mun's work verbatim (BL ADD 25115, 43–50).

[48] BL ADD 25115, 169–175.

[49] BL ADD 25115, 175. Charles's 1666 adoption of wearing a Turkish vest made of English cloth came as a response to similar advice that he promote English goods by setting the fashion. See E. S. De Beer, "King Charles II's Own Fashion: An Episode in Anglo–French Relations 1666–1670," *Journal of the Warburg Courtald Institute II* (1938).

nomic opponents and rivals could also reach the king. *Short Notes and Observations Drawn From the Present Decaying Condition of this Kingdom in Point of Trade*[50] exhibits apprehensions of too much access. The anonymous author expressed anxiety that the newly founded Royal Fishing Company (August, 1661) would lose its exemption from paying customs because of the actions of some

> busie . . . to perswade his majesty to deface his commission . . . whereby they would insinuate to his majesty how considerable his loss would be in his customs having no respect to the high and many advantages that his majesty, and the whole kingdom will receive, by the employment and the industry of so many thousands persons as will be concerned therein, abundantly transcending any such petty loss as they can make out will fall on the customs.[51]

Comprised almost entirely of courtiers, the Royal Fishery was an unlikely target to be harmed by whispers in the king's ear. The author of this tract, however, believed that even with such protection, the fishery had to fear custom agents, who could get access to the king, implanting "evil" ideas in the royal head. A concern with too much access, with too many people influencing the sovereign, prompted this author to publish his tract, and to argue his case in terms of the benefit of the nation, not exclusively the benefit of the king.[52]

The notion of the benefit of the realm was harnessed both by those in favor and those against specific monopolies. The fact that arguments based on national interest convinced the king to curtail the privileges granted to powerful financial interests illustrates the effect of Charles II's open access. In May, 1662, the Merchant Adventurers, despite their considerable resources, lost most of their privileges. The king, prompted by the complaints of woolen manufacturers against the company, proclaimed that "all woolens could be exported to any place beyond the sea except Dort and Hamburg from May 20 until December 25 on account of the decay of trade." While the king was careful to include the phrase, "but not thereby esteeming or lessening the Merchant Adventurers," one wonders whether investors could have retained confidence in the company's ability to maintain its monopoly.[53] Similarly on December 20 the king allowed the free import of nutmeg, cloves, and cinnamon, a move which violated the Act of Navigation and impinged on the rights of the East India Company.[54] Such actions probably reassured his

---

[50] Sel. 1662E Sh8.

[51] *Short Observations*, 3.

[52] The author, of course, argued that benefitting the nation inherently benefitted the king. The king, this tract claims, would receive more revenue in taxation from a wealthy country and therefore should be willing to lose some customs revenue to promote the Fishery.

[53] *CSPD*, vol. 2, 371 (May 14, 1662).

[54] The dispensation to import was to last only until the EIC was able to re-establish itself in the Spice Islands (*CSPD*, vol. 2, 446).

subjects that Charles II was not, like his father, trading monopolistic privileges for revenue; when necessary he dispensed with those privileges for the sake of the "national interest." Such actions did not considerably alienate the trading companies either. They could feel confident that they would regain their privileges if they proved that their rights benefitted the realm, an objective which they pursued before the Privy Council and in printed appeals to the nation.

Charles's commitment to open access helped revive trade, and did so in a manner which enhanced his authority to regulate trade by restoring confidence in the patrimonial system and the king's ability to supervise monopolies. In the following years war, foreign and domestic economic competition, and the politically inspired changes which Charles made in his system of regulating access all severely tested such confidence both in the patrimonial system and the king's ability to supervise monopolies.

## Monopolies, merchants, and the king: the Dutch War

Most historians have viewed the Dutch War as the prime example of mercantile influence on Restoration royal policy. By attacking the Dutch, Charles adapted the sort of blue water policy urged upon him by the ditty-chanting sailors during his pre-Coronation progress. Indeed, Sir Keith Feiling, Charles Wilson, and Jonathan Israel all subscribe to the premise that England's merchants convinced the monarch and Parliament that a war with the Netherlands would allow England to capture the Dutch trade.[55] But Steven Pincus's *Protestantism and Patriotism* has criticized this view, stressing that the war, as many merchants testified, was in fact against their financial interests. Pincus claims that ideological factors brought the court – and only secondarily the merchants – to press for military action against the United Provinces. "The English," Pincus asserts, "understood the recent success of the Dutch not in the context of twentieth century supply and demand curves, but in terms of the seventeenth century idiom of universal monarchy."[56]

This thesis has much merit. The assertion that royalist Anglican courtiers feared the Dutch primarily because they considered the Netherlands a seed-bed of dissent is particularly telling, as is the analysis of Orangist sentiment

---

[55] Keith Feiling, *British Foreign Policy, 1660–1672* (London: Macmillan and Co. Ltd., 1930). C. H. Wilson, *Profit and Power; a Study of England and the Dutch Wars* (London: Longmans, Green, 1957). Jonathan I. Israel, *Dutch Primacy in World Trade, 1585–1740* (Oxford: Clarendon Press, 1989).

[56] Steven Pincus, "Popery, Trade and Universal Monarchy: The Ideological Context of the Outbreak of the Second Anglo–Dutch War," *EHR* (January, 1992) 23. Pincus reiterates the argument he expresses in this article in *Protestantism and Patriotism* (Cambridge: Cambridge University Press, 1996), 198ff., 262.

among Charles and his advisors. Pincus, however, overreaches when he claims that both courtiers and merchants donned the garb of hawks because they feared Dutch aspirations of universal monarchy. Pincus makes this point by eliding the concepts of universal monarchy and monopoly. In the seventeenth century, he maintains, theorists such as William Coventry claimed that success in trade meant military might and naval power brought about international dominance. Within such a context, Pincus interprets merchants' claims of Dutch monopolistic practices as fears of universal monarchy.[57] Pincus's elision of monopoly and universal monarchy seems unnecessarily complicated. Merchants complained about the Dutch monopolistic actions because they were monopolistic. By reading such statements in the context of universal monarchy, Pincus both wrongly analyzes why merchants supported the war and severely downplays the importance of monopoly in mercantile thought. The diction which merchants employed to describe the Dutch actions in the South Seas does not correspond to the way previous generations described Habsburg attempts at world domination. Pincus cites merchants as saying: the Dutch would "Prohibit (sic) all nations whatsoever to trade with the Malabar coast"; their "utmost endeavours are to run over this coast and quite banish the English off the whole India trade"; "They would deny all traffic there to all ships, but their own"; "They seek a monopoly of trade which they make their interest." The merchants' repeated employment of mercantile terms suggests that they thought the Dutch were securing a monopoly. Even the royalists employed such diction when addressing merchants about the "nefarious" actions of the Dutch. William Coventry, Secretary to the Duke of York, commented to Andrew Riccard, Governor of the Levant Company, that the peace treaty the Dutch signed with Argiers signaled an attempt to "engross the whole trade of the Levant."[58] Certainly, there is much merit in the assertion that royalist Anglican courtiers feared the Dutch primarily because they considered the Netherlands a seed-bed of Presbyterianism and Republicanism. But the evidence gives little support to the assumption that the merchant community was apprehensive because it deemed the Dutch Charles V redux.

Rather, the companies believed they needed the government's help because they thought that the Dutch were securing a monopoly. For the trading companies, securing a monopoly went hand in hand with maximizing profits. Trading companies believed that demand was essentially inelastic and that therefore the only way to boost profits was to increase market share. Much of their striving for access to the king was to secure their privileges and to gain even more power against interlopers, thereby strengthening their control over product supply. The actions of the Dutch in Africa and Asia appeared to the British traders as using force to secure the control of product,

---

[57] Pincus, *Protestantism*, 260–262.
[58] PRO SP 105/152, 61.

an action remarkably similar to obtaining a monopoly from the king. The English merchants projected their economic views upon the Dutch and therefore thought the Netherlands intended to increase profits by tightening their stranglehold on supply. As the East India Company protested to the king in 1662, "the petitioners humbly conceive that it may be the result of the Dutch counsels to perfect at once their long-designed work of ruining the whole trade of the English in India and dispossessing the Portuguese of the little that still remains in their hands."[59] English companies viewed monopolies as Lenin did corporations, inevitably and constantly expanding, and believed that if the English did not resist forcefully they would completely lose their ability to trade.

The East India Company made this position clear to the king in countless petitions.[60] As Peter Loughead states, "right up to the opening of hostilities they [The East India Company] continued to press their demands without restraint. The committees continued with their alarmist tactics of presenting relatively minor incidents as part of a concerted Dutch threat to the company's entire position in the east."[61] The companies did so not out of some sort of naivety or inexperience, but because they actually did see these minor incidents as part of such a plan.

Pincus argues that the fact that only the East India Company and the Royal African Company had complained against Dutch practices prior to the Committee of Trade's inquiry testifies to the lack of widespread mercantile support for the war. True, English merchants feared Dutch monopoly primarily in the "underdeveloped" regions of the world. In Africa and South East Asia, the Dutch built forts to control shipping lanes and waged war with indigenous nations in order to gain exclusive trading privileges.[62] Such practices could not be carried out in the Levant or the North Seas, where they would have been resisted by considerable native military forces. In Africa and Indonesia

---

[59] Sainsbury, 82 (January 28, 1661).

[60] In 1661 and 1662 petitions were delivered to the king or representations made to the king about the perfidiousness of the Dutch on the following dates: January 28, 1661; February 1, 1661; February 22, 1661; August, 1661; October 23, 1661; March, 1662; April 2, 1662; May, 1662.

[61] Peter Loughead, "The East Indian Company in English Domestic Politics 1657–1688" (Oxford University D. Phil., 1981), 75.

[62] George Downing wrote, "This trick of the Hollanders to declare warre with the natives in the East Indies and upon the Coast of Africa, with whom His Majesty's subjects have any trade, and then thereupon to forbid them all trade with them, and to continue the warre till they have brought those natives to an agreement with them, to sell them upon all their commodities, and then to keep the English from trading, upon the account that the natives have agreed with them, to sell all to them; – this trick, I say, that not only bin the ruine of numbers of His Majesty's subjects, but beaten them out of mighty trades and will certainly in conclusion overthrow the English East Indian and African Companies, if nothing be applied for remedy but words." Quoted in Israel, *Dutch Primacy in World Trade*, 271.

the Dutch used force actively against the English, whether invading Amboyna, burning the spice trees on Pulo Run, or capturing ships which seemed to veer too close to their protected islands. Hence African and Indian merchants complained more about the Dutch than their counterparts in the Eastland or Levant Companies.

In the North Seas and the Mediterranean the Dutch rarely employed military might to out-compete the British; they were simply more efficient.[63] The Levant, Muscovy, and Eastland Companies could not ask the king to attack the Dutch because they had low insurance rates.[64] Still, when England negotiated with Sweden and Denmark the main concern of the Eastland and Muscovy Company was obtaining the same privileges of trade that the Dutch enjoyed.[65] The Levant Company did not initiate any anti-Dutch action, but its response to a suggestion by William Coventry speaks volumes. The *Journal of the Levant Company* records that in May, 1662 William Coventry intimated to Andrew Riccard "That upon consideration of the late peace made by the Netherlands with Argier (hereby they doe suppose to design engrossment of the whole trade of Levant into their own hands) his highness has resolved to secure the English trade into those parts by convoys."[66] The inclusion of the parenthesized statement is significant.

If the companies were so apprehensive of and incensed by the Dutch, why then did they grumble against the war? Pincus argues that all traders saw the war as a short-term disaster. He explains the companies' petitions to Parliament's Committee of Trade – petitions which blamed the Dutch for the "decay of trade" – as deriving in part from a momentary coup of the trading companies by their royalist Anglian members and in part as a result of "the merchants having been 'impelled by the cabals of the servants of the king.'"[67] Loughead explains that the companies wanted to have their cake and eat it too, urging the king on with constant complaints about the Dutch, but at the same time reluctant to wage war.

Companies grumbled against the war for a calculated reason. The East India Company did not want to seem the main proponent of the war because such a stance would oblige it to pay for the brunt of the cost. When the East India Company told the Lord Treasurer, "The worst of peace is better than

---

[63] Jonathan Israel mentions cheaper insurance and freight as the key reasons for this efficiency. The Dutch did, however, use their naval might to influence European nations to grant them trading privileges, but their use of force was much more subtle in Europe than in Africa or Asia.

[64] Still, many of the proposals about the Royal Fishery had competition with the Dutch as their subtext. The Dutch, these authors assumed, could hire sailors more cheaply because so many were trained in the seas.

[65] BL ADD 25115, 30, 35.

[66] PRO SP 105/152, 61.

[67] Pincus, "Popery," 15, 3. Pincus quotes the French ambassador Comminges to support his claim.

the best warr, by which they cannot expect but to bee present sufferers in one kinde or other," they did so in the midst of haggling with the crown over the price of saltpeter. Southampton assumed that the East India Company would benefit greatly from the war – a just assumption based on the company's repeated complaints against the Dutch – and should therefore sell saltpeter to the Treasury at a considerable discount. The EIC replied quite strongly to Southampton's assumption: "for the publicke concernment his lordship is pleased to hinte, the company hopes it is the interest of the kingdome, for as to their private concerne as merchants they must needs say that the worst of peace is better than the best warr."[68] By quoting this statement out of context, Pincus and Loughead have misunderstood the companies' motivation for protesting the war.[69]

Certainly, as Stephen Pincus reiterates, the war was not in the short-term interest of the merchants. Pincus's repeated use of the word *short term* begs the question that the merchants may have had their long-term interests in mind. Fearing that the Dutch, if left unfettered, would eventually chase England from trading with Africa and Asia, the merchants realized that they needed to sacrifice some short-term benefits for long-term security. If the English had been able to impose their demands upon the Dutch, particularly the right to trade freely "at any place in the East Indies not actually occupied and immediately governed by the Dutch,"[70] then the Dutch monopoly would be permanently dismantled.

Merchants often recognized the benefits of sacrificing short-term gains for long-term benefits. Immediately prior to the breakout of the third Dutch War (1672) the Venetian ambassador summarized the mood of the exchange: "The general opinion of the mart of London is that trade will suffer, though many merchants consider this desirable, as commerce being limited to experienced and capable persons, would thus rid itself of a crowd devoid of practical knowledge, who ruin it."[71] No doubt merchants also realized the benefits of sacrificing present profit to prevent the Dutch from engrossing trade.

The desire of these merchants to risk war, with its deleterious effects on their bottom line, in order to prevent the Dutch from securing a monopoly, testifies to the central place that monopoly held in the economic worldview of English businessmen. Many businessmen wanted not only to prevent the Dutch from complete control of product, they also desired monopolistic privileges for themselves. Both goals required access to the king.

---

[68] Sainsbury, vol. 7, 40 (May 25, 1664).
[69] Pincus, "Popery," 8, "*Protestantism*, 244. Loughead, 75.
[70] In the negotiations for the Triple Alliance the English made the following demands: the Dutch should not block access to an independent district by building forts, make exclusive contracts for trade, nor interfere with neutral Asiatic vessels carrying an English passport. Sainsbury, vol. 8, ix–x.
[71] *CSPV*, vol. 37, 121 (November 20, 1671).

## The Councils of Trade and economic regulation

Charles, by establishing the Council of Trade in 1660 and peopling it with merchants, in effect brought the arcana imperium into the full light of day. For economic regulation – especially coinage, foreign trade, and the bestowal of patents and monopolies – were very much the purview of the sovereign. Through such revealing action, Charles signaled his commitment to inclusive government. However, as the previous chapters have shown, Charles's commitment to inclusion did not last. The fate of the Council of Trade paralleled closely the king's varying sentiments towards access, obedience, and authority.

The king created the Council of Trade to provide the mercantile community with the means to communicate with him, but its function varied throughout Charles's reign; its role changed in accordance with the king's policy of accessibility. Only when the king was actively promoting his accessibility did the Council serve as a conduit for economic interests. More often the king used the Council as an advisory body. When the king turned decisively towards strict regulation of access, he abolished the Council of Trade, replacing it with a subcommittee of the Privy Council. The members of this subcommittee did not interact with merchants; they commanded, intent in securing in the economic world a mirror image of the patriarchal-hierarchical system that they saw in English society.

Although the membership of the Council of Trade[72] remained the same after Charles turned away from toleration and accessibility in late 1662 and 1663, the Council's function changed. Internal records of its proceedings dry up after 1662. The State Papers mention the Council only twice in 1663. On March 3, 1663 (n.s.) the king asked the Council of Trade for a report on coal importations[73] and, in December, 1663, George Duke, the Secretary of the Council, wrote Daniel O'Neal, Postmaster General and member of the Council, that the Council was to move to three or four rooms in Sir John Denham's buildings in Whitehall.[74] Moving to the palace may have enhanced the prestige of the Council, but it also rendered it less accessible. Access to the palace was restricted and a round trip from the Exchange to the palace took half a day.[75] The move to the palace, in conjunction with the fact that the Council's only activities in 1663 and 1664 were issuing two reports, suggests

---

[72] Some confusion does occur over the Committee of Trade which is a parliamentary body, and the Council of Trade, a body under the patent of the king. The Committee of Trade had a key role in the origins of the Dutch War, the Council of Trade slipped into the shadows.

[73] *CSPD*, vol. 3, 67 (March 3, 1663). In the summer of 1664 the council delivered a report on Scottish tariffs. *CSPD*, vol. 3, 651 (July, 1664).

[74] *CSPD*, vol. 13, 386 (December 23, 1663).

[75] Pepys, viii, 132 (March 27, 1667). For the segregation between Westminster and the city of London and the difficulty of traveling between them see Spurr, *1670s*, 160–161.

that the council no longer served as a conduit between mercantile interests and the monarch.[76] Now, when it was active, the Council operated as a royal advisory body; traders had to find other avenues of approach if they were not to be excluded from accessing the king.

The Dutch War ended all Council activity. Many members of the Council had other duties which took up their time and the war slowed foreign trade to a snail's pace. During the War and the plague, the king's person was inaccessible and the conduits which merchants had used to reach the king no longer existed.

After the war Charles re-established the Council of Trade as part of a general return to open access. The method of choosing members of the Council and the composition of the board differed from the first one: the king did not ask the established companies for nominations to the board as he had done in 1660, and, consequently, the 1668 Council was less representative of the London mercantile elite than its 1660 counterpart. In 1660 sixteen of the fifty-eight members belonged to livery companies, while in 1668 only six of forty-seven took the freedom from a London guild. Members of the overseas trading companies also constituted a larger proportion of the first Council.[77] On the other hand, the Council of 1668 had a higher percentage of nobles and government employees.[78] The king replaced traders with navy officials,[79] members of Buckingham's or Arlington's faction,[80] merchants who supplied the navy,[81] and diverse experts.[82] Such a configuration rendered the Council of Trade less of a mouthpiece of the large trading companies and more of a conduit for diverse economic interests, such as manufacturers and interlopers.[83]

---

[76] The two instances of Council activity from 1663 to 1667 inclusive are both cases of the Council reporting to the king: see note 73 above.

[77] 17/58 in 1660; 8/47 in 1668. I do not consider members of the Royal African Company which was not in existence in 1660, and was merely a holding company in 1668.

[78] The Council of 1660 had fourteen nobles (24 percent) and twenty employees of the administration (34 percent). The Council of 1668 had sixteen nobles (34 percent) and twenty-one government employees (45 percent).

[79] Thomas Littleton, Col. John Birch, Sir Thomas Osborne.

[80] William Garraway, Thomas Osborne, and Thomas Grey were all part of Buckingham's faction. Sir Thomas Littleton supported Arlington in the house of Commons.

[81] John Shorter, Josiah Child.

[82] Josiah Child and Benjamin Worsley had published a number of tracts on trade. Henry Blount was famous for a book he wrote on the Levant (*DNB*).

[83] In 1668 Lord Keeper Bridgeman believed that the Council of Trade could speak on behalf of the merchants. He wrote Joseph Williamson, "I cannot give instructions thereon [the marine treaty] until Lord Arlington's return, nor then without consulting the Council of Trade (whose commission is not yet passed), or some other merchants, for the states will expect that the English should putt in all their demands at once, and those already made only proceed from the East India Company" (Sainsbury, vol. 8, 101 (October 13, 1668)). Bridgeman's assumption, however, may have been based on his dealings with the Council picked in 1660.

Although almost half the Council consisted of royal officials, the remaining members represented a broad political–religious spectrum. Nonconformists, latitudinarians, officers in the Parliament's army, and former interregnum councilors of state all served on the Board.[84] So many "fanatics" belonged to the Council of Trade that the ultra-loyalist Roger North later claimed that the Council was a "project [meant] to straighten the king," and that "the commissioners considered, one may conclude that whatever interests were regarded, the public revenue coming to the crown out of trade was not their chief care unless it were to sink it by all the ways they could possibly contrive."[85] North saw conspiracy when Charles II was consciously reaching out to a broad public.

The letters patent which established the Council of Trade declare the king's intent both to listen to the needs of a wide spectrum of his population and for the Council to be independent of the large overseas trading companies. Along with enquiring into "the state of trade; means of preventing the export of wool and the cause in the decay of fishing," the Council was commanded to investigate "the usefulness or otherwise of the merchant company."[86] Although he still did not step on the other third rail of English mercantile policy, preventing the export of wool, Charles was willing to question the long-standing policy of conducting foreign trade via merchant companies whom the monarch empowered with exclusive rights.[87] Such open access to both persons and ideas encouraged communication to the king. Interloping merchants and theorists picked up this cue and intensified their campaign to convince the sovereign that opening up trade would benefit king and country.

When the king began to move towards a more hierarchical system of access in 1672 he created a new Council of Trade and Plantations (appointed September 27, 1672). This Council was more in line with the king's desire for tighter access to his person and stricter regulation of trade. As opposed to the two previous Councils whose diversity stood out, the homogeneity of the 1672 Council startles. Every member except three[88] sat in the House of Commons or the House of Lords. Virtually every member except Shaftesbury

---

[84] Thomson and Love were nonconformists. Child, Papillion, Holles, and Ashley favored toleration. Titus and Birch served in the Parliament's army. Love was a councilor of state.

[85] Roger North, *Examen*, (1740), 461.

[86] *CSPD*, 607 (September 28, 1668). The letters patent run for seven and a half pages; these are just a few of the orders.

[87] Charles II was not acting completely without precedent; foreign trade had been opened up before to Spain, France and Portugal.

[88] Sir John Finch and John Evelyn were the exceptions. Finch had served as ambassador to Venice, and soon after the commission (December 7, 1672) he resigned to serve as ambassador to Constantinople. Henry Slingsby, also not a Member of Parliament, took his place.

and Buckingham was Anglican,[89] intensely loyal,[90] and strongly against toleration.[91] Nine of the members received salaries of £500 per annum[92] which suggests that a place on the Board may have come more as a reward for past Parliamentary support of court measures than from any specific economic knowledge, especially since most members had little if any connection with trade. Lord Colepeper had written a number of tracts arguing for lower interest rates and some other members had tangential relationships with ventures such as draining fens,[93] but few had ties to any major mercantile interest in England and none had any practical knowledge of trade.

The lack of connection between Council members – most strikingly the non-noble Council members – and the mercantile community suggests that the Council served more as a filter than a conduit between king and businessmen. Unlike the first Council, which sat at the readily accessible Mercers Hall, or even the second Council, which sat at the less accessible but still public Whitehall, the council of 1672 met in the seclusion of the private

---

[89] There may have been some secret Catholics. Shaftesbury and Buckingham had leanings towards nonconformity.

[90] Thomas Osborne listed Allington and Hickman as independents who generally voted for supply. Henry Brouncker had served as groom to the Duke of York and perhaps his pimp. Thomas Culpeper's father and Robert Long accompanied the king in his exile during the interregnum. Richard Gorges was commended as loyal by Paston and Southampton. The Earl of Cleveland described Humphrey Winch as "a member of the House of Commons and a perfect honest gentlemen acting there with all sincerity for your majesty's service as he engaged me to perform before he was chosen." Silas Titus, after an initial stint with the interregnum forces, had served as a spy for the king. John Evelyn's loyalty is well known.

[91] Richard Gorges attacked toleration in 1668. Hickman was one of the key members in bringing about the "Clarendon Code." Humphrey Winch also explicitly opposed toleration.

[92] The Earl of Shaftesbury, Lord Colepeper, Lord Gorges, Lord Alington, Henry Brouncker, Humphrey Winch, William Hickman, Sir John Finch, Edmund Waller, Henry Slingsby, and Silas Titus received salaries. Those who did not receive salaries were employed by the administration in some other capacity. They included York, Rupert, Lauderdale, Ormonde, Halifax, Sir Thomas Osborne, Sir Robert Long, and Sir George Carteret (J. C. Sainty, *Officials of the Boards of Trade, 1660–1870* (London: Athlone Press, 1974), 23).

[93] Sir George Carteret and Shaftesbury were involved in the Carolina Plantation. William Hickman was the trustee of a sailcloth venture and supported high taxes on French linen. Henry Brouncker was Deputy Governor of the Royal Adventurers in Africa from 1665 to 1667, but probably received the position more for being the pimp of the Duke of York than for any business acumen. Silas Titus and the Duke of York were also involved in the Royal African Company. Robert Long was the auditor of the receipt of the Exchequer and was famed for his ability to understand balance sheets. Prince Rupert was Governor of the Hudson Bay Company. Gorges and Hickman were involved in fen drainage. These mostly ceremonial positions, however, had little to do with the bulk of trade in which English merchants participated.

house of the Duchess of Castlemaine on King Street near Whitehall.[94] Even the patent which authorized this council sounds more restrictive than the previous patents.

> We have thought fit to erect and establish a *select* council whose employment shall be to take care of the welfare of the said colonies and plantations and of the trade and navigation of these our kingdomes and of our said colonies and plantations and to *give us* a true and faithful account thereof from time to time with their opinions and advice therupon.[95]

In these patents the king lays out the council's role as an advisory body. Its function is to "give us" an account of trade and the plantations, not to help merchants. Like the Council in 1663, this group would not serve as a means of communication between merchants and monarchs.

Unlike the patent, the instructions drawn up by the Earl of Shaftesbury[96] resemble the patents of the 1668 Council in respect to investigating the merits of freer trade; for Shaftesbury did not view the economy as needing royal guidance to avoid glut. His political views naturally brought him into alliance with a group of economic theorists who viewed demand as elastic, saw toleration of all Protestants as a means to encourage trade, favored open trading companies, and advocated instituting an advisory council composed of merchants.[97] Shaftesbury, however, was alone in his tenets and as a founder of the Carolina Plantation concerned himself primarily with colonial affairs.[98] Not surprisingly most Council of Trade business dealt with running the crown's colonies. The Council's homogeneity and primary concern with the plantations discouraged English merchants from applying to it for redress of economic grievances.[99]

---

[94] *CSPD*, vol. 14, 48, 213. The Duchess of Cleveland received £200 rent per annum for leasing the house to the Council of Trade and Plantations. Charles M. Andrews, *British Committees, Commissions, and Councils of Trade and Plantations, 1622–1675, Johns Hopkins University Studies in Historical and Political Science* (series XXVI, Nos 1–3, 1908), 107.

[95] PRO CO 389/4, 70; emphasis added.

[96] For a copy of the instructions see Andrews, 127–132.

[97] See, for instance, Josiah Child, *A Treatise Wherein Is Demonstrated that the East India Trade is the Most National of All Foreign Trades* (1681), Sel. 1681 E C. [Slingsby Bethel], *Observations on the Letter Written to Sir Thomas Osborn upon the Reading of a Book Called the Present Interest of England Stated Written in a Letter to a Friend in London* (1673), Sel. 1673 E B46; *England Great Happiness or a Dialogue Between Content and Complaint Wherein Is Demonstrated That a Great Part of Our Complaints Are Causeless and We Have More Wealth Now than Ever We Had at Any Time Before the Restoration of His Sacred Majesty* (1677), Sel. 1677 E En 34.

[98] Haley, 255, 227–265.

[99] Most petitions sent to the council came from the plantations. The Gambia Adventurers, the English consul at Venice, and John Row were the only non-plantation petitioners. Andrews, Appendix IV; *CSPD, passim.*

Shaftesbury's influence as President did, however, combine with the pre-dominance of landowners on the Council to create an anti-monopolistic bias among the Council. It often found against monopolistic entities. For instance, John Row, a glover who had learned how to make shammy (chamois) gloves in Holland, successfully petitioned the Council to operate without paying fines to the Glovers Company.[100] The Guinea Adventurers[101] were unsuccessful in preventing the importation of sanders, a dying agent, from the Netherlands.[102] After enquiring with the Dyers Company, and establishing that the use of sanders greatly cheapened the price of dyed cloth without adversely affecting quality, the Council allowed the importation of sanders from the Netherlands, until the East India Company could import a sufficient quantity from the Indies. The royal administration, however, tended to side with the monopolists at this time.[103]

Partly due to the Council's anti-monopolist tendencies, but primarily as an aspect of Danby's urging Charles to restrict access, Charles dissolved the Council of Trade in December, 1674, ending any pretense of privileged access of the merchants as a class.[104] The Committee of Trade, a subdivision of the Privy Council, took the place of the Council of Trade. This Committee followed all the restrictive rules of access of the Privy Council. The Committee also tended to express economic views which correlated with Danby's and the Anglicans' hierarchical views of society.

The committee itself took measures to ensure that communication to the king occurred only through the proper channels. When John Haynes and other clothiers addressed a petition to the Earl of Danby in July, 1676 complaining about high French tariffs on English goods, the Committee of Trade rebuked Haynes for trying to bypass them and ordered "that if those petitioners have any thing to represent they must address themselves directly to the Committee of Trade (which they are acquainted with) upon this occasion the lords declare their opinion that this committee is capable of

---

[100] *CSPD*, vol. 14, 161.

[101] The Guinea Adventurers were licensed by the Royal African Company to trade with Northwest Africa.

[102] The Guinea Adventurers imported the dying agent redwood from North Africa, and the cheaper sanders cut into their market share.

[103] Those who petitioned the king and Council directly tended to have their requests for strict regulation of industry and trade granted. Felt hat makers petitioned successfully to establish a company for the stricter supervision of their product (*CSPD*, vol. 14, 108). The Royal African Company gained authorization both to stop ships ladened with goods vendible only in Africa and to command the Governors of the Caribbean Islands to make sure that the Royal African Company was the sole vendor of slaves (*CSPD*, vol. 13, 295). The king also issued a warrant to revoke the letters patent which had allowed the inhabitants of Cornwall to trade freely within the realms of the Merchant Adventurers, the Eastland Company, the Russia Company, and the Turkey Company (*CSPD*, vol. 16, 291 (June 26, 1674).)

[104] Individual merchants, of course, could gain privileged access in a variety of ways.

receiving any address relating to trade and plantations as shall be made them immediately and in the first instance in order to prepare the same for his majesty."[105] The Committee had little vested interest in protecting its turf; it was ensuring only that all communication follow the proper path.

Although the Committee of Trade did not appreciate Haynes's method, it sympathized with his message. Royalist-Anglican sentiment and restrictive access policies were perfectly compatible with anti-Catholicism, francophobia, and protectionism. On March 9, 1675/6, Sir George Downing addressed the Committee and explained that England had a £968,000 trade deficit with France.[106] Downing and a group of weavers blamed French impositions and English servitude to French fashion as the cause of this gap. Fashion, furthermore, was not seen as fickle and beyond human control: both Downing and the weavers believed that the French used fashion as an economic weapon, changing what was in vogue as soon as the English weavers set their looms to produce the fabric in style. The Committee did not think that preventing the exportation of wool or high imposts on French products would solve this problem; instead, they once again suggested that the king should wear only English cloth and use his personal wardrobe to "erect a fashion." The king seemed pleased with this idea. When Charles II entered the council chamber, the weavers and mercers were called in and showed the king a great variety of "silk stuffs and ribbons." Charles II rose to the occasion and announced "that he will give encouragement to the wearing of English manufactures by his own example & that he will recommend the same to the queen & cause the same to be observed generally in Whitehall."[107] These measures corresponded with the Anglican view of society as hierarchical: the monarch acted and the rest of the nation (according to their proximity to the king) followed to the benefit of the whole. Furthermore, it represents a trend of actual access being replaced with symbolic appearances and of display taking the place of communication.

In this hierarchical conception of society the king ordered and subjects obeyed. Such a concern with securing obedience or at least the show of obedience dominates the Committee of Trade's interaction with New England after 1675. Prior to 1675 the administration had left the colonies, and particularly New England, largely to their own devices. In 1675, however, the Committee of Trade began to question the economic and political policies of

---

[105] PRO CO 391/1, July 11, 1676.

[106] This was not the only case of the Committee addressing the issue of the French balance of trade. On June 9, 1676 Secretary Williamson argued for English retaliation against French high tariffs and Heneage Finch, The Lord Chancellor, claimed that the French, "in order to destroy our Levant trade have forbidden the import of silk into France by any other port than that of Toulon and . . . there is a particular company at Toulon . . . that has the whole monopoly of this trade and hinders the import of silk by stranger that way" (PRO CO 391/1, 1676).

[107] PRO CO 391/1, March, 9, 1675/6.

the colonies. This issue came to the fore when Robert Mason and Ferdinando Gorges (proprietors of New Hampshire and Maine respectively) petitioned the Committee against the Massachusetts Bay Company's encroachments on their lands. Mason and Gorges had previously petitioned the Council of Trade in 1671. The 1671 petition occasioned some debate, but the commissioners refrained from taking action, fearing, in the words of Evelyn," their [the Massachusetts Bay Company's] altogether breaking from all dependence upon this nation."[108]

Such concerns did not occur in 1675 when Mason and Gorges petitioned again. Because Holland and France were at war, the Committee, as they themselves testified, had no apprehension that a foreign country would use the opportunity of a rift between New England and its mother country to annex the colonies. Nevertheless, the committee – still somewhat wary of appearing to execute judgement before the Massachusetts Bay Company was heard – deemed it "much more advisable that his majesty should send the state of the complaint unto them and require their sending commissioners over to agree the difference by which his majesty would see the state of their *obedience* towards him";[109] Such concern with having colonies show obedience towards the king, indicative of the economic policies of the Danby years, was absent in the Council of Trade debates of 1671. As K. D. H. Haley states, Shaftesbury, the President of the 1671 Council of Trade, "was not interested like James [Duke of York] in the enforcement of royal authority as an end in itself."[110] The Committee of Trade of 1675, however, sided with James.

The desire to force the colonies to publicly display their dependence upon the king permeates the Committee of Trade's debates on Mason's and Gorges's petitions. When the Massachusetts Bay Company delayed sending commissioners, the Committee of Trade resolved, "it were necessary to have New England more in dependence upon his majesty as for example first in relation to the irregularity of their trade and secondly to bring them to such an acknowledgment of his majesty's authority as to submit and leave the final determination and last result of superior points to his majesty."[111] The Committee stressed the need for obedience when it refused to frame any rules for passes to be granted in New England. The Committee declared that "so that until his majesty come to a better understanding touching what degrees of dependence that government will acknowledge to his majesty their lordships have not fit to offer any rules for passes in that place."[112] The council meant to force from the colonies a public acknowledgment of their place within the hierarchy, under and dependent upon the king.

---

[108] Quoted in Haley, 261.
[109] PRO CO 391/1, 61, emphasis added.
[110] Haley, 263.
[111] PRO CO 390/1, 70; emphasis added.
[112] PRO CO 391/1, 291; emphasis added.

When commissioners from New England finally came in the summer of 1677, the committee once again highlighted the need for "the necessity of bringing those people under a more palpable declaration of their *obedience* to his majesty and *dependence* on his crown."[113] In a precursor to royal policy after 1681, the Committee of Trade decided to threaten the charter of the Massachusetts Bay Company, suggesting that the king issue a Quo Warranto. On July 30, 1678, the Committee of Trade threatened the commissioners: "their lordships tell them they do not declare their charter void, but only intimate to them the condition they are in that they might dispose themselves to pray of his majesty what their case requireth." The New England commissioner stated that they had kissed his majesty's hands and "promised to submit to his majesty in all things."[114]

Such diligence on the part of the Committee of Trade to secure obedience to his majesty was not what most merchants wanted from the governmental body assigned to commerce. They wanted the ability to shape and influence economic policy. Perhaps the clarion call for a new Council of Trade best demonstrates merchants' and manufacturers' lack of satisfaction with their inability to gain access to the king in the 1680s.

As early as 1674, Carew Reynell argued for the establishment of a Council of Trade "being mixt with the chief able merchants that understand trade."[115] Joseph Trevors's 1677 tract against illegal wool exports railed against the hierarchical system of access which prevented those hurt by smuggling from appealing to anyone outside the corrupt local magistracy who turned a blind eye to illegal exports of wool. To end corruption, Trevors suggested the formation of "a committee of clothiers . . . with merchant of the several cities, and some other tradesmen and artificers to be appointed"; A key function of this committee would be "to receive petitions or projections from work-men, which may any way tend to the increase and encouragement of trade."[116] Clearly Trevors felt that the current Committee of Trade was not accessible to clothiers. In a letter to Sir Joseph Williamson in 1675, Hugh Morrell also suggested a renewal of a Council of Trade that was independent of the Privy Council. When mentioning the types of people of whom the council should consist, he made sure to specify, "but no lords, being beneath their dignity and out of their element." The council in his mind would act as a conduit between economic interests and the king. He thought the establishment of a council would allay the trouble clothiers had in going to London to petition the king and also "free them [the Privy Council] from the laborious and intricate mysteries of clothing and

---

[113]  PRO CO 391/2, 95 (July 27, 1677); emphasis added.
[114]  PRO CO 391/2, 262ff. (July 30, 1678).
[115]  Reynell, *The True English Interest* (London: printed for Giles Widdowes, 1674), 16.
[116]  Joseph Trevors, *An Essay to the Restoring of Our Decayed Trade Wherein Is Described the Smugglers, Lawyers and Officers Fraud* (London: 1677), 40, 45.

commerce."[117] Six years later this trope emerges once again. The anonymous N. N.'s *The Trade of England Revived* also endorsed the founding of a council "made up of some eminent trades men of the city of London mixt with some of the country and some eminent clothiers, who might consider what might be necessary for the promotion of trade, and for the right setting thereof, and who might suggest the same to the Parliament when they do meet, that so they may have the less to do herein; for the whole structure of trade is very much out of frame at present." In this period where communication to the king became difficult, theorists and merchants looked back wistfully at the earlier Councils of Trade.

Merchants wanted the Council of Trade to serve as an intermediary between them and the administration because it made communicating with the king easier. It was possible for merchants to attempt to influence policy by speaking directly to the king when they wanted to circumvent the council or when the council was not active. But maintaining direct communication with the king was a feat which few mercantile entities could accomplish successfully.

## Companies and the king: a study in communication

The ruler's role as the focal point of the economic hierarchy is a basic tenet of the patrimonial economic system. Since the monarch was to both encourage beneficial innovation and curb abuse, the king or queen was seen as the target for complaints and suggestions. The Council of Trade facilitated the flow of such communication from economic entities to the king. Even without the Council of Trade, mercantile organizations could plead with the king, but such communication was difficult and costly. When Charles was relatively open to receiving pleas, organized economic interests surmounted these hurdles, in order to persuade the king to regulate the economy according to their interest. When access was difficult, however, many companies looked elsewhere, appealing to Parliament or public opinion. The facts that the king ceased to be the key recipient of economic pleas and that even those capable of reaching the king directed their entreaties elsewhere jeopardized the monarch's position as the focal point of the patriarchal economic system. Charles, however, partially reclaimed his role by monopolizing the power to effect economic change.

When Charles withdrew from courting the public in late 1662, large economic interests such as the East India Company (EIC) remained relatively unscathed. Small businessmen suffered because the Council of Trade no longer functioned as a conduit to the king, and the administration leaned more towards commanding than consulting businessmen. In one particularly striking example, the Levant Company was informed *post facto* that it should

---

[117] *CSPD*, vol. 17, 163 (June 14, 1675). N. N., *The Trade of England Revived* (1681), 51.

pay the expense of a naval expedition against Algiers, an expedition which they neither approved of nor even knew about.[118] But because Charles tightened access for private not public reasons and because the existence of monopolistic entities coincided with the hierarchical system that Charles and most economic pundits favored, large organized economic entities generally interacted successfully with the king. Two incidents involving spice and tin illustrate Charles's continued open access to organized and powerful groups.

After the Dutch had attacked Pulo Run and burned down that island's spice trees, the East India Company had no ready source for cloves, nutmeg, and cinnamon. To supply the want, two prominent courtiers Henry Bennet[119] and John Grenville[120] petitioned for a license to import spices from German cities and the United Provinces. Charles did not simply award the patent to his two intimate companions; he made sure to consult both Lord Treasurer Southampton and the East India Company. Southampton believed that there was a dearth of spice, but he could not see how giving the patent to only two people would benefit the nation and therefore suggested that the importation be open to all. The East India Company could not employ the usual arguments which they used against interlopers: the proposed license could not ruin the East India Company's relationship with Asian potentates, and the Dutch East India Company's careful regulation of the supply of spice rendered moot any fears of a glut. The East India Company's only recourse was to argue that it would soon import spices. The king appeased both Southampton and the East India Company by allowing anyone to import spices until the company found another source of supply.[121] The economic interests of the nation did not take a back seat to the greed of courtiers.

The ability of all major interest groups to reach the king is also shown by the attempt of the Cornish tinners to improve their ability to vent their product.[122] Enlisting the aid of William Godolphin[123] among others, the tinners petitioned

---

[118] PRO SP 105/109, 123.

[119] Secretary of State later created Earl of Arlington.

[120] The Groom of the Stool and Earl of Bath.

[121] Sainsbury, vol. 11, 233–259, 265. *CSPD*, vol. 2, 597 (December 20, 1662).

[122] Stannary law dictated that tinners could sell their product only twice a year at specific coinage houses. These laws caused a great deal of financial hardship: the tinners who were often strapped for cash had to borrow from merchants at 20 percent interest and sell to those merchants below market prices. When the laws were suspended during the interregnum, allowing the tinners to sell their tin whenever they wished, the price of tin doubled and the tin industry expanded. With the restoration, however, came a resumption of the laws which required tinners to sell their product at the coinages twice a year. (The tin mines were the property of the Duke of Cornwall. The institution of set coinages was designed to ensure that the Duke received his revenue.) The price of tin remained stable, but the tinners once again depended upon the capital advances of the merchants which rendered tin mining much less profitable (George Randall Lewis, *The Stannaries* (New York: Houghton Mifflin & Co., 1908), 218–220).

[123] Godolphin was a royalist of Cornish descent, Undersecretary of State and deputy warden of the Stannaries.

successfully to establish a new coinage house in Penzance. Their plea that the king suspend the laws which regulated the selling of tin did not fare as well. According to a letter William Godolphin received from his father, the tinners realized that "his majesty is the best friend they have at the council table" and that they needed the king to "preserve them from ruin so daily coming upon them from the contrivances of the merchants." The tinners, cognizant of their need to reach the king, solicited the support of the Earl of Bath who served as the Lord Warden of the Stannaries, Hugh Boscawen (MP for Tregony), and William Godolphin. But the tinners could not prevent their opponents from pleading their case in front of his majesty. As Francis Godolphin reported, "now in the meantime the officers of the coynages apprehending from the reason & neccessitie of the tynners desires some danger to their fees, have lately met at Truro & dispatched Mr. Catcher to London with all the suggestions they can raise in order to disparage & defeat the just endeavours of the tinners."[124] Charles had allowed both sides of the dispute to argue the merits of their case, and made a compromise by restoring the custom of selling tin at a fixed rate, known as pre-emption.[125] Appealing to the king, however, required a great deal of effort, money, and organization. When the patent of pre-emption expired in the midst of the Dutch War, the tinners could summon neither the will nor the resources to reach the king.

The time of the war proved a crucible in which to test the relationship of companies and the monarch. The years which witnessed the Dutch War, the great fire, and the plague were not propitious ones to try to get in contact with the king. The king stayed away from Whitehall, whether to visit the fleet or to escape the plague. Hearings before the king often had to be pushed off because of other emergencies.[126] During these years companies needed to expend more effort to maintain good relations with the king. The East India Company surmounted the challenge and began a mutually beneficial association. But others, in particular the Merchant Adventurers, the Bristol Merchants, and the tinners did not adapt to this environment of restricted access.

At the beginning of the war, The East India Company, cognizant of the need for convoys,[127] made extensive efforts to bestow a major gift upon the king. On July 12, 1664 Captain Prowd was "desired to inquire aboard the

---

[124] BL ADD MSS 28052, 2.

[125] Elizabeth originated pre-emption of tin in 1599 in order to "relieve (*sic*) the tinners from the necessity of dependence upon the tin dealers by a guarantee of a fixed price for their tin for a term of years in advance" (G. R. Lewis, The Stannaries (New York: Houghton Mifflin & Co., 1908), 218). The patent of pre-emption was given to a group of financiers led by Sir Richard Ford, yet another example of his access to the king yielding dividends.

[126] The Bristol merchants and the Levant Company, for instance, had a long-standing debate over the right of the Bristol merchants to trade in the Levant, but the hearing kept on being postponed because of the plague (see below, p. 151).

[127] The East India Company petitioned the king for convoys in September, 1664 (*CSPD*, vol. 4, 21) and for men on January 9, 1666.

several ships for rare birds, beasts, or other curiosities fit to present to the king." Unable to find "anything suitable as a present for the king, on the suggestion of the governor it was (*sic*) resolved to present his majesty with a silver case of oil of cinnamon which is to be had of Mr. Thomas Winter for £75 and some good tea."[128] Of more importance were the loans and advances of saltpeter. From 1664 until 1667 the East India company loaned the king a total of £244,000 and allowed him to purchase 45,700 pounds of saltpeter on credit.[129] At first The East India Company hesitated when asked to lend money to the administration. The committees feared that advancing money would establish a dangerous precedent.[130] Stockholders and the financial community would view such a precedent as rendering the resources of the East India Company a source of royal revenue. As Loughead observes, "from the company's point of view what mattered was the way agreement was reached with a minimum of pressure or overt manipulation."[131] If it was perceived that the monarch could raid the East India Company's coffers at will, then no investor would feel secure buying East Indian stock.[132] Charles was wary of too forceful an approach and carefully worded his requests. On April 16, 1666, he requested £50,000 "with all speed on good security to pay off the arrears of the seamen, without which it will be impossible for the fleet to put to sea." The king did not make the request a blunt one, nor did he threaten the company with a suspension of its monopoly. Rather he placed the request in the context of thanking the company "for the readiness with which they advanced a sum of money upon the East India prizes in a time of public calamity and sickness;" and was careful to note, "and this shall not be considered a precedent for future applications."[133] Advancing the money and the constant bestowal of gifts to the king gave the East India Company access to the king and influence upon the government. It could rely on royal officials to look out for its interests in negotiations with the Dutch and other foreign powers as opposed to the "double dealing which especially characterized Charles I's reign."[134]

The corporation of London likewise eagerly sought the good graces of the king.[135] In November, 1664 the city advanced a £100,000 loan to the king.

---

[128] Sainsbury (February 17, 1666). On February 17, 1666 the East India Company presented Charles II with rarities (£371); tea (22.75 lb. besides tea to the value of £6 15s given to his two chief attendants; a silver china cabinet (£100); spirit of cinnamon (£53); Indian dishes (£458); china dishes and jars (£58).

[129] Loughead, 101–107.

[130] The leaders of the East India Company were called the committees.

[131] Loughead, 107.

[132] Such practices on the part of Charles I had undermined the company's credit: Loughead 101–107.

[133] *CSPD*, vol. 6, 357 (April 9, 1666).

[134] Loughead, 92.

[135] Charles II's terminating the erection of a bridge between Lambeth and Westminster, which would have hurt the city by diverting traffic, reminded the city why it needed to retain his good graces. *CSPD*, vol. 4 (1664/5), 43.

When the Lord Mayor of London wrote a letter urging the Clothworkers to contribute their part of the £100,000 loan to the king, he emphasized, "how far your company with the whole city will hereby gain upon his majesty's favour your good understanding of the present agitations and unquestionable true affection to his majesty."[136] By this time, the Clothworkers did not represent those who teased and trimmed cloth so much as wealthy merchants[137] who needed the king's favor; they contributed readily to the loan.[138]

The war, however, strained the relationship between merchants and the king. Two years after relative success raising the £100,000 loan the city encountered difficulty trying to raise money to replace *The London*, a ship sunk by the Dutch. The subscription meant to raise £15,000 garnered only £4200. Even the Clothworkers had some trouble rallying their members. When asked to help raise £550 for the gift, the Clothworkers acquiesced but only after being urged by the mayor of the necessity of "promoting his ma^ties and the whole kingdom . . . and the honor of this cittie . . . you are required to use your utmost care and diligence therein that soe his ma^ties expectation to have her dispatched for present service (as hee hath pleased to intimate) may not bee frustrated nor the city's honor nor the repute of your particular company lessened by any neglect or remissness therein." Even after such exhortations the request occasioned "a long and serious debate and consideration."[139]

Considerably less wealthy and powerful than the Clothworkers, the Weavers did not think that they could reach the king during the Dutch War.[140] Instead, the Weavers looked to Parliament to defend their interests. In March, 1664, for instance, the four in place[141] were asked "to treat with the several members of Parliament whether it is best to present the bill to the Parliament this session or the next."[142] Since the king seemed unreachable, the Weavers did not feel compelled to please him. When the Weavers received the letter from Lord Mayor John Lawrence asking the Weavers to contribute £800 to the £100,000 that the city promised to loan Charles II, the Weavers loaned the money reluctantly. They claimed that their share should

---

[136] Clothworkers, 9 November 1664, 273b.

[137] The minutes of the guild's court discuss real estate more often than the handicraft workers' concerns.

[138] The king for his part chose a representative, the Earl of Manchester, who would be acceptable to the city elites (*CSPD*, vol. 4, 43).

[139] Clothworkers (March 6, 1665/6), 12.

[140] The Guild of Weavers was not one of the twelve major livery companies and consisted almost exclusively of actual weavers.

[141] The "four in place" was the phrase used to designate the four chief officers of the guild.

[142] Guildhall Library Weavers Company Records, 4655–3, 192 (March 26, 1664). The Weavers were not alone in assuming that during this period of restricted access only those with wealth and sway could influence the sovereign. The tin miners did not even attempt to approach Charles II.

be only £350, but agreed to forward £500. The city of London insisted that the Weavers give the full £800 which they eventually did. Throughout the negotiations the Weavers display no concern over how their reluctance would appear to the king.[143]

The Weavers assumed rightly that any attempt to contact the king would be fruitless. The tin farmers did not have to assume that trying to contact the king would be a waste of time; they were told so by the king himself. The tin farmers – who were well enough connected to employ Williamson and Ashley on their behalf[144] – received a royal missive which commanded them, "The king having determined to raise money beyond the seas by sale of tin has authorized the Duke of Albemarle and Sir George Carteret to treat with them for the sale or deposit of 500 tons on good security of their forbearance. The occasion being pressing admits of no return or reply." Charles denied them the right of communication.[145] The Bristol Merchants, mistakenly, thought they could gain the king's support. In 1643 Charles I had granted the merchants of Bristol – who had remained loyal – the right to trade freely in the domain of the Merchant Adventurers, Levant Company, and Eastlands Company. In February, 1665, after a dispute with the Levant Company, the Bristol Merchants petitioned Charles II to confirm those rights.[146] It took the merchants fifteen months to receive a hearing at which they failed to convince the Council of the merits of their case.[147] The Bristol merchants were denied the privilege of trading with the Ottoman Empire,[148] and could not prevent the Levant Company from trying repeatedly to exclude the Bristol Merchants from trading with the rest of the Levant. So the Bristol Merchants also tried their luck in Parliament, to no avail. Companies with fewer resources than the Clothworkers and the East India Company had to struggle to get in touch with the king. Many simply turned away from Charles, looking to Parliament for a solution to economic quandaries such as the importation of Irish cattle and the decay of trade. This concentration on Parliament as the source of economic reform damaged the image of the king as the head of the patrimonial economic system.

---

[143] Ibid., 147–148. Although the Weavers, whose monopolistic privileges pertained only to the city of London, did not need the kind of royal support that the EIC did; nevertheless they wanted the king to prevent the imports of foreign cloth and the export of wool.

[144] *CSPD*, vol. 4, 495 (July 31, 1665)

[145] *CSPD*, vol. 4, 509 (August 8, 1665).

[146] Patrick McGrath, *Records Relating to the Society of Merchant Adventurers of the City of Bristol in the Seventeenth Century* (Bristol: Bristol Record Society, 1952, 16 (February 10, 1665)) hereafter referred to as *Bristol Merchant Adventurers*.

[147] The Bristol Merchants were allowed a few rights to trade in the Mediterranean and exemption from paying impositions on goods from Zante and Venice (*Bristol Merchant Adventurers*, 218 [May 1666]).

[148] In 1668 the Bristol Merchants explained that they could not trade in the Levant "in regard of the restrictions thereon and the capitulation of peace made with the grand signor only for that company" (*Bristol Merchant Adventurers*, 219).

After the Dutch War, perhaps to regain some of that authority, Charles returned to his previous policy of openness, an openness to ideas as well as to persons. Charles, for the first time in his reign, countenanced the notion of elastic demand and questioned the need for monopolies to stave off glut.[149] The dissemination of anti-monopolist theory – combined with the ease with which anti-monopolists could present their ideas to the king – pressured the large trading companies to both change the nature of their arguments and strengthen their ties to the king.

The East India Company reacted to this openness by endeavoring to establish direct conduits to the king. Sir William Morrice, the Secretary of State, acted as their agent. In 1668 the committees asked Morrice if it was a propitious time to petition the king. Receiving a positive answer, the company asked the king, "to recommend to the States-General . . . that this company may carry on their trade in the Indies without interruption, and that the Dutch generals and commanders may . . . take an oath to religiously to observe the peace."[150] Morrice was "directed to draw up a letter from His Majesty to the states general accordingly." The company obtained its desire with extraordinary speed. It first approached Morrice on January 20 and the letter was sent on January 25, 1668. Ten days later, the governor thanked the Secretary of State and asked further "that Sir William Temple should be reminded to procure an answer to the same; also that notice might be given to the company when the treaty marine comes on that they may make their addresses to his majesty concerning it; all this Sir William promised should be done."[151]

After Morrice's retirement (September 29, 1668) the company endeavored to maintain its conduits of access. It tried to gratify Charles II's key advisors by giving jobs to their clients. Arlington,[152] the Duke of York,[153] and Ashley[154] all secured positions for their clients. The East India Company continued to give the king exotic presents, including spotted deer and small green parrots.[155] Furthermore, the company agreed to a beneficial arrangement

---

[149] See the instructions to the Council of Trade above, p. 139.

[150] Sainsbury, vol. 8, 10–11, 13.

[151] Sainsbury, 19 (February 4, 1668).

[152] Henry Grey and Ensign Rice received prominent positions (Grey was President at Surat). (Sainsbury, 32 (February 25, 1668)). Although Mr. Boreman did not immediately receive a position, Arlington was informed that he would be considered when there was occasion for a person of his qualifications (Sainsbury, vol. 9, 103 (January 24, 1672)).

[153] The Duke of York's solicitor, Charles Porter, was admitted to the company gratis. Sainsbury, 46.

[154] "Samuel South, a young man related to and recommended by Lord Ashley, is entertained to work in the company's office and is promised that, when he shall be sent to India, a salary shall be given him" (Sainsbury, vol. 8, 310), 1670.

[155] Sainsbury, 310.

where the Treasury could buy saltpeter not at the candle[156] – which royal agents deemed "not honorable or decent for the king" – but at a prearranged contract and on credit.

These measures paid off. The East India Company not only defeated the "interlopers",[157] but also had a major say in foreign treaties. The treaty with Spain included the right to water and victual English ships in Manila. In 1671 the king wrote to the Sultan of Bantam on behalf of the East India Company to reinforce the company's position as the sole representative of the king in all matters to foreign powers beyond the Cape of Good Hope.[158] The company was consulted in negotiations with the Dutch, as well as with Asian powers. In 1668 Sir William Morrice kept the EIC well informed. In 1672 the king, after being petitioned by the East India Company, instructed Arlington and Buckingham[159] "to procure an adjustment of trade in the East Indies as we have desired formerly."[160] The pressures upon the East India Company were different in times of strict and easy access, but as long as the regulation of access did not have a political dimension, the EIC and other companies with considerable resources maintained lines of access and, consequently, influenced economic policy.

In July, 1675, Alderman Patience Ward wrote Secretary Williamson on behalf of the woolen industry. Ward opened his letter with the phrase, "the free

---

[156]  It was customary for the East India Company to auction its goods by having prospective buyers bid until a candle burned down to a certain mark. Auctioning by candle was a relatively common practice in Restoration England.

[157]  The company, for instance, quashed an attempt to allow pepper to be imported. When the company learned "that considerable quantities of pepper have been offered for sale and are to be brought from Holland by licenses granted or endeavored to be obtained from the king," they ordered "Certain committees . . . to wait on the Secretaries of State, [and] inform them . . . of the great inconveniences that may arise not only to the Company but also to the whole kingdom if such licenses prove effective." The secretaries replied that no such license had been given. Sainsbury, 107.

[158]  The letter reads, "The measures by which friendship with him and his country do and must always subsist. His royal predecessors by their charters granted to the East India Company sole traffic to all the kingdoms and places of the east beyond the Cape of Good Hope with full power to correspond with all emperors, kings and princes in those parts in order to trade with them which power and authority his present majesty has confirmed by renewing the said company's charter, therefore though the sultan's letter and present has been willingly accepted as a testimony of friendship, yet it must be understood that all power and authority has been transferred to the said company to trade and correspond with the sultan and all other princes and kings in those parts without reserving any distinct correspondence to ourselves." It appears that this message was much needed because of "great inconvenience having been caused through the King of Bantam's 'insinuations with some of the commanders', and the sending of presents to England which has proved troublesome and inconvenient, and caused expectations of returns of much greater value" (Sainsbury, vol. 9, 38, 45 (May 24, 1671, June 23, 1671)).

[159]  They were ambassadors to negotiate a treaty in Holland.

[160]  Sainsbury, 138 (June 20, 1672).

access I have ever had with your honour has encouraged this, though, when I reflect on my fruitless solicitations in the French treaty of commerce my heart fails."[161] Ward's phrase reflects contemporary experience with access. For most of the previous fifteen years, access to the king and his officers had been free which encouraged petitioners to approach the royal administration. But Thomas Osborne's rise to power (1673) occasioned a strong shift towards a strict and hierarchical system of access. Danby instituted this system to ensure that royalist Anglicans, and only royalist Anglicans, would benefit from being conduits between the king and his subjects. Many contemporary thinkers considered such a policy as the best means to secure a well-ordered and obedient nation. However, the relative open access of the previous years had accustomed Englishmen such as Ward to express their views and the now restricted access simply encouraged the discontented to air their complaints in other forums. This system of closed access also damaged Charles II's reputation as an accessible king which in turn harmed the ideological framework underpinning the king's rights to grant monopolistic privileges.

The new hierarchical system of access forced companies to strive harder to keep the channels of access open. The East India Company set up a slush fund of £2000 for "those who have countenanced and given furtherance to the company's affairs."[162] The Clothworkers, looking for ties to the administration, elected Sir Joseph Williamson as their master in November, 1675 and Samuel Pepys in November, 1677. Advertising their powerful connections, the Clothworkers set up the Williamson arms in their hall.[163] Doddington a member of the royal diplomatic corps, sensed Charles II's current approval of proper hierarchical systems. When Doddington proposed banning the import of currants from Venice, he appealed to Charles II's sense of proper hierarchy, arguing that "their [Venetian] executive power being in the hands of persons of the same order and degree with those who have the legislature" inevitably led to corrupt officials.[164]

---

[161] CSPD, vol. 17, 276–277.
[162] Sainsbury, vol. 9, 207.
[163] Clothworkers (1665/83), 419, 420, 451, 454.
[164] The argument went as follows: "But as if these disadvantages were too few, our trade and traders lie under other and very great discouragements; all which proceed principally from the exorbitant uncontrollable avarice, insolence and oppression of their noblemen whom they send abroad to Levant and Cessolonia, to be judges and magistrates; but whose actions bespeak them rather butchers than shepherds, but this proceeds from a defect in their very government their executive power being in the hands of persons of the same order and degree with those who have the legislature; so as if all in one and the same degree are to be considered as one man, here is then no way left to obtain reason against any offender of that degree; and in fact no noble Venetian was ever punished for whatever crime or offense committed which makes them as bold to kill and rob his majesty's subjects as if they were their own" (PRO SP 105/145, 46).

Many, however could not adapt to this new, tighter, hierarchical form of access to the king. Stymied at the center of power, they aired their complaints elsewhere. Leather workers and clothiers complained in print and in Parliament against the exportation of leather and wool. Weavers took to the streets after they did not receive any response to their complaints about engine ribbon looms.[165]

The king, cut off from the sentiment of the nation, showed little concern for popular protests. The monopolistic system fitted very well with his attempts to render English society more hierarchical and the king therefore continued to support the East India Company, the Merchant Adventurers, the Royal African Company, and the Hudson Bay Company. The Royal African Company was even allowed to treat with the Dutch in order to stop interlopers.[166] Even those with good ties to the king, such as Sir John Bankes, lost out against monopolistic interests.[167]

Charles's tactics which he adopted to survive the exclusion crisis soured the cozy relationship that monopolistic trading companies enjoyed with the administration. Charles II frequently changed men and measures. These rapid alterations confused merchants: they knew neither whom to apply to in order to get the monarch's ear nor what arguments to use to sway the king. This confusion led merchants to take actions which they later regretted.

At the beginning of 1681, for instance, The East India Company elected Josiah Child and Thomas Papillion as governor and sub-governor. At first glance, one would think that the members of the East India Company would avoid this pair whose candidacy in 1676 had provoked the king's ire.[168] Political conditions in the first few months of 1681, however, illuminate the company's choice of this Whig duo. Before the dissolution of the Oxford Parliament (March, 1681) it looked to all the world as if Shaftesbury, Hollis, and Russell would guide the king. Papillion and Child supported the political agenda of those individuals, and members of the East India Company chose Child and Papillion to establish good ties with the new administration. The king was sufficiently preoccupied with other matters to take any overt notice of Papillion's and Child's election. However, after the dissolution of the Oxford Parliament, competitors noted the weakened position of the East India Company.

The Levant Company, allied with clothiers and Bristol Merchants, attacked the privileges of the East India Company. The dispute began when

---

[165] *CSPD*, October 1675, 369–376. Harris, *Crowds*, 194–195.

[166] *CSPD*, vol. 18, 530 (February 1, 1677).

[167] The Merchant Adventurers petitioned successfully against Bankes continuing to trade with Leipzig. Bankes had been given this right due to the naval conditions of the third Dutch War. *CSPD*, vol. 18, 437, 444, 501.

[168] See below, pp. 161–162.

the East India Company seized a Levant Company ship sailing from Mocha for interloping.[169] This dispute quickly escalated as the Levant Company, eager to expand its turf at the EIC's expense, criticized the company's practices as adversely affecting the balance of trade and, when those tactics failed, attacked their monopolistic privileges. After a long protracted debate, the EIC won.[170]

The East India Company's eventual success does not surprise the historian as much as the length of time it took to quash the Levant Company's attack. Before the exclusion crisis, the links between crown and company were quite strong. Between 1669 and 1678 the East India Company advanced the crown £160,000-worth of saltpeter and a considerable amount of money.[171] But the election of Child and Papillion caused Charles II to fear that the company's resources would come to serve his political enemies and he seriously considered using the Levant Company's offering of stock to "guarantee that the power may be in the hands of such only as shall be well affected to the present government."[172]

Such fears were not allayed by the East India Company's tactics to win its dispute with the Levant Company. Sensing that Charles faced a hostile Parliament which would curtail his ability to regulate the economy, Child and Papillion targeted their arguments towards the public. In a pamphlet defending the East India Company, Child denounced the very principle of monopoly: "All monopolies are destructive of trade and consequently obstructive to the increase of the value of our lands";[173] Child used the Levant Company's anti-monopolistic argument against them. He claimed that the Turkey merchants hindered trade far more than the East India Company because the Levant Company restricted who could participate in its regulated trade while anyone could buy East India Company stock. Child ably disparaged his opponents, but complaining about monopolies came dangerously close to a condemnation of the king's prerogative. The East India Company could have taken a different tack and espoused an argument which agreed with monarchical and hierarchical principles. The Royal African Company, when under attack in 1680, made just such an argument:

> but trade and commerce cannot be maintained or increased without government, order, and regular discipline; for in all confused traffique it must necessarily happen that while every single person pursues his own particular interest, the publique is

---

[169] Mocha, a seaport in present-day Yemen, lay within the East India Company's monopoly.
[170] For details of the debate see Loughead, 138–150 and *CSPD*, vol. 22, 427 (August 30, 1681); vol. 23, 194 (May 2, 1682), 242.
[171] Coleman, 72. In 1678 the East India Company advanced £20,000 to the crown.
[172] Loughead, paraphrasing Roger North, 174.
[173] Josiah Child, *A Treatise*, 1681. Sel. 1681 E C.

deserted by all, and consequently must fall to ruine. for which reason the crown hath erected and established fraternities or companies of merchants with grant of privileges exclusive to all others, as his majesties ancestors and himself by their royal charters have been graciously pleased to do.[174]

The Royal African Company never had any difficulty in getting the administration to support it.[175]

Although the East India Company had alienated the king by electing Child and Papillion, nevertheless they successfully regained his affection and support. Once it was clear that Parliament was not to meet again, the EIC had no other recourse than to court the monarch's favor. The old-fashioned method of gifts did not obtain immediate results. Seeking to appear impartial, Charles II refused a £10,000 gift from the company and told it "that it was not fit to offer this subscription when we made the present but that the king should be made acquainted with it, and in due time we should hear from him."[176] Gifts to those around the king may have gained the East India Company swift access to the king's ear. Macaulay described Child as ensuring that "all who would help or hurt at court, ministers, mistresses, priests were kept in a good humour by presents of shawls, silks, birds' nests, and atar of roses . . . diamonds, and bags of guineas."[177]

But persons more than presents allayed the fears of the king and brought him to the side of the East India Company. The company sought systematically to make its governing body more appealing to the king. Ashe and Banks, who had very close ties to the king, negotiated on behalf of the company.[178] Child himself experienced a conversion to the royalist cause. Like Andrew Riccard twenty years earlier, Child used a marriage to ally himself to the Tories. His daughter married the strongly royalist Marquess of Worcester

---

[174] *Certain Considerations Relating to the Royal African Company of England to Which National Advantages Are Demonstrated Must be in a Joint Stock,* Sel. 1680e, c337.

[175] K. G. Davis, *The Royal African Company* (New York: Longman, 1957), 115. The Royal African Company was not alone in its call for increased order and discipline. In *The Trade of England Revived* (Sel. 1681 E T675) the author known only by the initials N. N. blames the "decay of trade "not from the total defect or want of trade but from the irregularity or disorder thereof" (1). He further supports establishing companies to regulate trade, suppressing an over-abundance of shopkeepers and making sure those free of a company practice the trade of the company. Curiously, this avid royalist may have felt that access to the king was limited, for he called for the re-establishment of the Council of Trade.

[176] Loughead, 138.

[177] Quoted in A. F. W. Papillion, *Memoires of Thomas Papillion of London, Merchant* (Reading: 1887), 81.

[178] Banks, besides having negotiated the details of East India Company loans to the king, had financial dealings with Killigrew, Chiffinch, Cartaret, Charles Bertie, York, Danby, Chicherly, Clifford, and married Heneage Finch's daughter (Coleman, 22, 24, 76, 82, *passim.*).

with a portion of £30,000.[179] To enhance their relationship with the king the governors of the East India Company purged itself of Whigs: only four of the twenty-six directors from ten years earlier remained.[180]

The East India Company, cognizant of its dependence upon the sovereign, voluntarily remodeled itself according to the Anglican hierarchical structure which Charles had been endeavoring to obtain in local government. The royal administration used the device of Quo Warranto to purge those companies that were not willing to follow the EIC's lead. Charles in effect was denying communication to any who did not agree with his political agenda. Economic concerns, the ability of those who created wealth to reach the king and represent their needs to him, had taken a back seat to political concerns. In some sense, Charles had re-formed the patrimonial economic system: instead of placing social order, the ability to feed the people, in front of economic growth, at the end of Charles's reign, the political-economical system subordinated economic growth to partisan politics.

## Politics and economics

Although the total subordination of economics to politics occurred only after 1681, a tension between political goals and economic growth existed through-out the reign. Because of the prominent role which nonconformists and their sympathizers played in the London financial world, whenever Charles tried to establish an Anglian predominance in politics and exclude dissenters from access to the king – in 1662, under Danby, and after the dissolution at Oxford – he used his power to grant monopolies to influence the composition of the mercantile elite. Charles's first moves in this direction were indirect, for he needed the support of the merchants and he feared that denying them communication to the king might wreak havoc on the economic system. At the end of his reign, Charles–more financially secure and more resolute in his political objectives – forced guilds and trading companies to ensure that only those who agreed with his political agenda would have the benefits and authority associated with monopolistic privileges.

The creation of the Royal Adventurers in Africa demonstrates Charles II's endeavor to change both the way mercantile interests communicated with the crown and the very makeup of the mercantile community. Urged by Prince Rupert and the Duke of York, Charles II gave the Royal Adventurers a monopoly of trade with the west coast of Africa. Steven Pincus has deemed

---

[179] Coleman, 85. For more on Worcester see Molly Mcclain, "The Wentwood Forest Riot: Property Rights and Political Culture in Restoration England," in *Political Culture and Cultural Politics In Early Modern Europe*, ed. M. Kishlansky and S. Amussen (Manchester: Manchester University Press, 1995).
[180] Coleman, 87.

the African Adventurers royalist-Anglican shock troops, fighting against the republican and tolerant Dutch. Pincus has a great deal of evidence to support this aspect of his thesis, not least of which is the later recollection of the Duke of York that the whole purpose of founding the company was "to hinder the Dutch from being absolute masters of the whole Guinea Trade." The chief members of the company all fit the royalist Anglican profile, and the actions of the company before the Dutch War appear contrary to their financial interest.[181] Before losing its right to trade with West Africa, The East India Company traded with the Dutch forts on the Guinea Coast and made a hefty profit doing so. In fact, in April, 1662, the East India Company, realizing the benefit of a triangular trade between England, Africa, and India, offered a merger to the Duke of York. Citing "the advantage of experienced hands, the cheapest terms and the reputation of the east India stock [which] joined with his royal highness's name would prove a greater security against any intruders English or others," the East India Company claimed justly that combining the two companies would be more profitable to the Duke than venturing on his own. But the Duke of York refused such overtures, which suggests that political more than economic motives prompted him to support the company.[182] For the Duke of York and Prince Rupert wanted to attack both their enemies abroad, the Dutch, and their perceived antagonists at home, Presbyterian merchants. The trade interests of the African Company directly opposed the royalists' adversaries. The slave-trade was a virtual Dutch monopoly and the formation of the company took away trade from Barbados merchants, who were the most radical sector of the mercantile community.[183] By creating the African trading company and packing it with royalists, Charles II tried to offset the power of the predominantly Presbyterian merchants.

A list of stockholders in the company reads like a who's who of the royal court;[184] many key members of the administration participated actively in the affairs of the company. The Duke of York's strong interest in the company and his use of his position at his brother's side to advance its interests show

---

[181] Pincus, 246, *passim*.

[182] Sainsbury, 202, 262. The EIC's claims had merit: the Royal Adventurers in Africa were a financial disaster.

[183] Robert Brenner, *Merchants and Revolution: Commercial Change, Political Conflict, and London's Overseas Traders, 1550–1653* (Princeton, NJ: Princeton University Press, 1993), 184.

[184] Members of the company at a meeting on March 8, 1664 include James Duke of York, sub- governor Lord Berkeley, Sir George Cartaret, Mr. Ashburnham, John Wolstenhome, Sir Richard Ford, Sir William Ryder, Col. Ashburnham, Col. Found, Mr. Ayres, Mr. Cutler, Mr. Povey, Alderman Blackwell, Mr. Seymour, Prince Rupert, Lord Craven, Mr. Bronherd [Brounchard], Capt. Cock, Mr. Killigrew, Mr. Benes, Sir John Shaw, Sir Nicholas Crispe, Mr. Williamson, Martin Noell, Mr. Props, Mr. Wren, Mr. Middleton, Alderman Maynell, Mr. Buckworth, Sir Ellis Leigton, and Mr. Bence. PRO T70, 1.

that James placed a large premium on the successful fulfillment of their mission. Whenever the company came into conflict with another business concern, the royal administration rallied to the support of the African company.[185] The sway of the company is amply demonstrated by the casual nature of a letter which George Duke wrote to Joseph Williamson[186] to obtain the king's signature for the company.[187]

Charles's sponsorship of the African company, his attempt to alter the makeup of the mercantile elite, soured the relationship between the king and the other trading companies. Soon after losing its privileges to the African company, the East India Company replied evasively to the king's request for a loan and implied that the generality would object strongly to extending credit to the king.[188] Charles, strapped for cash, needed the support of the merchants, and consequentially refrained from meddling with the composition of the mercantile elite for close to ten years.

As 1671 drew to a close royal policy turned towards stricter regulation of access. Access became more limited, and communication to the king took on a more hierarchical form. This preference for hierarchy was echoed in Charles's support for new trading companies with extensive monopolies.[189] The new Royal African Company which replaced the Royal Adventurers[190] received broad powers including the right to try interlopers in Africa. According to K. G. Davies, "in effect the crown was sanctioning a court with power over the property of English subjects and leaving its composition to be determined by a body which would be an interested party in every important matter that came before it. The monarch could scarcely have given a more emphatic demonstration of his favour towards the African Company."[191] The

---

[185] PRO CO 389/2 (November 4, 1663).

[186] At this point Williamson was the chief aid to Henry Bennet, Secretary of State.

[187] BL ADD 22920 (September 25, 1663).

[188] The court books of the EIC records: "Sir Geo. Cartaret presents the kings [letter] of the 9th instant desiring the loan of £30,000 to be secured; this is read, but, there not being a full court Sir George is told that nothing can be decided until there is; therefore he leaves, and suddenly the court fills up and the matter is debated, but no means found to do the king the desired service, though some suggest that each committee should lend £500 on his own account. Finally, the governor, the deputy and some of the committees are desired to wait on Sir George and give a verbal answer to the effect that the company are willing on all occasions to do his majesty any service in accordance with their ability, but are so unprepared for what he now asks that they have neither the power nor means to comply, for the committees have no power to lend the adventurers money, which is only entrusted to them to manage the stock in trade without the consent of the generality, and if they are called together it is feared that the consequences would not be satisfactory to the king and may cause many and great inconveniences to the company" (Sainsbury (May, 1662), 320).

[189] For more on the stop see Andrew Browning, "The Stop of the Exchequer," *History*, vol. 14 (January 1930), 333–337.

[190] The Royal Adventurers in Africa had lapsed into selling licenses to trade.

[191] Davies, 99.

king also demonstrated his favor to his cousin Prince Rupert and The Hudson Bay Company by granting them a charter which included "a grant of all of Canada to be held as of the manor of East Greenwich on rent of 2 elks and 2 black beavers yearly."[192] By sponsoring these companies, Charles indicated his preference for orderly trade and, by installing strong royalists at their head, showed his inclination to place the hierarchical system of trade under the control of his supporters.

After the Compton Census (1676), Charles moved more decisively towards the establishment of an Anglican hierarchy, and to some degree attempted to establish that hierarchy in economic entities. For the first time, Charles meddled in the internal affairs of established companies in order to ensure that the leadership remained committed to the administration's agenda. In 1676 Charles II attempted to influence the East India Company elections. Since 1671 Josiah Child and Thomas Papillion had been accumulating East Indian Company stock.[193] In 1676 they stood for election as governor and sub-governor which prompted a reaction against these newcomers. Child's opponents paid Mr. Guy, one of the gentlemen of the bedchamber, £500 to convince the king to write a letter to the Governor of the East India Company attesting to Charles II's dislike of Papillion and Child.[194] At the behest of these members of the company, Charles's Secretary of State, Joseph Williamson, wrote Nathaniel Herne, the Governor of the East India Company, on April 17, 1676:

> His majesty being informed that endeavors are using to have Mr. Childe and Mr. Papillion chosen governor and sub governor of the company for the ensuing year, has commanded me to let you know they have behaved very ill towards him, and that therefore he should take it very ill from the company, if they should choose them, which I am commanded to signify to you, to be forthwith communicated to the company as by his majesty's order.[195]

On the following day, Herne and his deputies waited on Charles II, who said "that he did not wish to reduce the company's privileges in any way but he expected that they would not disoblige him so much as to choose Mr. Child and Mr. Papillion who had acted very ill towards him." The company at large, apprehending an end to its good relations with the king, was shaken by this incident. Realizing the damage his letter had done, Williamson wrote Herne four days later: "but that they find themselves in great difficulties by reason of that incident in his tender care for the privileges of the company, which

---

[192] *CSPD*, vol. 9, 543.

[193] In four years Child had acquired enough stock (£15,000) to make him the largest shareholder and was elected as a committee in 1674.

[194] Unlike the gentlemen of the *privy chamber* who lost influence under Charles II's open access policy, the gentlemen of the *bedchamber* retained considerable influence.

[195] *CSPD*, vol. 18, 75.

his meaning was not in the least to infringe, and which he will preserve and protect as commanded me to signify that you proceed in the election now depending in your usual form according to your charter." A majority of the stockholders, although "allowed" to choose whomever they wished, realized that electing those whom the king disliked was not in their best interest, and voted Sir William Langhorne the next governor. They sent a delegation to the king to underscore their obedience. The delegation expressed the sentiment that Charles II "being the sun who influences all their actions, and if he should withdraw the beams of his favour from them, they must wither and decay." Such statements were not simple flattery, for, without the king's support of their charter, the company would lose all its monopolistic privileges and be unable to function. Charles "expressed his pleasure at the results of the election and his hope that they would continue to take care to choose men acceptable to him."[196]

Charles II may not have entered into internal company politics without an invitation. As his conciliatory letter to the company suggests, he did not yet claim the authority to freely manipulate corporate structures at his whim. Where the opportunity presented itself, however, he took action to have men who were loyal to him. The motivation of those who sought Guy's aid is complex, but they may have anticipated an unfavorable reaction on the part of the king to Child's election and acted to prevent such ill consequences. The king's letters made the entire company cognizant of the reality of those fears.

Although in 1676 Charles hesitated to manipulate corporate structures for political ends, the higher political stakes after the exclusion crisis and the very real fear of rebellion led the king to ensure that all economic organizations supported his Tory agenda. Those who fully conformed to his design received royal support, but those who resisted suffered a steady attack. In the Quo Warranto proceedings and their aftermath, almost 80 percent of Londoners lost their liveried status along with the right to vote in parliamentary elections.[197] The anarchy of the popish plot brought Charles II firmly into the camp of those that supported strict regulation of trade, but he was willing to sacrifice the ability to regulate to ensure that all organs of political representation were strictly under his thumb.

The London livery companies were split along partisan lines. Most of the companies were led by and composed of Whigs,[198] and Charles II wanted to replace the self-perpetuating oligarchic system of government in these guilds with a hierarchical system, wherein officers of the companies depended on the king, not their fellow members, for their position. Charles II used the

[196] Loughead, 110–124.
[197] Arthur Giffen Smith, "London and the Crown" (University of Wisconsin Ph.D. dissertation, 1967), 339.
[198] Approximately 60 percent of the liveried members of the companies were Whigs: A. G. Smith, 341.

device of Quo Warranto to attack the charters of thirty-nine guilds. Those companies which could rely on Tory contacts for access to the court fared better than those associated with Whig interests. The Clothworkers, for instance, emerged virtually unscathed. They consulted with their members who had privy knowledge (Pepys and Williamson) and resolved immediately to surrender their charter to Charles II, thereby demonstrating their trust and dependence upon him. During the time their charter was in limbo, the Clothworkers took steps to show their devotion to the Tory cause by admitting William Hewer and William Bridgeman free of the company.[199] Bridgeman soon began to work for the company as a messenger to the king. Bridgeman informed his boss, Secretary of State Sunderland, that the company wished to demonstrate its loyalty by erecting a statue of James I in the exchange. The Clothworkers wished Charles II to see them as exemplars to the other companies. Sunderland apprized the king that the company hoped that "their act would bee a president and encouragement to other companies of this city to sett up the rest of the former kings as they stood before the late dreadful fire of London."[200] When the Clothworkers received their new charter, none of their assistants[201] were replaced.[202]

Most of the other guilds fared worse. The ruling body of the Haberdashers was replaced.[203] The new charters called for a spring-clean of liverymen[204] as well as assistants. Each new charter contained a clause stipulating that all liverymen must be "loyal churchmen who do not frequent conventicles, approved by the lord mayor and court of aldermen and must take all oaths required by assistants."[205] Among the twelve great livery companies these stipulations led to a 53 percent reduction in the livery. The lesser companies were harder hit. Their new charters only permitted them to call a number of livery men equal to the number of assistants and other officers. The Weavers suffered a 63 percent reduction and the Cordwainers a 73 percent reduction. In total, the number of London livery dropped from approximately 8000 to less than 2000. This reduction in size rendered the London livery a

---

[199] William Hewer, Samuel Pepys's good friend, served as Treasurer of the Tangier company and Judge Advocate General of the Navy. Bridgeman was Under-secretary of State.

[200] Clothworkers Hall, Orders of Courts, 1683–1712, 37 (October 11, 1684). The Tory companies opted to replace statues of the Stuarts while the Whig companies chose Tudor or medieval kings. The Grocers erected Charles II (Charles I was already there). The Mercers erected Queen Mary and Elizabeth. The Drapers erected Edward VI. London Guildhall Library MSS 17087.

[201] The governing body of twenty-four.

[202] Clothworkers 1683–1712, 20–45.

[203] GL MSS 15842, 270–280.

[204] Those called to the livery had some say in major issues of a particular guild and the right to vote in parliamentary elections.

[205] A. G. Smith, 336.

**Table 3** Livery companies and the Quo Warranto

| Livery company | Members: 1682 | Members: 1685 | Percentage left |
|---|---|---|---|
| Clothworkers | 174 | 96 | 55 |
| Drapers | 164 | 85 | 52 |
| Fishmongers | 261 | 120 | 46 |
| Goldsmiths | 200 | 123 | 62 |
| Grocers | 277 | 166 | 60 |
| Haberdashers | 407 | 114 | 28 |
| Ironmongers | 75 | 65 | 87 |
| Mercers | 174 | 81 | 47 |
| Merchant tailors | 391 | 103 | 26 |
| Salters | 128 | 61 | 48 |
| Skinners | 172 | 77 | 45 |
| Vintners | 198 | 139 | 70 |
| Total great companies | 2621 | 1230 | 47 |
| Lesser companies | | | |
| Apothecaries | 141 | 82 | 58 |
| Barber/surgeons | 201 | 64 | 32 |
| Blacksmiths | 148 | 48 | 32 |
| Coopers | 162 | 34 | 21 |
| Cordwainers | 104 | 28 | 27 |
| Innholders | 91 | 48 | 53 |
| Stationers | 174 | 58 | 33 |
| Weavers | 165 | 61 | 37 |

more manageable group. Since Lord Justice Jeffries supervised the process, Tories dominated the remaining Livery, as the next election amply demonstrated.[206]

This process had powerful ramifications for the means of access to the monarch. Merchants could no longer select who represented their interests; the king, not the liverymen, chose who would serve as conduits for requests, advice, and communication. In fact, many former representatives were stripped of all public offices. Nine former aldermen and twenty deputy aldermen were removed from the rolls of livery along with countless assistants and wardens.[207] Furthermore, there was no way for most merchants to bypass these outwardly imposed officers. Even these royally selected intermediaries had only one channel to approach the king. As the Lord Mayor Sir James Smith told Sir John Reresby, "he [the mayor] had the title of Lord Mayor, but my Lord Chief Justice Jeffreys usurped the power, that they had no access to the king, nor any message or direction from him as to any business but by that

[206] Ibid., 322–349. London elected four Tories to serve in the first Parliament of James II's reign.
[207] A. G. Smith, 340.

lord."[208] After Sir George Jeffries accepted a case on behalf of interlopers, the Earl of Conway wrote Jeffries that "his Majesty being informed that in a suit between the company of Merchant Adventurers and certain interlopers he is retained as counsel against the said company, signifying his pleasure that he do not appear in any manner against the said company, his majesty intending by all lawful means to encourage the trade of the said company."[209] Charles II wanted not only to deprive the interlopers of the able counsel of Jeffries, but also to ensure that it did not appear that the king supported the interlopers. In the past, each member of the administration interpreted policy to his own benefit, which sent out conflicting signals.[210] When diverse members of the administration came out on different sides of an issue, it was unclear where the king stood and therefore easier to take a stance opposed to the monarch. Now, the king and his secretaries strove to ensure that the administration presented a united front, thereby making it extremely difficult for those against current policy to claim that they were in conflict with ministers but not with the king. The absence of alternate paths of access created a deferential economic hierarchy.

Once a company submitted to Charles, he fully supported its calls for an extension of its monopoly. The Grocers, for instance, received the right to govern confectioners, druggists, tobacconists, and tobacco cutters. The innkeepers extended the area of their control to a twelve-mile radius around London.[211] The East India Company, which by 1683 was completely Tory, received a new charter which granted them the right to hold their own courts in India and to seize the ships of interlopers.[212] The East India Company also benefitted from the king's influence in the Sandys case. On May 10 The Earl of Sunderland wrote the Lord Chief Justice, "The king, having been acquainted with the enclosed paper relating to the East India Company, has commanded me to transmit it to you, and he would have you show them all the favour you can so far as may be consistent with the law and the practice of the court."[213] Charles willingly extended these companies, privileges because it would create, in the words of the Royal African Company, "Government, order and regular discipline."[214]

---

[208] Reresby, 380.

[209] *CSPD*, vol. 24, 27 (January 24, 1684).

[210] For examples of conflict within the administration over economic policy see the case of the tinners where Williamson and Ashley favored the tin farmers and Bath and Godolphin favored the tin miners and the different attitudes to monopoly expressed by, on the one hand, the 1672 Council of Trade led by Shaftesbury and, on the other hand, the Privy Council (see pp. 147–148, 141–142 above).

[211] *CSPD*, 1684/5, 164 (October 3, 1684), Warner, *History of InnHolders*, 31, quoted in A. G. Smith, 334.

[212] *CSPD*, vol. 25, 183 (July 21, 1683).

[213] *CSPD*, vol. 27, 8 (May 10, 1684).

[214] See above, p. 156.

Political ends drove Charles to a view of the economy where regulation and monopoly were the keystones to creating an ordered society. As a reaction to the chaos of the exclusion crisis the king wanted order in all dimensions of his realm, both economical and political. Such an economic philosophy presupposed a reality where demand is inelastic and where wronged parties could contact the king. But Charles's policies of access had brought theorists to question that reality and the benefits of strict regulation of trade.

## Access and economic theory

The reign of Charles II was a heady time for the development of economic theory. Mun's radical ideas on free trade came into print. The rapid change of economic policy in the 1640s and 1650s inspired theorists to come to grips with the nature of the patrimonial economic system. Some economic pundits looked abroad to the Netherlands to advocate the financial benefits of toleration and low interest rates; others, in reaction to Colbert's mercantilistic policies in France, issued a clarion call for the protection of English manufactures.[215] In this atmosphere an intense debate erupted between those who saw demand as finite and therefore monopolies as an essential component of economic regulation, and those who viewed demand as elastic and endorsed freedom of trade. Such economic arguments, however, had political derivations, for the king's regulation of access shaped this debate.

At the Restoration, theorists universally called for the re-establishment of monopolistic trading companies to establish order and combat glut. For Hide and Bland, workers and merchants needed to be organized in fraternities to prevent economic chaos.[216] But consensus failed to last: the king's accessibility during the reign of the Cabal encouraged a non-hierarchical view of society which created the space to view the economic system as capable of functioning without extensive strictures. However, when the king retreated from his embrace of diversity he allied himself with those who claimed to fear glut, or "overcloying" the market. Charles took this position, in part, because those who posited inelastic demand successfully maintained access to the king. But the monarch also sided with them because their economic ideology reinforced a conception of society as a hierarchal system with the king necessarily on top, thus truly endearing their cause to a monarch very conscious of enhancing his legitimacy.

Samuel Fortrey's *England's Interest and Improvement* (1663) demonstrates the nexus between strict access to the king, a hierarchical view of the econ-

---

[215] Joyce Appleby's *Economic Thought and Ideology in Seventeenth Century England* remains the best analysis of the economic theory of this period.
[216] See above, pp. 122–123.

omy, and a firm conception of the limited nature of demand. Samuel Fortrey's work is best known to posterity for his attempt to estimate the balance of trade with France. His primary concern, however, was to demonstrate how England could multiply its wealth. Fortrey claimed that to raise prices of English goods abroad merchants should limit domestic production by forming companies. Fortrey believed that "the prejudice that may happen by them [combinations] to the workmen, or home chapmen, is fully recompensed by the clear profit they return to the publick."[217] Since, in the eyes of this theorist, foreign demand was extremely limited, the best way to increase profit was to create a hierarchical structure of trading companies to limit supply and stop exports.

Fortrey argued further for the importance of the king resisting entreaties from private interests. To Fortrey, private interests, like the chapmen, often forced the government to regulate contrary to the national interest. "Private advantages are often impediments of publick profit." Hence, Fortrey asserted that only a king, "a single power to direct whose interest is only the benefit of the whole" can govern for the wealth of the nation.[218] If Fortrey had considered the effects of dislocation his logic would suggest the need for an accessible sovereign. But Fortrey wanted a monarch who could resist individual pleas, who need not be importuned by those thrown off their lands by enclosures or those displaced from work by immigrants. In other words, the king should not respond to individual entreaties but should only take into account the narrowly construed wealth of the nation. As a gentleman of the privy chamber, a position which "the assault on the bed-chamber" had rendered virtually powerless, Fortrey's desire for the restriction of access makes some sense.[219] Later theorists often quoted Fortrey's francophobe account of the balance of trade, but his narrowly constructed idea of the wealth of the nation, which did not take into account the distribution of wealth, failed to catch on.

In 1667 and 1668 Charles clearly disregarded the advice of Fortrey. Instead of taking into account a strict definition of national interest, Charles – in line with his desire to be everybody's king – made sure to take into account as many particular interests as possible. This return to open access had a marked effect on economic theory. The king's regard for free communication may have spurred a corollary regard for free trade. One theorist, at least, saw a connection between free access to a person and free access to trade. In the dedication of *A Discourse on Trade* (1670) Roger Coke predicted that his tract would meet in the person of Sir Charles Harbourd "besides a well

---

[217] Samuel Fortrey, *England's Interest and Improvement* (1663), 41, *passim*.
[218] Fortrey, 3–4.
[219] I use David Starkey's terminology here (Starkey, *The English Court.*) Fortrey's leaning towards a lack of access coincides with his call for a narrow church and no toleration: Fortrey, 10–11.

weighed understanding . . . an open and free access (which are the principles from whence trade is best generated and increased)."[220] The king's open access policy also meant that Charles now listened to the complaints of producers which prompted him to consider the possibility that demand was elastic. Royal countenance of such ideas spurred theorists to posit the benefits of free trade and even brought monopolistic interests to concede that glut was not a major problem, forcing them to find new justifications for their privileges.

Charles's openness was displayed in the events surrounding the Merchant Adventurers's bid to renew their charter. In May, 1670 the Merchant Adventurers petitioned the king for the restoration of their charter which had been suspended since 1662. The king demonstrated his commitment to open access by summoning William Kiffen and other interlopers to the Council to debate the merits of the charter.[221] While Kiffen was willing to enter the Merchant Adventurers,[222] he could not speak for all interlopers. When realizing that no agreement could be easily made between the interlopers and the Merchant Adventurers, the government did not renew the charter.[223] The fact that interlopers had a valid say in the negotiations of the Adventurers' charter indicates both the openness of the administration and the fact that the king was not wedded to the idea that all trade must be carried on by fraternities.[224]

As early as 1668 the king had expressed his willingness to question the efficacy of trading companies.[225] The Bristol Merchants, picking up on this signal, petitioned the king, at some considerable expense,[226] to allow them to trade in the domain of the Levant Company. Their petition focused exclusively on the benefits of free trade. They claimed, "surely where there is a free trade, Riches flowes in, and the poore wants not, But if there is noe exportation there can be noe Importation, And where commerce languishes

---

[220] Roger Coke, *A Discourse of Trade In Two Parts* (London, 1670), A2.

[221] *CSPD*, vol. 10, 202, 281.

[222] The Merchant Adventurers had lost a fortune loaning money to the government of the interregnum. Kiffen was willing to enter the company only if he did not have to help pay off the company's debts.

[223] *CSPD*, 281 (June 17, 1670).

[224] At times, the administration independently adopted the interlopers' view, that "nothing conduceth further to the improvement of trade than plenty of merchandise and a multitude of merchants" (see below, p. 000). The king relaxed regulation by allowing merchants to buy ships in order to import timber, contrary to the Act of Navigation (*CSPD*, vol. 9, 290 (April 23, 1669)).

[225] See instructions to Trade Council.

[226] Their agent Sir Richard Ellsworth was paid £125 to defray his expenses of £182; £14 were paid for sack sent to the Attorney-general and £6 for Mr. Robert Aldworth the town clerk and William Meredith for procuring the charter (*Merchant Adventurers of Bristol*, 25).

the poore is in penury."[227] The Merchant Adventurers of Bristol had no fear of glutted markets; they asserted that "cheapness gives [sic] occasion of its greater consumption."[228] The petition claimed that "their charters confirmation will help his majesty more than themselves" because it would raise revenue, enlarge the clothing trade, and advance the price of wool. If we accept Clive Holmes's assertion that even Fenmen tailored their request to please the administration[229] we could expect no less from the well-connected Bristolians.

In this effort to overcome the Levant and Hamburg companies the merchants of Bristol sought the aid of the other out-ports. The response of the Newcastle Merchants to the Bristol traders indicates that in 1668 the Bristol Merchants' conception of demand was far from universal.[230] Although the London Merchant Adventurers inspired no love on the part of the Newcastle Adventurers,[231] the Newcastle Merchants held on strongly to the tenet that only a strict control of trade would enable England and they themselves to prosper. They praised the much maligned London Merchant Adventurers for supporting English manufacturers "by their stock, trade, and credit." Despite the treatment they received from the London Merchant Adventurers, they explained, "yett, in this case, we doe hold it more conducing to the common good of trade, and the maintaining of our general privileges to joyne with the Marchants of London, rather than these interlopers." Calling the Bristol Merchants "interlopers" reveals that the Merchants of Newcastle saw the world of trade as divided into companies who through strict regulation prevented glut and secured maximum prices for English goods and interlopers who destroyed markets by selling too many goods at inopportune times. For these Newcastle merchants demand was finite. The fear of interlopers brought them not only to deny Bristol's request for aid, but to offer their aid to the Londoners.[232]

---

[227] *Merchant Adventurers of Bristol*, 21.

[228] The merchants also appealed to Charles II's sense of honor, claiming that he should uphold the memory of his father, "that Mirror of Kings," by reconfirming the charter that he granted (*Merchant Adventurers of Bristol*, 19–24). McGrath notes that Ellsworth may have had a hand in these preliminary suggestions.

[229] Clive Holmes, "Drainers and Fenmen: The Problem of Popular Political Consciousness in the Seventeenth Century" in *Order and Disorder in Early Modern England*, ed. A. Fletcher and D. Stevenson, (Cambridge: Cambridge University Press, 1987).

[230] The Bristol Merchants' conception of trade being the best when free may have had some relation to the predominance of the Atlantic trade in their city.

[231] F.W. Dendy, *Extracts from Records of Merchant Adventurers of Newcastle Upon Tyne*, vol. 2 (Surtees Society, CI, 1899), 137. The Newcastle Adventurers claimed that the London branch "has (sic) dealt very unkindly with us (to give it no worse term) and put us to very much and needless charge." The London Merchant Adventurers, among other misdeeds, tried to set up a branch in Newcastle, ignoring the patent of the Newcastle Adventurers.

[232] The Newcastle Adventurers informed their agent that "if wee can help by petitioning with them [the London branch], or for them wee shall perhaps be readily drawne

In 1668 and 1669 the Newcastle Adventurers had good company. The Levant Company, most merchants, and economic theorists asserted that a strict regulation best sustains trade. When the House of Lords called members of the Council of Trade to testify about the decay of rents and trade, any mention of increasing foreign sales by increasing the number of merchants was muted. Josiah Child did say that "another cause of the decay of the Eastland Trade, the straitness of trade, they admit none unless they give £20." And Thomas Papillion uttered the ambiguous phrase, "If we will carry on trade we must make it easy." But for the most part, the members of the Council of Trade discussed manipulating interest rates and preventing the export of wool to maintain England's natural monopoly.[233] Most other theorists found the cause of the decay of trade to be a problem of too much supply as opposed to artificial restraints preventing vent. William Coventry, for instance, thought that English land yielded too much produce and urged reforestation.[234] Sir Edward Dering, like Coventry, bemoaned the problem of overproduction.[235]

Clothiers who disparaged monopolies and posited the benefits of free trade attacked this near universal belief that overproduction was damaging trade. The petition of the Bristol merchants summarized the complaints of clothiers

> They cannot many tymes in 2 or 3 months sell a cloth by reason of the merchants design in forbearing to buy that soe they may be driven of necessities sake to sell of their clothes at the cheaper or at such prices as the merchants themselves will be pleased to give for the same, many tymes for less then they stood them out of purse, soe that several clothiers of very considerable stock have of late years . . . left of that their trade rather then they would run such hazards and inconveniences.[236]

In *Reasons Humbly Offered Against the Merchant Adventurers* clothiers attacked

---

to it, notwithstanding our former differences. . . . And if you finde them desirous of it, if York and Hull will doe the like, we shall joyne our force against those enemies of our trade" (*Newcastle Merchant Adventurers*, 137). Newcastle was careful to explain that they would not agree to help the Merchant Adventurers with the cost of their legal battle.

[233] J. Thirsk and J. P. Cooper, *Seventeenth Century Economic Documents* (Oxford: Oxford University Press, 1972), 68–78. The House of Lords chose Sir Henry Blunt, Capt. Titus, Josiah Child, Doctor Worsley, and Thomas Papillion to testify.

[234] Thirsk and Cooper, *Documents*, 79–84, excerpted from BL Sloane MS 3828, ff205–210. Coventry also cited a lack of supervision of goods, the high interest the king had to pay on debts, and the concentration of people in London as reasons for the decay of trade and rents.

[235] Thirsk and Cooper, *Documents*, 85–88. Excerpted from Bod. Lib. M. Top. Kent, a1, f.26.

[236] *Merchant Adventurers of Bristol*, 142.

monopoly as harmful to the country since "nothing conduceth further to the improvement of trade than plenty of merchandise and a multitude of merchants."[237] The author of this pamphlet did not see trading companies as staving off glut, as reducing exports in order to sell abroad at higher prices, but rather claimed that the incorporation of many merchants into one cartel forced producers to sell at artificially low prices. Reducing exports would not increase prices abroad, this author argued, because the Dutch would produce more to supply the unsatisfied demand.[238]

The success of this argument may be seen in the fact that monopolistic entities conceded the point of the general benefits of free trade and argued that their privileges constituted a special case. The Merchant Adventurers claimed they would be unable to renew their privileges with the city of Dort without a monopoly and the Levant Company claimed that the treaty with the Grand Signor allowed only the Levant Company and no other English organization to trade with Turkey.[239] The East India Company highlighted the need for a unified power to deal with foreign potentates and in response to Captain Mynor's petition to the king asking for permission to transport his family and goods from India to England on a private ship.

> Any petition presented to the king for leave to send out any ship or ships to the Indies under any pretence whatever is contrary to the company's charter from His Majesty, and in the highest manner destructive to them and conducive to the overthrow of their trade. For all piracies or injuries committed by any Englishmen or by any ships carrying the English flag against the subjects of any Indian kings or princes have always been paid for by the Company, they being compelled to do so by the imprisonment of their president, agents or factors; and often the asserted damage is five times as much as it is in reality. . . . If the commander of such a ship as Minor's wishes to go to the Indies were to die, who could give security that his successor and the men would not turn pirates or act dishonestly?[240]

For the EIC, organization and control was still necessary, if not to prevent overcloying the market, then at least to deal with foreigners.

In the debate over the privileges of monopolies which occurred from 1668 to 1672, an echo of the Charles's desire to be everybody's king emerges.

---

[237] *Reasons Humbly Offered Against the Merchant Adventurers* (1670), Sel.1670 E r23, IX.

[238] As further proof the pamphlet argues that after the suspension of the Merchant Adventurers' privileges in 1625, English trade increased and Dutch production decreased. *Reasons*, IX, XII. For an example of an unabashed argument for free trade in 1670 see Roger Coke's *A Discourse on Trade*.

[239] *Bristol Merchant Adventurers*, 219.

[240] Sainsbury, vol. 8, 182.

Just as the king wanted to right every interest,[241] theorists and petitioners highlighted the benefits their proposal would have for a variety of segments in the nation;[242] unlike Fortrey, these theorists and petitioners specified the individual groups which their proposals would benefit. In their petition, the Bristol Merchants stressed how renewing their charter would aid clothiers. The East India Company mentioned the possibility of selling woolen goods to China and Japan to convince the king to negotiate for victualing rights in Manilla.[243] In William Carter's plea to stop the exportation of wool he illustrated how "the manufacture of wool" was a precious commodity to the entire country.

> [wool] is the richest treasure in his majesties dominions, the flower strength and sinews of this nation; a band uniting the people into societies for their own utility: It is the milk and Honey to the Grazier and country farmer; the Gold and spices of the East and West Indies, to the merchant, and citizens; the continued supply of bread to the poor; and, in a word, the exchequer of wealth, and staple of protection to the whole, both abroad and at home; and therefore of full merit to be had in a perpetual remembrance, defense and encouragement, for the most advantageous improvements thereof.[244]

The king's desire to be everybody's king was recognized by theorists who tailored their arguments to demonstrate how their proposals would benefit the entire nation.

Charles II's turn towards a strict regulation of access in 1672 may have played a small part in the anti-French sentiment behind the balance of trade controversy.[245] Although the negative balance of trade with France had been an issue of contention since Samuel Fortrey calculated its extent in 1663, when France and England became allies in the third Dutch War the issue took on new meaning. As Margaret Priestley has explained, the war convinced those who saw France as an economic, political, and religious threat that English foreign policy had gone astray.[246] Furthermore, merchants' lack of access – they were no longer represented on the Council of Trade – made them doubt that they could influence the king against the French.

---

[241] For Charles's concern to right every interest see *CSPD*, 607 (September 28, 1668).
[242] While such rhetoric was not new, it appears much more frequently and with more intensity in this literature than in prior economic texts.
[243] *Merchant Adventurers of Bristol*, 142. Sainsbury, vol. 8, 65.
[244] Carter, *England's Interest by Trade Asserted*, 1671, 2.
[245] *CSPD*, vol. 16, 374. For the controversy over undyed cloths see *CSPD*, vol. 16, 314–316 (July 24, 1674). See *CSPD*, vol. 14, 323, 379, 382, 170.
[246] Margaret Priestley, "London Merchants and Opposition Politics in Charles II's Reign," *BIHR* (1956). For an analysis of the actual balance of trade see her "Anglo–French Trade and the Unfavorable Balance Controversy: 1660–1685," *EHR* (1951).

Such cynicism was not aided by the general belief that strict access was part and parcel of arbitrary government. Since France was seen as the premier example of Christian arbitrary government, a move towards strict access may have made some think that Charles II meant to adopt French principles of governance along with a French alliance. The financial community feared arbitrary government for many reasons, not least of which was the strong belief that arbitrary government stymied economic growth.[247]

Charles's strict regulation of access not only provoked the anti-French sentiment which lay underneath much of the balance of trade controversy; it also prompted anti-monopolistic rhetoric. By stripping away the patrimonial image of the accessible king, the introduction of a strict policy of access tore down a key bulwark for the ideological legitimization of monopoly; the king no longer seemed willing to receive complaints against engrossers abusing their privileges. Protests against particular monopolies mushroomed. Pewterers declaimed the monopoly of tin.[248] Clothiers denounced "the great restraint on trade by the East India and Guinea Companies, they having monopolized the sole trade of above half the world, and utterly excluding all other subjects from trading to any places within their charter."[249] Economic theorists also attacked trading companies. Carew Reynell claimed, "The Guinny Trade would be much advanced by being freer."[250] One anonymous theorist used the king's intervention in the East India Company's election as a literary pretense to question the very idea of monopoly. In *Two Letters Concerning the East India Company* a barrister proclaims to his country correspondent that "all grants of monopolies are against the antient and fundamental laws of this kingdom."[251]

The strength of anti-monopolistic sentiment is shown by the fact that even those who benefitted from monopoly or supported the king argued against monopoly as a concept. Thomas Papillion replied to the author of *Two Letters* to defend the East India Company's right to trade. He did not theoretically defend the king's prerogative, and in fact stated that monopoly is in most cases deleterious to the economy. Rather, he contended pragmatically that the exigencies of the East India trade necessitated a monopolistic joint stock company.[252] Similarly an anonymous piece entitled *England's Great Happiness*

---

[247] See Carew Reynell, *The True English Interest* (London, 1674), 6. (Slingsby Bethel), *Observations on the Letter Written to Sir Thomas Osborn upon the Reading of a Book Called the Present Interest of England Stated Written in a Letter to a Friend* (London 1673), Sel. 1673 e b46. John Locke, "Notes on Trade" in Thirsk and Cooper, 96, reprint of Bod. Lib. MS Locke, c30, f.18.

[248] *CSPD*, vol. 20, 31 (March 11, 1678).

[249] *CSPD*, vol. 17, 374 (October, 1675).

[250] Reynell, 11.

[251] *Two Letters Concerning the East India Company* (1676), 2. Sel. 1676 E T 93.

[252] Thomas Papillion, *The East India Trade a Most Profitable Trade to the Kingdom and Best Secured and Improved in a Company and a Joint Stock Represented in a Letter Written*

*or a Dialogue Between Content and Complaint (1677)*[253] has the loyalist speaker express the anti-monopolist sentiment that a multitude of tradesmen greatly benefits the economy.

In the late 1670s and 1680s, however, such arguments failed to persuade the king. Even when economic data pointed to the contrary, Charles favored monopolistic entities. The Levant Company, in 1681 and 1682, for instance, desired to trade with India and Arabia, both within the exclusive domain of the EIC. The Levant Company argued before the Council that the amount of capital the East Indian Company employed in trade, and therefore the amount of exports, was significantly below what the market could bear. To prove its point, the Levant Company opened up a new subscription for the East India trade and received £1,000,000 in less than a week.[254] Despite the Levant Company's evidence that there was sufficient capital to expand trade, the king decided in favor of the East India Company.[255] It appears that political concerns brought the king to appreciate the order generated by organized companies, regardless of economic benefits.

The king's return to very strict regulation of access after the dissolution of the Oxford Parliament had an additional effect: it stifled the expression of economic thought. In this atmosphere, where the king appeared immovable and where Parliament ceased to meet, few economic tracts came off the presses.[256] One of the few, *A Treatise of Wool* by George Clark, argued that factors were destroying the market. Clark cited verbatim the presentment of the Grand Jury at the General Quarter Sessions at Brereton, Somerset. The Grand Jury called for more regulation, in particular banning the import of Spanish wool by the factors. The Grand Jury couched its appeal in terms which enhanced and glorified Charles II's power: "Item, we present that this honorable bench will be pleased to implore the royal power and prerogative of his sacred majesty for conveying remedies of these great abuses and that

---

*upon the Occasion of Two Letters Lately Published Insinuating the Contrary* (1677), Sel. 1677E, 19.

[253] Sel. 1677 E En 34.

[254] Loughead, 150.

[255] A newsletter reported that "The new subscribers as well as the old East India Company were at Windsor, where they had a hearing before his majesty and council. He declared after a long hearing on both sides that he did not find it convenient to make any alteration in the charter of the old company or to grant any new one to the new subscribers" (*CSPD*, vol. 23, 194 (May 2, 1682)).

[256] In the Seligman collection there are a few tracts on the establishment of a bank and setting up fire insurance as well as one tract which criticizes bankers and scriveners. There is also a curious piece which calls for the introduction of cloth manufacture in Scotland. According to the tract the Duke of York was the moving force behind this push for industrialization. Likewise, a search of the word "trade" in *Early English Books Online* for the years 1682 to 1685 rendered thirty-six titles. Of these, eight were official proclamations of the state, seven were advice books for young men commencing professions, six had nothing to do with trade, four were published after Charles's death, two were books recounting

this presentment may be with submission presented to his majesty as the grievance and compliant of the whole county." The lack of any alternative routes to governmental power forced the gentry to petition the king and in so doing to rely on and glorify his prerogative.[257]

Charles had, in effect, created a royal monopoly on economic theory. By eliminating alternative fora to present economic grievances he had restored his place as the focal point of the patriarchal economic system. But the genie was out of the bottle. His previous open access had led his subjects to question the benefits of organized and regular trade. As soon as economic opinion could present itself in the form of a Parliament the monopolistic trading companies came under attack.[258]

someone's travels, and two dealt with Irish trade. The remaining six books were a curious group. Of these only two had anything to do with trade: a defense of the East India Company and a book about various credit devices.

[257] Soon after the presentment Charles II died. The pamphlet states that the presentment "[supposed to be delivered by George Clarke] should have been delivered to his majesty king Charles II, but by his sudden death it was prevented and now comes more properly to be considered of and redress'd in Parliament." Clearly the Somerset gentry had rather address Parliament than the king with their complaints (Clarke, *A Treatise of Wool* (London: William Crooke, 1685), 8).

[258] Henry Horwitz, *Parliament, Policy and Politics in the Reign of William III* (Newark: University of Delaware Press, 1977), 58, 75, 112–113.

# Conclusion
## The merrie monarch?

The image of the merrie monarch is powerful. Thanks to Evelyn, Rochester, and Pepys, the conception of Charles as amorous, affable, and accessible, as everybody's king, has a near strangle-hold on our consideration of his reign. The image has much validity, especially for the first half of his reign, but by making accessibility seem an inherent part of Charles's nature, it obscures his use of the regulation of access and style of rule as potent political implements. The detection of marked vacillations in the king's policies of access, however, sets forth a new image of the restored monarch: not as the Venetian resident described Charles as "unable to shake off the habits formed under necessity during so many years of private life,"[1] but as a wily king – all too aware of the limits of his resources and the politically possible – maximizing the effectiveness of one of the few resources over which he had total control, the regulation of access to and the presentation of his person.

Charles's vacillations in accessibility and his subjects' reactions to those vacillations elucidate the crucial role that the interaction between monarch and subject, and the perception of such interaction, played in the formation of obedience and authority. The formula relating accessibility to authority is not as simple as Newcastle would have us believe:[2] it was contingent upon the goals of the king, and the social, religious, and political makeup of the nation. The relationship between accessibility and authority is complicated further by the fact that there were different modes of interaction between king and subject as well as different kinds of authority gained through such interactions. Charles's sponsorship of the Council of Trade, for instance, and the ease of communication between merchants and monarchs that the Council of Trade created, legitimized the royal authority to dispense monopolies. Yet accessibility did not always work in the king's favor. His openness to a variety of political factions, while mollifying some of his more radical opponents, rendered his will indeterminate and therefore an impotent weapon to shape legislation. For the most part, however, Charles successfully deployed the tool of access to garner the kind of authority necessary for his political goals.

[1] CSPV, vol. 33, 84.
[2] See above, pp. 16–17.

Charles used his control over access to great effect, both to placate former rebels in the first years of his reign and to galvanize the Tories in the late 1670s and 1680s. But perhaps his intense concentration on the political effects of access caused the king to overlook the social and economic ramifications of his policies of access. This is particularly true of the end of his reign. Spurred by a desire both to adhere to Anglican-Tory principles of proper hierarchical order and to assure his ultra-supporters that he would not abandon them, Charles strictly regulated access and communication.

But such regulation made the court a less inviting and therefore a less attractive place. If Charles had successfully moved the court to Winchester, he would have become the central focus of the society that developed there, but a society formed in the restrictive atmosphere of Winchester would probably have been small and dull. Such a society would not reflect the elite of the nation, which would forgo the ardors of trying to speak to the king in favor of the attractions of London.

Likewise, the king's concern with order and hierarchy prompted him to favor conducting the nation's trade by means of monopolistic entities. However, over time, such a policy could cause economic stagnation, because monopolistic entities tend to artificially limit trade to maximize return on capital, and because hierarchical economic systems discourage entrepreneurial behavior. Both the social and the economic ramifications of closed access could have adversely affected Charles's political agenda. Economic stagnation would cause a decline in royal revenue. The creation of a separate society at Winchester would drive a wedge between Charles and his subjects, alienating them from him.

In 1685 such problems lay in the distant future, and it is unfortunate – at least for the purposes of this study – that we cannot observe how the policies of access would have played out if Charles had lived longer. Once James came to the throne, his Catholicism and his stubborn zeal to obtain some religious freedom for Catholics so overwhelmed the national conscience that his policies of access had only minor consequences. Nevertheless, comparing Charles's reign with that of his less fortunate brother will yield some results, for James also tried to change his style of rule.

Unable to convince the Anglican royalists to tolerate papists, James embarked on a campaign to create a political alliance between Catholics and dissenters. To accomplish this goal, James abandoned the policy of strict access to which he had been adhering and began to press the flesh, traveling through the countryside to speak face to face with nonconformist ministers.[3] However, unlike his brother, James failed in his attempt to use access to change the makeup of the governing class. For dissenters viewed his current policies through the lens of his previous stance against accessible monarchy.

---

[3] John Miller, *James II: A Study in Kingship* (Hove: Wayland, 1977), 173.

For Charles as well as for James, the residual effects of his prior accessibility played a role in the conception that subjects had of their sovereign. Just as historians have been unable to shake off the image of the merrie monarch, Charles's contemporaries had difficulty readjusting their perception of the king. In contrast to James, Charles capitalized upon the residual effects of his accessibility. He survived the exclusion crisis, in no small part, by using his previous reputation for openness to convince his political opponents that he would welcome and duly consider their counsel. Charles's successful deployment of the promise of access in his most dire time of need testifies both to the power that the promise of access to the king held and the deftness with which this not always merrie monarch wielded the most potent implement at his disposal: the regulation of access to his person.

# *Appendix*
## Charles's itinerary 1661 to 1684

### 1661

January 1 Hampton Court; January 2–9 Portsmouth; January 10 to March 14 Whitehall; March 15–17 Windsor; March 18 to September 14 Whitehall; September 15 Cornbury; September 16 to December 31 Whitehall.

### 1662

January 1 to May 29 Whitehall; May 30 to August 22 Hampton Court; August 23 to December 31 Whitehall.

### 1663

January 1 to July 24 Whitehall; July 25 to July 28 Tunbridge Wells; July 29 to August 25 Whitehall; August 26 to September 21 Bath; September 22 to September 30 Oxford; October 1 to December 31 Whitehall.

### 1664

January 1 to February 17 Whitehall; February 18 Hinchinbrook; February 19 to May 23 Whitehall; May 24 to May 27 Chatworth; May 28 to December 31 Whitehall.

### 1665

January 1 to April 10 Whitehall; April 11 Deptford; April 12 to June 27 Whitehall; June 28 Windsor; June 29 to July 8 Isleworth; July 9 to July 25 Hampton Court; July 26 Greenwich; July 27 Hampton Court; July 28 to September 22 Salisbury; September 23 to December 31 Oxford.

## 1666

January 1–26 Oxford; January 27–31 Hampton Court; February 1 to March 7 Whitehall; March 8–12 Audley End; March 13–27 Whitehall; March 27–29 Deptford; March 30 to May 5 Whitehall; May 6–7 Yacht; May 8 to June 15 Whitehall; June 15–16 Yacht; June 17 to July 30 Whitehall; July 31 to August 1 Tunbridge Wells; August 2 to December 31 Whitehall.

## 1667

January 1 to December 31 Whitehall.

## 1668

January 1 to March 2 Whitehall; March 3 Deptford; March 4 to June 21 Whitehall; June 22–4 Yacht; June 25 to July 3 Whitehall; July 4 Hampton Court; July 5–6 Whitehall; July 7 Hampton Court; July 8–14 Whitehall; July 15 Vauxhall; July 16 to August 8 Whitehall; August 9–10 Bagshott; August 11–25 Whitehall; August 26 Huntingdon; August 27 Dover; August 28–31 Whitehall; September 1–9 Bagshott; September 10–13 Portsmouth; September 14?; September 15–28 Whitehall; September 29 to October 5 Newmarket; October 6–12 Audley End; October 13–16 Newmarket; October 17 to December 31 Whitehall.

## 1669

January 1 to March 7 Whitehall; March 8–19 Newmarket; March 20 to April 25 Whitehall; April 26 to May 2 Newmarket; May 3 to July 29 Whitehall; July 30–31 Yacht; August 1–29 Whitehall; August 30 to September 5 Southampton; September 6–17 Hampton Court; September 18 to December 31 Whitehall.

## 1670

January 1 to March 13 Whitehall; March 14 Woolwich; March 15 to April 13 Whitehall; April 14–28 Newmarket; April 29 to May 13 Whitehall; May 14 Gravesend; May 15 to June 2 Dover; June 3–26 Whitehall; June 27 Gravesend; June 28 to July 23 Whitehall; July 24 Woolwich; July 25 to August 20 Whitehall; August 21 to September 7 Windsor; September 8–25 Whitehall; September 26 to October 13 Newmarket; October 14 to December 31 Whitehall.

## 1671

January 1 to May 4 Whitehall; May 5 Chetham; May 6–25 Whitehall; May 26 to July 12 Windsor; July 13 Portsmouth; July 14–15 Yacht; July 16–19 Plymouth; July 20 Yacht; July 21 Dartmouth; July 22 *en route* from Devon to London; July 23–31 Whitehall; August 1–2 Windsor; August 3–7 Whitehall; August 8 Guildford; August 9 Whitehall; August 10 Windsor; August 11–14 Whitehall; August 15 Tilbury; August 16 to October 3 Whitehall; October 4 Cambridge; October 5–8 Norfolk; October 9–19 Newmarket; October 20 to December 31 Whitehall.

## 1672

January 1 to April 21 Whitehall; April 22 Yacht; April 23 to May 6 Whitehall; May 7 Deptford; May 8 to June 4 Whitehall; June 5–8 Yacht; June 9–18 Whitehall; June 19–20 Yacht; June 21–23 Whitehall; June 24–6 Yacht; June 27 to July 1 Whitehall; July 2 Yacht; July 3 to October 2 Whitehall; October 3–11 Newmarket; October 12–13 Euston; October 14–18 Newmarket; October 19 to December 31 Whitehall.

## 1673

January 1 to April 14 Whitehall; April 15–18 Woolwich; April 19–21 Whitehall; April 22–23 Sheerness; April 24 to May 15 Whitehall; May 16–19 Rye; May 20 to August 3 Whitehall; August 4–5 Bagshott; August 6 to December 31 Whitehall.

## 1674

January 1 to April 5 Whitehall; April 6–8 Newmarket; April 9 to May 25 Whitehall; May 26 to August 25 Windsor; August 26 to October 3 Whitehall; October 4–17 Newmarket; October 18 to December 31 Whitehall.

## 1675

January 1 to March 10 Whitehall; March 11–27 Newmarket; March 28 to June 13 Whitehall; June 14 Portsmouth; June 15–24 Whitehall; June 25 to July 1 Yacht; July 2 Portsmouth; July 3–4 Yacht; July 5 Whitehall; July 6 to September 9 Windsor; September 10 to December 31 Whitehall.

## 1676

January 1 to March 31 Whitehall; April 1–6 Newmarket; April 7–9 Euston; April 10–14 Newmarket; April 15 to October 3 Whitehall; October 4–18 Newmarket; October 19 to December 31 Whitehall.

## 1677

January 1–15 Whitehall; January 16 Woolwich; January 17–24 Whitehall; January 25 Greenwich; January 26 to April 6 Whitehall; April 7 Newmarket; April 8 to August 4 Whitehall; August 5–15 Yacht; August 16–18 Plymouth; August 19 Yacht; August 20 Dover; August 21 Yacht; August 22 to September 24 Whitehall; September 25 to October 11 Newmarket; October 12 to December 31 Whitehall.

## 1678

January 1 to August 13 Whitehall; August 14 to September 24 Windsor; September 25 to October 4 Whitehall; October 5–15 Newmarket; October 16 to December 31 Whitehall.

## 1679

January 1 to June 29 Whitehall; June 30 to July 28 Windsor; July 29 to August 4 Yacht; August 5–6 Windsor; August 7–8 Hampton Court; August 9 to September 25 Windsor; September 26 to October 12 Newmarket; October 13 to December 31 Whitehall.

## 1680

January 1 to February 11 Whitehall; February 12–17 Windsor; February 18 to March 9 Whitehall; March 10–30 Newmarket; March 31 to May 5 Whitehall; May 6 to September 9 Windsor; September 10–16 Whitehall; September 17 ?; September 18–21 Newmarket; September 22–3 Euston; September 24 to October 7 Newmarket; October 8 to December 31 Whitehall.

## 1681

January 1 to March 12 Whitehall; March 13–14 Burford; March 15–28 Oxford; March 29 Windsor; March 30 to April 28 Whitehall; April 29 to

September 5 Windsor; September 6–26 Newmarket; September 27 Chetham; September 28 to October 11 Newmarket; October 12 to December 31 Whitehall.

## 1682

January 1 to March 5 Whitehall; March 6 to April 5 Newmarket; April 6–10 ?; April 11–21 Whitehall; April 22 to May 10 Windsor; May 11 Hampton Court; May 12–22 Windsor; May 23 Hampton Court; May 24 to June 16 Windsor; June 17 Hampton Court; June 18 to July 12 Windsor; July 13–16 Whitehall; July 17 Windsor; July 18 Hampton; July 19–26 Windsor; July 27 Hampton Court; July 28 to September 8 Windsor; September 9–16 Whitehall; September 17 Yacht; September 18 to October 3 Whitehall; October 4–20 Newmarket; October 21 to December 31 Whitehall.

## 1683

January 1 to March 2 Whitehall; March 3–21 Newmarket; March 22 Suffolk; March 23–26 Newmarket; March 27 to April 13 Whitehall; April 14 to July 20 Windsor; July 21–29 Whitehall; July 30 to August 28 Windsor; August 29 to September 4 Winchester; Sep 5–6 Portsmouth; September 7–24 Winchester; September 25 to October 8 Whitehall; October 9–20 Newmarket; October 21 to December 31 Whitehall.

## 1684

January 1 to February 28 Whitehall; March 1–22 Newmarket; March 23–26 Whitehall; March 27 to June 10 Windsor; June 11 Hampton Court; June 12 to July 10 Windsor; July 11 Hampton Court; July 12 to August 27 Windsor; August 28 to September 9 Winchester; September 10–12 Portsmouth; September 13–25 Winchester; September 26 to December 31 Whitehall.

Sources: *CSPD*, *Pepys Diary*, *The Gazette*, *Evelyn's Diary*, *The Lord Chamberlain Books* PRO LC 5/137–46.

# Bibliography

**Manuscripts**

*British Library*

Additional Manuscripts
 976, 5017, 5759 (Gervase Holles's Notebook), 8499, 8867–8868,
 10613–101614, 14269, 15632 (Gervase Holles's Notebook), 15894, 18447,
 18730, 19399, 21484, 21947, 21948, 22185, 22578, 22919, 23114, 23213,
 23214, 23215, 25115 (Records of the Council of Trade 1660–1620, 25125,
 27396, 27447–27448 (Letters of the Paston Family), 28040–28052 (Danby
 and Godolphin Manuscripts), 28569, 28875 (Correspondence of John
 Ellis), 32093–32095 (Malet Papers), 33233, 33589, 33579, 33589, 34217,
 34727, 34889, 35104, 36540, 36916, 36988, 38091, 38847, 38861, 38891,
 40711, 40713, 40860, 41803, 41254 (Lord Fauconberg's Letter Book),
 41806, 41809–41811, 41832, 41834, 41835, 63743, 63744
Althorp Manuscripts
 B5, C5–7
Egerton Manucsrips
 806, 2043, 2537, 2555,3043 3328–3338 (Danby Manuscripts)
Landsdowne Manuscripts
 1152
Sloane Manuscripts
 1003, 1808, 3828
Stowe Manuscripts
 489, 562, 744–746 (Dering Correspondence), 770
SWT
 39–43, 71

*Bodleian Library*

Additional Manuscripts
 c302, c308
Carte Manuscripts
 38, 72, 217
MS Wood
 39–45

MS English History
  c196, c712, c2693, e308–311, g22–23
MS English Letters
  c130
Tanner Manuscripts
  35, 48

## Cheshire County Record Office

DCH/K/3/3, DCH/L/51, DCH/L/58, DSS/1/1/1

## Chester City Record Office

Cowper MSS Vol 1, Mayors Letters Ml3/386u

## Clothworkers Hall

Orders of Courts

## Coventry City Record Office

ba/h/k/1/2, ba/h/c/7/1, ba/h/c/17/2 (Coventry City Minute Book),
ba/h/d/3/1, ba/h/c20/2

## Devon Record Office

1262M, 1329M, Act Books X–XI, Exeter Letter Book DRO Q/60/f

## House of Lords Record Office

Earl of Manchester MSS, Willcocks Selection, Section 2.

## London Guildhall Library

17807
Merchant Tailor Records
Weaver Records 4655/3–7
Skinner Company Records 30708/5

## Norfolk Record Office

Bradfer Lawrence MSS, COL 13/210, Hare 5653, King's Lynn KL/c7/11, King's Lynn MFRO 430/1, King's Lynn MFRO 430/4, MC 107/1, Norfolk Records MFRO 82/2, WKC Norwich

## Public Record Office

CO 77, 134–135, 388–391
LC 2–8, LC 5/2, LC 5/12, LC 5/81–82, LC 5/108, LC 5/118–122, LC 5/137–145, LC 5/191, LC 5/196, LC 5/201
Shaftesbury Papers 30/24/7/601
SP 29, 105/144–152
T 70–76
Works Works 5/1 fol. 121v 133r

## Warwickshire Record Office

1216w203, Session Order Book, CR 136

## Printed primary sources

Aubrey, John. *Brief Lives*. Edited by A. Clark. Oxford: Clarendon Press, 1898.
Bate, George. *Elenchus Motuum Nuperorum in Anglia*. London: 1663.
Bayntun, Edward. *The Commonplace Book of Sir Edward Bayntun of Bromham*. Edited by Jane Freeman. Devizes: Wiltshire Record Society, vol. 43, 1988.
Blount, Thomas. *Boscobel* (1660). An expanded version was published in 1662.
Broadley, A.M. *The Royal Miracle*. London: Stanley Paul & Co., 1907.
Browning, Andrew (ed.) *English Historical Documents Volume 8 1660–1714*. London: Eyre & Spottiswoode, 1953.
*Calendar of the Clarendon State Papers in the Bodleian Library*, ed. F. J. Routledge, vol. 5 of 5. Oxford: Clarendon Press, 1970.
Cartwright, Thomas. *Diary of Dr Thomas Cartwright Bishop of Chester 1686–7*. London: Camden Society First Series, 1843.
Castiglione, Balsadare. *The Book of the Courtier*. Translated by George Bull. New York: Penguin, 1976.
*A Collection of Ordinances and Regulations for the Government of the Royal Household*. London: 1790.
Corie, Thomas. *The Correspondence of Sir Thomas Corrie*. Norwich: Norfolk Record Society, 1956.

Crouch, John. *A Mixt Poem, Partly Historical*. London: Thomas Bettertun, 1660.

Dauncey, John. *The History of His Sacred Majesty Charles II*. London: James Davies, 1660.

Day, W. G. (ed.). *The Pepys Ballads*. Cambridge: D. S. Brewer, 1987.

Dendy, F.W. *Extracts from Records of Merchant Adventurers of Newcastle Upon Tyne*, volume 2. Surtees Society, CI, 1899.

Eglesfield, Francis. *The Life and Reigne of our Sovereign Lord, King Charles II*. London: R. Daniel, 1660.

Einhard and Notker the Stammerer. *Two Lives of Charlemagne*. Edited and translated by Lewis Thorpe. New York: Penguin, 1987.

Erasmus, Desiderius. *The Education of a Christian Prince*. New York: Columbia University Press, 1936.

Evelyn, John. *The Diary of John Evelyn*. Edited by E. S. De Beer, 6 vols. Oxford: Oxford University Press, 1955.

Gerbier, Balthazar. *A Brief Discourse Concerning the Three Chief Principles of Magnificent Building*. London, 1662.

Halifax, Marquis of. *Complete Works*. Edited by J.P. Kenyon. New York: Penguin, 1969.

Herbert. Sir Henry. *The Dramatic Records of Sir Henry Herbert Master of the Revels 1623–1673*. Cornell Studies in English. Edited by J. Q. Adams. New Haven, CT: Yale University Press, 1917.

Hill, R.H. (ed.). *The Correspondence of Thomas Corie, Town Clerk of Norwich, 1664–1687*. Norwich: Norfolk Record Society, 27, 1956.

Howard, Edward. *The British Princes*. London, 1669.

—— *The Change of Crownes A Tragi-Comedy*. Edited by F. S. Boas. London: Oxford University Press, 1949.

Howard, Robert. *The Duke of Lerma*. In *Dryden and Howard 1664–8*. Edited by D. D. Arundell. Cambridge: Cambridge University Press, 1929.

*An Imperfect Portraiture of His Sacred Majesty Charles II*. London, 1660.

James VI. *Basilikon Doron*. Edited by James Craigie. *Scottish Text Society*, 1944.

Jennings, Abraham. *Miraculum Basilcon*. London, 1664.

Joinville, Jean de. *The Life of St. Louis*. In *Memoirs of the Crusades*. Translated by Frank T. Marzials. New York: EP Dutton, 1911.

Lauderdale, Earl of. *Lauderdale Papers*. London: Camden Society, 1895.

*Letters Addressed to Sir Joseph Williamson*. London: Camden Society, 1874.

Lloyd, David. *Eikon Basiike. Or, The True Pourtraiture of [.] Charles II*. London: H. Brome, 1660.

Lord, G. De F. (ed.). *Poems on Affairs of State*, vols 1–3. New Haven, CT: Yale University Press, 1963–1958.

Macray, W. D. (ed.). *Notes Which Passed at Meetings of the Privy Council*. 1896.

McGrath, Patrick. *Records Relating to the Society of Merchant Adventurers of the City of Bristol in the Seventeenth Century*. Bristol: Bristol Record Society, 1952.

"A Mad Designe: or A description of The King of Scots marching in his Disguise." London, 1651.

Magalotti, Lorenzo. *Lorenzo Magalotti at the Court of Charles II*. Edited and translated by W. E. Knowles Middleton. Waterloo, Ontario: Wilfrid Laurier University Press, 1980.

Martindale, Adam. *Life of Adam Martindale*. London: Chetham Society, vol. 4, 1845.

Matthews, William (ed.). *Charles II's Escape from Worcester*. Berkeley: University of California Press, 1966.

Montpensier, Duchesse de. *Memoires of Le Grande Mademoiselle Duchesse de Montpensier*. Translated by Grace Hart Seely. New York: The Century Company, 1928.

Newcastle, Marquis of. *Ideology and Politics on the Eve of the Restoration: Newcastle's Advice to Charles II*. Edited by T. P. Slaughter. Philadelphia, PA, 1984.

Ogilby, John. *The Entertainment of Charles II,*. Edited by Ronald Knowles. Binghamton: Medieval and Renaissance Texts & Studies, 1988.

Pepys, Samuel. *The Diary of Samuel Pepys*. Edited by R. C. Latham and W. Matthews (11 vols). London: HarperCollins, 1995.

Reresby, John. *Memoirs*. Edited by Andrew Browning. Glasgow: Jackson, 1936.

Rich, E. E. (ed.). *Hudson Bay Co. Minutes 1671–84*. 1943–1946.

Rosenheim, J. M. (ed.). *The Notebook of Robert Doughty 1662–1665*. Norwich: Norfolk Record Society, 1991.

Rugg, Thomas. *Diurnal of Thomas Rugge*. Edited by W. L. Sachse. London: Naval Society, 1961.

Rye, Walter (ed.). *Extracts from City of Norwich*. Norwich: Norwich and Norfolk Archeological Society, 1905.

Sadler, Anthony. *Maiestie Irradiant*. London, 1660.

Sainsbury, Bruce Ethel. *A Calendar of The Court Minutes etc. of the East India Company*. Oxford: Clarendon Press, 1929.

Sidney, Henry. *Diary of the Times of Charles II* (2 vols). Edited by R. W. Blencowc. London: Henry Colburn, 1843.

Stockey, H. (ed.). *Records of the Borough of Leicester*. Cambridge, 1923.

Terry, Edward. *A Character of his Most Sacred Majesty King Charles II*. London: D. Maxwell, 1660.

*The Royal Pilgrimage, or The Progress and Travels of King Charles the Second Through the Most and Greatest Courts of Europe By An Eye Witness*. London, 1659.

Tuke, Sir Samuel. *A Character of Charles the Second*. London, 1660.

Turner, George Lyon. *Original Records of Early Nonconformity under Persecution and Indulgence* (3 vols). London: T.F. Unwin, 1911–1914.

Yonge, James. *The Journal of James Yonge*. Edited by F. N. L. Poynter. London: Longman, 1863.

## Economic tracts

[Bethel, Slingsby]. *Observations on the Letter Written to Sir Thomas Osborn upon the Reading of a Book Called the Present Interest of England Stated Written in a Letter to a Friend in London.* 1673.

—— *England's Improvement.* 1675.

Bland, John. *Trade Revived.* 1660.

Carter, William. *England's Interest by Trade Asserted.* 1671.

*Certain Considerations Relating to the Royal African Company of England to Which National Advantages Are Demonstrated Must be in a Joint Stock.* 1680.

Child, Josiah. *A Treatise Wherein is Demonstrated that the East India Trade is the Most National of All Foreign Trades.* 1681.

Coke, Roger. *A Discourse of Trade In Two Parts.* 1670.

*England Great Happiness or a Dialogue Between Content and Complaint Wherein Is Demonstrated That a Great Part of Our Complaints Are Causeless and We Have More Wealth Now than Ever We Had at Any Time Before the Restoration of His Sacred Majesty.* 1677.

Fortrey, Samuel. *England's Interest and Improvement.* 1663.

Hide, Ralph. *A State of Discourse in Honor and for the Advance of Trade for Woolen Manufacturers.* 1660.

Markham, Gervase. *A Way to Get Wealth.* 1683.

N. N. *The Trade of England Revived.* 1681.

Parker, Henry. *The Vintners Answer.* 1642.

Petty, William, Sir. *The Economic Writings of Sir William Petty.* Edited by Charles Graunt. Fairfield, NJ: A. M. Kelley, 1986.

*Reasons for the Bill for the Improvement of Woolen Manufacturers and Preventing the Exportation of Wool.* 1660.

Reynell, Carew. *The True English Interest.* 1674.

*Short Notes and Observations Drawn From the Present Decaying Condition of this Kingdom in Point of Trade.* 1662.

Smith, John. *England's Improvement Reviv'd.* 1670.

*The Vindication of The Clothiers of the Old and New Draperies.* 1660.

Thirsk, Joan and Cooper, J. P. *Seventeenth Century Economic Documents.* Oxford: Oxford University Press, 1972.

Trevors, Joseph. *An Essay to the Restoring of Our Decayed Trade Wherein Is Described the Smugglers, Lawyers and Officers Fraud.* 1677.

Verney, Robert. *England's Interest or The Great Benefit to Trade.* 1682.

Yarranton, Andrew. *England's Improvement by Sea and Land.* 1677.

## Secondary sources

Allen, David. "The Political Function of Charles II's Chiffinch." *Huntington Lib Q,* 39 (1976): 277–290.

Andrews, Charles M. *British Committees, Commissions, and Councils of Trade and Plantations, 1622–1675, Johns Hopkins University Studies in Historical and Political Science.* Series XXVI, Nos 1–3, 1908.

Appleby, Joyce Oldham. *Economic Thought and Ideology in Seventeenth Century England.* Princeton, NJ: Princeton University Press, 1978.

Asch and Birke (eds). *Princes, Patronage and the Nobility.* Oxford: Oxford University Press, 1991.

Aylmer, G. E. *The King's Servants.* London: Routledge & Kegan Paul, 1974.

Backscheider, Paula. *Spectacular Politics: Theatrical Power and Mass Culture in Early Modern England.* Baltimore, MD: Johns Hopkins University Press, 1993.

Baille H. M. "Etiquette and the Planning of the State Apartments in Baroque Palaces." *Archaelogia 101,*169–199.

Barbour, Violet. *Henry Bennet, Earl of Arlington Secretary of State to Charles II.* Washington, DC: AHA, 1914.

Barton, Anne. "The King Disguised." In *The Triple Bond.* Edited by Joseph Price. University Park, PA: Pennsylvania State University Press, 1975.

Beaver, Daniel. "Conscience and Context: The Popish Plot and the Politics of Ritual 1678–1682." *HJ* 34 (1994).

Becket, J. C. "The Irish Viceroyalty in the Restoration Period." *TRHS* 10 (1970): 53–72.

Bergeron, David. "Gilbert Dugdale and the Royal Entry of James I." *Journal of Medieval and Renaissance Studies* 13 (1983): 111–125.

Bold, John. *John Webb: Architectural Theory and Practice in the Seventeenth Century.* Oxford: Clarendon Press, 1989.

Brenner, Robert. *Merchants and Revolution: Commercial Change, Political Conflict, and London's Overseas Traders, 1550–1653.* Princeton, NJ: Princeton University Press, 1993.

Brinkman, C. "England and the Hanse Under Charles II." *EHR* 23 (1908).

Brown, Jonathan and Elliott, J. H. *A Palace for a King the Buen Retiro and the Court of Philip IV.* New Haven, CT: Yale University Press, 1980.

Browning, Andrew. *Thomas Osborne, Earl of Danby and Duke of Leeds* (3 vols). Glasgow: Jackson, 1944.

—— "The Stop of the Exchequer." *History* 14 (1930): 333–337.

Bruce, S. and Yearley, S. "The Restoration Portraits and the Kings of Scotland. In *Making of Scotland.* Edited by D. McCrone, S. Kendrick, P. and Straw. Edinburgh: Edinburgh University Press, 1989.

Burckhardt, Jacob. *The Civilization of the Renaissance in Italy.* New York: Harper & Row, 1958.

Butt, Ronald. *A History of Parliament The Middle Ages.* London: Constable, 1989.

Cacicedo, Alberto. "Seeing the King: Biblical and Classical Texts in Astreas Redux." *Studies in English Literature* 32 (1992): 407–427.

Cannadine, D. and Price, J.M. (eds). *Rituals of Royalty.* Cambridge: Cambridge University Press, 1992.

Carte, T. *Life of James Duke of Ormonde* (6 vols). Oxford, 1851.

Challinor, P. J. "Restoration and Exclusion in the County of Cheshire." *Bulletin of the John Rylands Library* 64 (2) (1981–1982): 360–385.

Chandamon, C. D. *The English Public Revenue*. Oxford: Clarendon Press, 1975.

Cockburn, J. S. *A History of the English Assizes, 1558–1714*. Cambridge: Cambridge University Press, 1972.

Coleby, Andrew. *Central Government and the Localities*. Cambridge: Cambridge University Press, 1987.

Coleman, D. C. *Sir John Banks: Baronet and Businessman*. Oxford: Clarendon University Press, 1963.

Colvin, H. M. *A Biographical Dictionary of English Architects 1660–1840*. London: John Murray, 1954.

Colvin, H. M. *The History of the King's Works*, Vol. 5. London: HMSO, 1976.

Conquest, Richard., Crook, J. M., Downes, K. and Newman, J. "The State and Commercial Expansion: England in the Years 1642–1688." *J. of Euro. Econ. Hist.* 14 (1) (1985): 155–172.

Cooper, J. P. "Economic Regulation and the Cloth Industry in Seventeenth Century England." *TRHS*, 5th series 20 (1970): 73–99.

Cornfield, Penelope. "A Provincial Capital in the Late Seventeenth Century: The Case of Norwich." In *Crisis And Order In English Towns*, edited by Clark and Slack. Toronto: University of Toronto Press, 1972.

Cruickshanks, Eveline (ed.). *The Stuart Courts*. Stroud, Glos: Sutton Press, 2000.

Cuddy, Neil. "Anglo Scottish Union and the Court of James I 1603–1625." *TRHS* (1988): 107–124.

Cust, Richard. "Politics and the Electorate." In *Conflict in Early Stuart England*, edited by R. Cust and D. Hughes. New York: Longman, 1989.

—— "News and Politics in Early Seventeenth Century England." *Past & Present* 112 (August, 1986): 60–90.

Davies, Julian. *The Caroline Captivity of the Church*. Oxford: Clarendon Press, 1992.

Davies, K. G. *The Royal African Company*. New York: Longman, 1957.

Davis, Ralph. "English Foreign Trade, 1660–1700." *Economic History Review*, 2nd series 7 (2) 1954): 150–166.

De Beer, E. S. "King Charles II's Own Fashion: An Episode in Anglo–French Relations 1666–1670." *Journal of the Warburg Courtald Institute* II (1938).

Dickens, A. G. (ed.). *The Courts of Europe: Politics, Patronage, and Royalty 1400–1800*. New York, McGraw-Hill, 1977.

Edie, Caroline. "The Public Face of Royal Ritual: Sermons, Medals, and Civic Ceremony in Later Stuart Coronations." *Huntington Library Quarterly* 53 (autumn, 1990): 311–336.

Elias, Norbert. *Court Society*, translated by Edmund Jephcott. Oxford: Blackwell, 1983.

Elliott, J. H. *Richelieu and Olivares*. Cambridge: Cambridge University Press, 1984.

Elton, G. R. "The Points of Contact." In *Studies in Tudor and Stuart Politics and Government* (3 vols). Cambridge: Cambridge University Press, 1974–1983: vol. III, 3–57.

Evans, John T. *Seventeenth-Century Norwich: Politics Religion and Government 1620–1690*. Oxford: Clarendon Press, 1974.

Feiling, Keith. *British Foreign Policy, 1660–1672*. London: Macmillan 1930.

Fletcher, Anthony. *Reform in the Provinces*. New Haven, CT: Yale University Press, 1986.

—— "The Enforcement of the Conventicle Acts 1664–1679." In *Persecution and Toleration: Studies in Church History*, vol. 21, edited by W. J. Sheils. Oxford: Blackwell, 1984.

—— "National and Local Awareness in the County Communities." In *Before the Civil War*, edited by Howard Tomlinson. New York: St. Martins Press, 1983.

Fletcher, A. and Stevenson, D. (eds). *Order and Disorder in Early Modern England*. Cambridge: Cambridge University Press, 1987.

Foster, G. C. F. "Government in Provincial England Under the Later Stuarts." *TRHS* 33 (1982): 29–48.

Fraser, Antonia. *Royal Charles*. New York: Knopf, 1979.

Fremantle, Katherine. *The Baroque Town Hall of Amsterdam*. Utrecht: Haentjens, Dekker & Gumbert, 1959.

Gardner-Medwin, A. "Views of King and People in Sixteenth and Seventeenth Century Ballads." In *Bryght Laternis*, edited by J. D. McClure and R. G. Spiller. Aberdeen: Aberdeen University Press, 1983.

Gauci, Perry. *Politics and Society in Great Yarmouth 1660–1772*. Oxford: Clarendon Press, 1996.

Girouard, Mark. *Windsor, the Most Romantic Castle*. London: Hodder & Stoughton, 1993.

Glassey, Lionel K. J. *Politics and the Appointment of Justices of the Peace*. Oxford: Oxford University Press, 1979.

Gough, Barry M. "The Adventurers of England Trading into Hudson's Bay: A Study of the Founding Members of the Hudson's Bay Corporation 1665–1670." *Albion* 2 (1) (1970): 35–47.

Grassby, Richard. "English Merchant Capitalism in the Late Seventeenth Century." *Past and Present* 46 (1970): 97–107.

—— *The English Gentlemen in Trade*. Oxford: Oxford University Press, 1994.

Green, Ian. *The Re-establishment of the Church of England 1660–1663*. Oxford: Oxford University Press, 1978.

Greenblatt, Stephen. *Shakespearean Negotiations*. Berkeley: University of California Press, 1985.

Haley, K. H. D. *The First Earl of Shaftesbury*. Oxford: Clarendon Press, 1968.

Halliday, Paul. *Dismembering the Body Politic*. Cambridge: Cambridge University Press, 1998.

Hammond, Paul. "The King's Two Bodies: Representations of Charles II." *Culture, Politics, and Society in Britain 1660–1800*, edited by Jeremy Black and Jeremy Gregory. Manchester: Manchester University Press, 1991.

Harris, Tim, Seaward, Paul and Goldie, Mark (eds). *The Politics of Religion in Restoration England*. Cambridge, MA: Blackwell, 1990.

Harris, Tim. *London Crowds in the Reign of Charles II*. Cambridge: Cambridge University Press, 1990.

Henning, Basil Duke (ed.). *The House of Commons 1660–90* (3 vols). London: Secker & Warburg, 1983.

Herbarge, Alfred. "Elizabethan-Restoration Palimpsest." *Modern Language Review* 35 (3) (1940).

Hinton, R. W. K. *The Eastland Trade and the Commonweal in the Seventeenth Century*. Cambridge: Cambridge University Press, 1959.

Hirst, Derek. *Authority and Conflict*. London: Arnold, 1987.

—— "Court, Country and Politics before 1629." In *Faction in Parliament*, edited by Kevin Sharpe. Oxford: Oxford University Press, 1978.

—— "The Conciliatoriness of the Cavalier Commons Reconsidered," *Parliamentary History* 6 (2), (1987).

—— *The Representative of the People?* Cambridge: Cambridge University Press, 1975.

Horwitz, Henry. *Parliament, Policy and Politics in the Reign of William III*. Newark: University of Delaware Press, 1977.

Hughes, Anne. *Politics, Society, and Civil War in Warwickshire, 1620–1660*. Cambridge: Cambridge University Press, 1987.

Hughes, Derek. *English Drama 1660–1700*. Oxford: Clarendon Press, 1996.

Huisken, Jacobine. *Jacob van Campen: The Classical Ideal in the Golden Age*. Amsterdam: Architectura and Natura Pers, 1995.

Hume, Robert (ed.). *The London Theatre World 1660–1800*. Carbondale: Southern Illinois University Press, 1980.

Hurwich, Judith. "A Fanatick Town." *Midland History* 4 (1) (1977): 15–44.

—— "Dissent and Catholicisn in English Society: A Study of Warwickshire, 1660–1720." *JBS* 16 (1976): 25–43.

Hutton, Ronald. "The Making of the Secret Treaty of Dover." *HJ* 29 (2) (1986): 297–318.

—— *Charles II King of England, Scotland and Ireland*. Oxford: Clarendon Press, 1989.

—— *The Restoration: A Political and Religious History of England and Wales, 1658–1667*. Oxford: Clarendon Press, 1985.

Israel, Jonathan I. *Dutch Primacy in World Trade, 1585–1740*. Oxford: Clarendon Press, 1989.

Johnson, A. M. "Politics in Cheshire 1640–1662." In *Crisis and Order in English Towns*, edited by P. Clark and P. Slack. Toronto: University of Toronto Press, 1972.

Jones, J. R. (ed.). *The Restored Monarchy*. Totawa, NJ: Rowman & Littlefield, 1979.

—— *Charles II: Royal Politician*. Boston, MA: Allen & Unwin, 1986.

Jouhaud, Christian. "Printing the Event: From La Rochelle to Paris." In *The Culture of Print; Power and the Uses of Print in Early Modern Europe*, edited by Roger Chartier. Oxford: Oxford University Press, 1989.

Justice, Stephen. *Writing and Rebellion*. Berkeley: University of California Press, 1994.

Kantorowicz, Ernst. *The King's Two Bodies*. Princeton: Princeton University Press, 1981.

Kent, Joan. "The Centre and the Localities: State Formation and Parish Government in England." *HJ* 38 (2) (1995): 363–404.

Kenyon, J. P. *Stuart England*. New York: Penguin, 1975.

Kettering, Sharon. "Brokerage at the Court of Louis XIV." *HJ* 36 (1993): 69–87.

Kirby, Joan W. "Restoration Leads and the Alderman of the Corporation, 1661–1700." *Northern History* 22 (1986): 123–174.

Knights, Mark. *Politics and Opinion in Crisis: 1678–1681*. Cambridge: Cambridge University Press, 1994.

Kunze, B. Y. and Bautigam, D.D. (eds). *Court, Country and Culture*. Rochester: University of Rochester Press, 1992.

Lake, Peter. "Anti-Popery: The Structure of a Prejudice." In *Conflict in Early Stuart England*, edited by R. Cust and D. Hughes. New York: Longman, 1989.

Landau, Norma. *The Justices of the Peace 1679–1760*. Berkeley: University of California Press, 1984.

Larminie, Vivienne. *Wealth, Kinship and Culture: The 17th Century Newdigates of Arbury and Their World*. Woodbridge, Suffolk: The Royal Historical Society, The Boydell Press, 1995.

Lee, Colin. "'Fanatic Magistrates': Religious and Political Conflict in Three Kent Boroughs, 1680–1684." *HJ* 35 (1) (March, 1992): 43–61.

Lee, Maurice. *The Cabal*. Urbana: University of Illinois Press, 1965.

Lewis, George Randall. *The Stannaries*. New York: Houghton Mifflin & Co., 1908.

Lindley, Keith. *Fenland Riots and the English Revolution*. London: Heinemann, 1982.

Lytel, G. F. and Orgel, S. (eds). *Patronage in the Restoration*. Princeton, NJ: Princeton University Press, 1981.

MacCaffrey, Wallace. "Place and Patronage in Elizabethan Politics." In *Elizabethan Government and Society*, edited by S. T. Bindoff, J. Hurstfield and C. Williams. London: Athlone, 1961.

Mcclain, Molly. "The Wentwood Forest Riot: Property Rights and Political Culture in Restoration England." In *Political Culture and Cultural Politics In Early Modern Europe*, edited by Mark Kishlansky and Susan Amussen. Manchester: Manchester University Press, 1995.

Maclean, Gerald (ed.). *Culture and Society in the Stuart Restoration*. Cambridge: Cambridge University Press, 1995.

Maguire, Nancy Klein. "The Whole Truth of Restoration Tragicomedy." In *Renaissance Tragicomedy*, edited by N. K. Maguire. New York: AMSP, 1987.

—— *Regicide and Restoration*. Cambridge: Cambridge University Press, 1992.

Makepeace, Margaret. "English Traders on the Guinea Coast 1657–1688." *History in Africa* 16 (1989): 237–284.

Malcolm, Joyce Lee. "A King in Search of Soldiers: Charles I in 1642." *HJ* (1978): 307–330.

—— "Charles II and the Reconstruction of Royal Power." *HJ* 35 (2) (1992): 307–330.

Marshall, Alan. *Intelligence and Espionage in the Reign of Charles II*. Cambridge: Cambridge University Press, 1994.

—— *The Age of Faction*. Manchester: Manchester University Press, 1999.

Miller, John. *Charles II*. London: Weidenfeld & Nicholson, 1989.

—— "The Crown and the Borough Charters in the Reign of Charles II." *EHR* 100 (January 1985): 53–84.

—— James II: *A Study in Kingship*. Hove: Wayland, 1977.

Moote, Alan Lloyd. *Louis XIII: The Just*. Los Angeles: University of California Press, 1989.

Morrill, John. *Cheshire 1630–1660: County Government And Society During The Puritan Revolution*. Oxford: Oxford University Press, 1974.

Moulton, Ian. *Before Pornography*. New York: Oxford University Press, 2000.

Mullett, M. A. "'Men of Known Loyalty': The Politics of the Lancashire Borough of Clitheroe, 1660–1689." *Northern History* 21 (1985): 100–111.

Neale, Sir John. *The Elizabethan House of Commons*. London Cape, 1949.

Newmann, Peter C. *Company of Adventurers*. New York: Viking Press 1985.

Norrey, P. J. "The Restoration Regime in Action: Relations between Central and Local Government in Somerset, Dorset and Wiltshire, 1660–1678." *HJ* 31 (1988): 789–812.

Oliver, H. J. *The Problem of John Ford*. Melbourne: Melbourne University Press, 1955.

—— *Sir Robert Howard*. Durham, NC: Duke University Press, 1973.

Ollard, Richard. *The Escape of Charles II After the Battle of Worcester*. New York: Scribner, 1966.

Orgel, Stephen. *The Illusion of Power*. Berkeley: University of California Press, 1991.

Papillion, A. F. W. *Memoires of Thomas Papillion of London, Merchant*. Reading: Addison-Wesley, 1887.

Patterson, Annabel. *Reading Between the Lines*. Madison: University of Wisconsin Press, 1993.

Peck, Linda Levy. *Court Patronage and Corruption in Early Stuart England*. New York: Routledge, 1993.

Pincus, Steven. "'Coffee Politicians Does Create': Coffee Houses and Restoration Political Culture." *JMH* 67 (December, 1995): 807–834.

—— "Popery, Trade and Universal Monarchy: The Ideological Context of the Outbreak of the Second Anglo-Dutch War." *EHR* (January, 1992).

—— *Protestantism and Patriotism*. New York: Cambridge University Press, 1996.

Price, Jacob M. "What Did Merchants Do? Reflections on British Overseas Trade 1660–1790." *Journal of Economic History*. 49 (2) (1989): 267–284.

Priestley, Margaret. "Anglo-French Trade and the Unfavorable Balance Controversy: 1660–1685." *Economic History Review* (1951).

—— "London Merchants and Opposition Politics in Charles II's Reign." *BIHR* (1956).

Pyne, W. H. *History of the Royal Residences*. London, 1817.

Ranum, Orest. "Courtesy, Absolutism and the French State." *JMH* (September, 1980): 426–451.

—— *The Fronde*. New York: W. W. Norton, 1993.

Reedy, Gerard. "Mystical Politics: the Imagery of Charles II's Coronation." *Studies in Change and Revolution*, edited by Paul Korshin. Menston, Yorkshire: Scolar Press Ltd. 1972.

Richards, Judith. "His Nowe Majestie and the English Monarchy: The Kingship of Charles I before 1640." *Past and Present* 113 (November, 1986): 70–96.

Robert, Rudolph. *Chartered Companies*. London: G. Bell, 1969.

Roberts, Clayon. *The Growth of Responsible Government in England*. 1966.

Roberts, Stephen K. *Recovery and Restoration in an English County: Devon Local Administration 1646–1670*. Exeter: Exeter University Press, 1985.

—— "Party Organization at the Local Level: The Norfolk Sheriff's Subscripion of 1676." *HJ* 29 (September 1986): 713–722.

Rosenheim, James. *The Townshends of Raynham*. Middletown, CT: Wesleyan University Press, 1989.

Roseveare, Henry. "Crafty and Fawning: Downing of Downing Street." *History T* 34 (July, 1984): 10–14.

Sacret, J. H. "The Restoration Government and the Municipal Corporations." *EHR* 45 (1930): 232–259.

Sainty, J. C. *Lists of Lieutenants of Counties 1660–1974*. London: List and Index Society Special Series, vol. 12, 1979.

Sainty, J. C. and Bucholz, R. O. *Officials of the Royal Household, 1660–1837*. London: University of London Press, 1997.

Saul, Nigel. *Richard II*. New Haven, CT: Yale University Press, 1997.

Sawday, Jonathan. "Rewriting a Revolution: History, Symbol and Text in the Restoration." *Seventeenth Century* 7 (2) (1992).

Seaward, Paul. "The House of Commons Committee for Trade and the Origins of the Second Dutch War, 1664." *HJ* 30(2) (1987).

—— *The Cavalier Parliament and the Reconstruction of the Old Regime: 1661–1667*. Cambridge: Cambridge University Press, 1989.

Sharp, Buchanan. "Popular Political Opinion in England 1660–1685." *History of Modern European Ideas* 10 (1) (1989): 13–29.

Sharpe, Kevin (ed.). *Faction in Parliament*. Oxford: Oxford University Press, 1978.

—— *The Personal Rule of Charles I*. New Haven, CT: Yale University Press, 1992.

Shils, Edward. *Center and Periphery: Essays in Macrosociology*. Chicago, IL: University of Chicago Press, 1975.

Simpson, P. "Die handelsniederlassung der Englishe Kaufleute in Elbing." *Haniische Geschichtsblatter* 22 (1916).

Skinner, Quentin. "History and Ideology in the English Revolution." *Journal of the History of Ideas* 8 (2) (1965): 151–177.

Smuts, Malcolm. *Court Culture and the Origins of a Royalist Tradition in Early Stuart England*. Philadelphia, PA: University of Pennsylvania Press, 1987.

—— (ed.). *The Stuart Court in Europe*. Cambridge: Cambridge University Press, 1996.

Solomon, Harry M. "The Rhetoric of Redressing Grievances: Court Propaganda and the Hermeneutical Key to Venice Preservd." *ELH* 53 (2) (1986).

Spurr, John. *The Restoration Church of England*. New Haven, CT: Yale University Press, 1991.

—— *The 1670s*. Oxford: Blackwell, 2000.

Starkey, David. *The English Court*. New York: Longman, 1987.

Stater, Victor. *Noble Government*. Athens, GA: University of Georgia Press, 1994.

Stevenson, David. "The English Devil of Keeping State: Elite Manners and the Downfall of Charles I in Scotland." In *People and Power in Scotland*, edited by Roger Mason and Norman Macdougall. Edinburgh: J. Donald, 1992.

Strong, Roy. *Art & Power: Renaissance Festivals 1450–1650*. Los Angeles: University of California Press, 1973, 1984.

Summerson, John. *Architecture in Britain 1530–1830*. New Haven, CT: Yale University Press, 1993.

Swatland, Andrew. *The House of Lords in the Reign of Charles II*. Cambridge: Cambridge University Press, 1996

Terwin, J. J. "The Buildings of Johann Maurits van Nassau." In *Johan Maurits van Nassau-Siegen 1604–1679*, edited by E. van de Boogart. The Hague: Johan Maurits van Nassan Stichting, 1979.

Thornton, Peter. *Seventeenth Century Interior Decoration in England, France and Holland*. New Haven, CT: Yale University Press, 1978.

Thurley, Simon. "The Lost Palace of Whitehall." *History Today* (January, 1988).

—— *Whitehall Palace: An Architectural History of the Royal Apartments, 1240–1698*. New Haven, CT: Yale University Press, 1999.

Tucker, Norman. "Col. Roger Whitley." *Journal of Flintshire Historical Society* 22 (1965–1966): 9–24.

Turner, E. R. *The Privy Council 1603–1784* (2 vols). Baltimore, MD: Johns Hopkins University Press, 1927.

Turner, Victor. *Dramas, Fields, and Metaphors*. Ithaca, NY: Cornell University Press, 1974.

—— *The Ritual Process*. Chicago, IL: 1969.

Vale, V. "Clarendon, Coventry and the Sale of Naval Offices." *Cambridge Historical Journal* 13 (2) (1956).

Vaughn, Richard. *A History of Valois Burgundy* (4 vols). New York: Archon, 1962–1973.

Visser, Colin. "Theatrical Scandal in the Letters of Colbert de Croissy, 1669." *Restoration* 7 (2) (1983): 54–57.

Warmington, A. R. *Civil War, Interregnum, and Restoration in Gloucestershire 1640–72*. Rochester, NY: Royal Historical Society, The Boydell Press, 1997.

Watt, Tessa. *Cheap Print and Popular Piety 1550–1640*. Cambridge: Cambridge University Press, 1994.

Weber, Harold. *Paper Bullets: Print and Kingship under Charles II*. Lexington: University of Kentucky Press, 1996.

—— "Representations of the King: Charles II and His Escape from Worcester." *Studies in Philology* 85 (4) (1988): 489–509.

Weil, Rachel. "Sometimes a Scepter is only a Scepter." In *The Invention of Pornography*, edited by Lynn Hunt. New York: Zone, 1993.

Weiser, Brian. "A Call for Order." *The Court Historian* 6 (2) (September, 2001): 151–156.

—— "Owning the King's Story: The Escape from Worcester." *Seventeenth Century* 14 (1) (spring, 1999): 43–62.

—— "The Politics and Representation of Access in Edward Howard's *The Change in Crownes*." *Restoration* 24 (1) (spring, 2000): 1–10.

Weiss, Allan S. *Mirrors of Infinity*. New York: Princeton Architectural Press, 1995.

Whiteman, Anne. *The Compton Census of 1676: A Critical Study*. London: British Academy Oxford University Press, 1986.

Williams, Penry. *The Tudor Regime*. Oxford: Clarendon Press, 1979.

Wilson, C. H. *Profit and Power; A Study of England and the Dutch Wars*. London: Longmans, Green, 1957.

Woodhead, J. R. *The Rulers of London, 1660–1689*. London: London and Middlesex Archaeological Society, 1965.

*Wren Society VII: The Royal Palaces of Winchester, Whitehall, Kensington and St James 1660–1715*. Oxford, 1930.

Yardley, Bruce. "George Villiers, Second Duke of Buckingham and the Politics of Toleration." *HLQ* 55 (2) (1992): 317–357.

Yates, Francis. *Astrea*. London: Pimlico, 1975.

Zwicker, Steven. "The King and Christ: Figural Imagery in Dryden's Restoration Panegyrics." *Philological Quarterly* 50 (4) (October, 1971): 582–598.

—— *Lines of Authority*. Ithaca, NY: Cornell University Press, 1993.

## Unpublished dissertations

Challinor, P. J. "The Structure of Politics in Cheshire, 1660–1715." Ph.D. diss., Wolverhampton Polytechnic, 1982.

Emmons, Julia Vorhees. "The Politics of Faction in the Early Restoration Court of Charles II 1660–1667." Ph.D. diss., Emory University, 1984.

Gauci, P. "The Corporation and the Country: Great Yarmouth 1660–1722." D.Phil., Oxford University, 1991.

Heap, P. C. "The Politics of Stuart Warwickshire." Ph.D. diss., Yale University, 1975.

Jones, Bunny Paine. "The Cully of Britain." Ph.D. diss, University of Houston, 1980.

Key, Newton Eldrege. "Politics Beyond Parliament: Unity and Party in the Herefordshire Region During the Restoration." Ph.D. diss, Cornell University, 1989.

Loughead, Peter. "The East India Company in English Domestic Politics 1657–1688." D.Phil., Oxford University, 1981.

Patterson, Catherine. "Urban Patronage in Early Modern England: Corporate Boroughs, the Landed Elite and the Crown, 1580–1640." Ph.D. diss., University of Chicago, 1994.

Rosenheim, J. M. "An Examination of Oligarchy: The Gentry of Restoration Norfolk, 1660–1720." Ph.D. diss., Princeton University, 1981.

Sinner, Robert John. "Charles II and Local Government: The Quo Warranto Proceedings, 1681–1685." Ph.D. diss., Rutgers University, 1976.

Smith, Arthur Giffen. "London and the Crown." Ph.D. diss., University of Wisconsin, 1967.

Weiser, Brian "Reconstruction of Monarchy." Ph.D. diss., University of Washington, 1999.

# Index